P9-CRW-912

e Pr

V
1/87

SAMBO

SAMBO

*The Rise & Demise
of an American Jester*

JOSEPH BOSKIN

New York   Oxford
OXFORD UNIVERSITY PRESS
1986

Oxford University Press

Oxford   New York   Toronto
Delhi   Bombay   Calcutta   Madras   Karachi
Petaling Jaya   Singapore   Hong Kong   Tokyo
Nairobi   Dar es Salaam   Cape Town
Melbourne   Auckland

and associated companies in
Beirut   Berlin   Ibadan   Nicosia

Published by Oxford University Press, Inc.,
200 Madison Avenue, New York, New York 10016

Oxford is the registered trademark of Oxford University Press

Library of Congress Cataloging-in-Publication Data
Boskin, Joseph.
Sambo: the rise & demise of an American jester.
Bibliography: p.
Includes index.
1. Sambo (Fictitious character)   2. Afro-American entertainers—Biography.
3. Afro-Americans in the performing arts.   4. Fools and jesters—
United States. 5. United States—Popular culture.   6. United States—
Race relations.   7. Stereotype (Psychology) I. Title.
II. Title: Sambo: the rise and demise of an American jester.
PN2286.B67   1986   306'.484'08996073   86-8451
ISBN 0-19-504074-0

Excerpt from "Gerontion" in *Collected Poems 1909–1962* by T. S. Eliot, copyright 1936 by
Harcourt Brace Jovanovich, Inc.; copyright © 1963, 1964 by T. S. Eliot. Reprinted by
permission of the publisher.

9 8 7 6 5 4 3 2 1

Printed in the United States of America
on acid-free paper

*In the ancient quest of reaching
into the mosaic of experiences
seeking the unity that binds us all,
there has always been Claire*

An Appreciation

To express my deepest gratitude to those who expanded my sensitivity to the subject—who, in addition to critical comments, also sent materials, suggestions, and reminiscences and hummed a tune of support despite occasional surliness—clearly goes beyond the written word. I was enlightened by Cecilia Tichi, a remarkable person, who volunteered to read the entire manuscript despite her own writing and personal commitments, and in her gentle and buoyant manner made me smile through criticisms always but always on the mark; by William Tuttle, whose incisive reading prodded me toward a better comprehension of the subject; by Murray Levin, who daily filled my plate with a humor permitting constant creativity; by Karl Fortress, who proffered his prints, postcards, and cynical experiences; by Herbert Hill, who not only constantly prodded in his certain way but connected me to movement people; by David Kunzle, who had an unflagging eye for Sambo's early relatives on the European continent; by Richard Newman, who offered a stream of biographical sources; by Helen MacLam, who vigilantly scanned for contemporary stereotypes; by David Mors, Bert Geyer and Gary Geyer, who sent artifactual sources from their various travels; by Tom Glick, who pointed the direction toward theoretical constructs; by Sam Bass Warner, who, in his incisive way, posed the right questions regarding my approach; by David Hall, James Henretta, and Howard Zinn, who read various chapters and recommended important changes; by Arnold Shapiro, who offered his interviewing skills; by Dorsay Dujon, who shared her extensive Sambo collection; by Matthew Boskin, who scrounged and carried a four-foot nineteenth-century Sambo lawn statue into my study; by Sheldon Benjamin, who offered a rare volume of Helen Bannerman's *Little Black Sambo* as a symbol of completion; by Holly Wallace, who encountered a messy manuscript but typed and edited it with marvelous cheerfulness; by Gilda Abramowitz, whose superb editing not only saved me from many embarrassing errors but made possible a finer work through her various suggestions. To Sheldon Meyer, who kept the faith over the years, a testimony to his deserved reputation as a truly caring person.

I am indebted to the Russell Sage Foundation for their generous grant in 1977–78 and Boston University for administrative support in completing the manuscript. And I am indebted to the Academy of Motion Pictures; Boston Public Library: Print Department, Rare Books; Boston University: Special Collections; Howard University: Moorland Collection; Library of Congress; National Archives; National Gallery of Art: Print Division; New York Public Library: Rare Book Division, Manuscripts and Archives, and the Schomburg Collection; University of California, Los Angeles: Radio and Film Collections; University of Southern California: Special Collections; and the Memorabilia Collections of Dartmouth College, Los Angeles, and New York City.

For their participation in interviews, dialogues, and correspondence, I deeply thank Roger Abrahams, John J. Appel, J. Herman Blake, Horace Cayton, Irving Fein, Adelaide Gulliver, Mary Jane Hewitt, Herbert Hill, Mort Lewis, Carleton Moss, Joan R. Perkal, Jim Quart, Saunders Redding, Timmy Rogers, Lou Smith, Phil Sterling, James Tolbert, Vic Walter, and Whitney Young.

Moreover, throughout the years of sometimes disjointed

efforts, the presence of many friends made possible the solitariness of it all. To Sheldon Benjamin, Mark Friedman, David Kunzle, Murray Levin and Helen Jacobson, Rita and Max Lawrence, Jason and Pat Finkle, Lilliann and Marvin Rosenberg, Nancy and Herb Bernhard, Herb Boskin, Joseph Nyomarkay, Marion and Bob Ross, William, Polia and Boris Pillin, William Tuttle, Joel and Tova Tarr, Bob Rosenstone and Cheri Pann, Stan Coben, Denny Thompson and Betsy Broadman, Trevor and Jackie Kaye, Sara Minden and Jim Miller, Mitch and Renee Geffen, Honey and Leon Geyer, Linda and Gary Geyer, Arnold Shapiro, Marilyn and Mel Boskin, Helen Maclam, Ruth Chad, Sam Hurst, Damon Lawrence, and Bob and Sue Erwin, I am the better for your embrace; to my daughters, Julie, Lori, and Deborah, I have never ceased to be enormously touched by your patience and presence; and to Sheila Brenner, you made me laugh even when I didn't want to, and by a smile made the entire effort possible.

Brookline   J. B.
1986

Various portions of the book appeared in the following articles: "Goodbye, Mr. Bones," *New York Times Magazine* (May 1, 1966): 30–31, 84–92; "Sambo: The National Jester in the Popular Culture," in *The Great Fear: Race in the Mind of America*, Gary Nash and Richard Weiss, eds. (New York: Holt, Rinehart and Winston, 1970), Chapter 8, pp. 165–85; "Humor in the Civil Rights Movement: Laughter in the Outer Sanctuaries," *Boston University Journal* XVIII (Spring 1970): 2–7; "The Life and Death of Sambo: Overview of an Historical Hang-up," *Journal of Popular Culture* IV (Winter 1971): 647–57.

Contents

SAMBO

The past is full of life, eager to irritate us, provoke and insult us, tempt us to destroy or repaint it.

The only reason people want to be masters of the future is to change the past.

—Milan Kundera, *The Book of Laughter and Forgetting*

1

An Epitaph Read Backward in Time

The Inscription

At a particular juncture in the post–World War II period—it may have occurred in 1955 with the black boycott that followed Rosa Parks's refusal to relinquish her bus seat to a white man in Montgomery, Alabama, or with the emergence of black comedians in the mass culture, or with the sudden violent uprisings in black urban communities throughout the country in the mid-1960s— somewhere among these events, an American icon was readied for burial. Yet the cause may not have been one of these unusual events but rather a series of many smaller, unheralded incidents that had steadily acquired meaning over time. Whatever the overlapping occurrences, after centuries of an incredibly active and energetic existence, Sambo was lowered into the cultural grave. Had such an event been observed at the time and a ceremony convened, an epitaph would have been written:

HERE INTERRED
LIE THE REMAINS
OF THE MAN
SAMBO

Born three hundred–odd years ago,
the exact date obscured by distorted memories:

danced and pranced and laughed
across the stages of American life
in blackface and bravado;

An image born in the inner reaches of white minds,
extending in childlike grin and gait,
entertaining and regaling
all who came into contact:
that pearly smile, those rounded eyes, rhythmical steps,
that rollicking laughter;

Gone, gone but hardly forgotten,
his name etched on cultural arches:
Tambo, Bones, Jim Crow, Uncle Remus, John, Sam, Boy,
   Sambo:
the national jester in the popular culture;

May he rest in Peace,
Never to be Resurrected.

Amen.

Five Portraits

Sambo was, in his lengthy stay in American culture, the enduring
comic image. Mirth and merriment were his trademark in a society
in which entertainment came to assume major proportions in the
lives of the people. His travels through American history were a
mixture of reality and stereotype, but in time he became what Walter Lippmann in his seminal work on public images termed the
"perfect stereotype." Its hallmark, he noted, is that "it precedes
reason" and, "as a form of perception, imposes a certain character
on the data of our senses. . . ."[1]

So fixed was the image, in fact, that dislodging it from its
preeminent place in American popular culture seemed, especially
to Afro-Americans over the long haul, virtually impossible. Sambo
would undergo changes over the centuries, the image reflecting
time and place, eventually to crack and disintegrate. But through
it all he was always what he started out as: a comic performer *par
excellence.*

1850s   Plantation Darkies

The place is a river plantation in South Carolina, but it could be any plantation throughout the South. Preparations for a large wedding are under way. Slave oarsmen are dispatched to the opposite wharf to row the bride and her maid to the plantation house. The oarsmen's shining skins are set off to the "greatest advantage" by the contrast of red woolen shirts, red woolen turbans, blue woolen coats, and white woolen pantaloons. Jovial work songs ring out, "their eyes glistened with fun," and when they meet their new mistress two oarsmen cross their hands to make a sedan chair and carry her into the boat. Watching from the plantation are two hundred slaves, who join in the clamor and chorus and joyfully receive the bride as she alights from the boat. The ceremony is extravagant, and as it nears completion all the slaves are given glasses of wine and toast the couple in song and dance:

> Lettle Miss bride, us wish you big joy:
> Ebery year one gal and one boy.[2]

1860s   Minstrel Man

The place is New York, but it could be any city or village in the North or West. A white man sits before a mirror, dips into a jar of theatrical paint, and gradually spreads it over his face, watching his whiteness give way to total black, except for the eyes, surrounded by white circles, and the mouth, turned upward into a perpetual grin. Then a kinky wig, a multicolored set of pants and shirt, a cutaway and top hat—behold, the minstrel man, Tambo. He bows before the delighted audience left and right, takes out a long sheet, and in thick dialect delivers a "Burlesque Political," a stump speech. The topic is the issue of slavery:

> FELLER CITIZENS:—Correspondin' to your unanimous call I shall now hab de pleasure ob ondressin ebery one of you: an I'm gwine to stick to de pints and de confluence where by I am myself annihilated.

When in de course ob human events it becomes necessary fur de colored portion ob dis pop'lation to look into and enquire into dis inexpressible conflict. It is—it is—it is—to return to our subject.

Dis is a day to be lookin' up, like a bob-tailed pullet on a rickety henroost, or—or, any other man![3]

1890s–1900s   Negro Jokes

The colored boy was up for the fifth time on a charge of chicken stealing. This time the Judge decided to appeal to the boy's father. "Now see here, Abe," he said to the older colored man, "this boy of yours has been up here in court so many times for stealing chickens, that I'm sick of seeing him up here!"

"I don't blame you, Jedge," replied the father. "I'm sick of seein' him up here myself."

"Then why don't you teach him how to act? Show him the right way, and he won't be coming before me!"

"I know it, Jedge; an' I's told him so, many a time. I has showed him de right way, sah," the old man said earnestly, "I certainly showed him de right way; but he somehow keeps gittin caught comin' away wid de chickens!"

A Negro applied at a stable for the job as helper.

"I suppose you know everything about horses?"

"Oh, yas, suh. I been handlin' hawses all mah life."

"Know how to feed 'em, kep 'em in condition, hitch up a rig an' all?"

"Yas suh ree bob!"

"I suppose you're familiar with mules?"

The Negro shook his head impressively. "Boss, I know too much about mules to get familiar wid *dem*."[4]

1920s   Postcard Buffoon

The place is any drugstore or stationery store. A man, woman, or child enters, goes to the penny-postcard section, scans the pickings, and decides to send an orange-colored card with a black figure on it. Standing next to an old-fashioned oblong mailbox attached to a small tree stump on a small patch of green lawn is a small black man. He is totally naked except for a green loincloth held up by an oversized safety pin. His downturned lips are totally surrounded by bright red; his white eyes are oblong saucers; his hair is braided with red, blue, and green ribbons; and his large feet protrude, while his hands are hidden behind his back. His message is capitalized in black: "I'SE PINNIN' A LOT OF HOPES ON GITTIN' A LETTAH FROM YO' ALL . . . WHY DON'T YO' WRITE?"

1930s   Movie Chauffeur

The place is any movie theatre in America. The film is one of thousands of "B" movies—a detective story in which a series of murders have occurred. The detective is aided by a young son and a valet, who accompany him throughout the story and constantly get into minor trouble. The valet is respectably dressed in a dark suit and cap. He has circular eyes, a round face, whitish teeth, and a short rotund body. His patter is quick and voluble. Invariably he enters a house inhabited by "spooks." There he encounters unexplained voices or movements. Quickly his eyes bulge, teeth chatter, body shakes, feet begin to twitch, and swoosh, he is *off*, emphatically declaring:

"Feets don't fail me now."

"Git out de way an' let a man run whut can *run*."

The Icon

The life of Sambo began with the early colonization efforts in the seventeenth century, if not considerably earlier. In all probability, the American Sambo was conceived in Europe, particularly in England, and drew his first breath with the initial contact with West Africans during the early slave-trading years. Sambo was a concept long before assuming a specific identity. Sambo's existence gradually evolved as Western Europeans directed the energies of blacks on the sugar plantations in the West Indies and the tobacco fields in the tidewater regions of Virginia and Maryland—

and later in the northern American colonies as well. Over a period of time Sambo became an integral part of the colonial family, particularly as worker but as entertainer, too. Heralded for his mirthfulness, the figure eventually emerged as a full-scale humorist and an icon in the popular culture. It would not be exaggeration to say that Sambo was the first truly indigenous American humor character throughout the culture, transcending region and ethnicity.

This work is an exploration into Sambo, his image and form, and his institutionalization in the popular culture. It is a history deeply involved with the elusive association between images and social behavior on the one hand and the ties between stereotyping and humor on the other. Attempted here is an unraveling of the origins, development, and demise of the figure as a public art form.

Once fully formed, Sambo was elevated in the folk and popular arts as the closest figure to a court jester the culture would permit, an ironic development in a society committed to an antifeudal future. In an earlier period, the role of Jester was one of influence and status. Not only did the Jester or Fool perform his various functions before the Crown, including dispensing advice and eliciting laughter, he was also included in the entourages of the wealthy families of the realm. The extensive demand for the Jester's services reflected a certain recognition of the connection between wisdom and folly, perspective and humor. Fools were consulted because it was widely assumed that mirth was of the utmost importance to the mind's deliberations and the body's digestive functions. The ancient adage "Laughter is the best medicine" was a widely accepted folk expression that reflected a holistic approach to healing. Robert Burton, in *The Anatomy of Melancholy*, quoted contemporary authorities for his claim that mirth "purges the blood, confirms health, causes a fresh, pleasing, and fine colour, prolongs life, whets the wit, makes the body young, lively and fit for any manner of employment. The merrier the heart the longer the life."[5]

Although the Jester never appeared in the role before the president's court, the American version, Sambo, was similarly located in the great houses and plantations of colonial and antebellum society. Sambo was the descendant of a long line of Fools who played an important role in medieval Europe. With considerable "tenacity and vigour" did the Fool survive for over five centuries, as Sandra Billington reminds us, because he mastered both wit and tricks: "both arts of the entertainer."[6] Yet it was much more than wit and tricks that enabled the Fool to perform before both the bourgeois families and royal courts. The tricks he played on others and the laughter he evoked was always "excused beforehand due to the state of his mind," Anton C. Zijderveld noted in his work on Fools; "the grin on his face—stupid and cunning at once—and his unremitting loyalty to the masters of the house, were doubtlessly the main ingredients out of which the great court and household fools were made. . . ."[7]

Similar to his predecessor, Sambo possessed the natural gift of humor, but it was the humor of a stranger—in this world but not of it. Their identities were never in doubt, however, because both were adorned by costumes, the Fool with cap and bells, attired in lively colors, while Sambo was draped in plantation garb or in the foppish dress of an urbanite. Both figures merrily performed before small and large audiences, holding them fast with tricky body movements, quick repartee, and an ingratiating grin.

Yet differences existed between the two figures. The American Sambo lacked certain qualities ascribed to the Fool. A separate set of responsibilities distinguished the Jester from Sambo, who was denied the Fool's touch of wisdom and perspective—and thus the ability to manipulate humor for higher ends. While the Jester was often chosen for his acumen, Sambo was only occasionally accorded such a rational function. The Jester's advice was to quicken decision making. Sambo's role was far more circumscribed and only occasionally affected major issues. While both initiated and received laughter, the intent of their humor was quite distinct: the Jester was accorded the beauty of wisdom, Sambo accorded the follies of foolishness.

Nonetheless, to deny Sambo the qualities of rationality and

responsibility was not to cast him out. On the contrary, Sambo became the figure unrivaled in the culture for producing and accepting laughter, for being both the prodder and butt of the joke. Sambo was clearly the more complex of the two historic Fools. He was represented throughout the culture in an incredible array of diverse and curious forms, as image, as artifact, as circus and stage performer, as worker, and as athlete. This diversity helps to explain Sambo's unusual reach and longevity.

The rollicking applause heard throughout the land for over two and a half centuries was in large part a consequence of the seeming *naturalness* of it all. Our Sambo could not be outdone or matched. No comic figure played to wider audiences, received more thunderous applause, or lasted as long in the popular theatre. No other immigrant stereotype came close to Sambo's popularity or expressive grin: not Pat and Mike, the "foolish" Irishmen; or Yonny Yonson, the "dumb" Swede; or Jakey, the "scheming" Jew; or Carlo, the "greasy" Italian; or José, the "lazy" Mexican; or even the no-name "stupid" Pole. At times these comic representatives laid them in the aisles, and often came close to toppling Sambo from top billing, but their reigns were relatively short. "Long live Jim Crow, Esquire," rang out the interlocutor in endless minstrel shows, the first popular theatrical form, which captivated audiences for a full century; and all had to agree that he was the funniest, most endearing, and certainly most enduring of all the ethnic performers. Humor poured forth from his antics. Few saw him crying. Few ever recognized that they were to a considerable extent laughing at themselves; such was the beauty of his performance!

Sambo was the undisputed lord of humor itself. He was at once both the instigator and the butt of humor. He played to both sides, a feat few comics have achieved. Sambo accomplished this dubious distinction because only he performed in both public *and* private places. He could be seen on stages, in the streets, even in business establishments, but long before the electronic media made it possible, he could also be found in the homes of strangers.

As the American jester, Sambo was found everywhere, in every nook and cranny of the popular culture. In journals, weeklies, newpapers, magazines, travel reports, diaries, brochures, and broadsides, there was Sambo, cited for his antics. His style filled the literary field in novels, short stories, children's tales, dime novels, essays, pamphlets, and leaflets. Visually, Sambo appeared in posters, on sheet music covers, postcards, wooden pegboards, in illustrations, paintings, cartoons, comic strips, children's games, on postage stamps, in advertisements, on magazine covers, playing cards, stereoscopic slides—the last of which were enlarged by the electrical and electronic media, including the projector and nickelodeon, movies, and television. On stages, in skits, marches, musicals, in street theatre, circuses, plays, radio shows, and at impromptu gatherings, at least one Sambo figure pranced across the lights before audiences cued to his actions. Dressed half in yellow, half in blue, Sambo mascots paraded before cheering crowds at college football games. In public schools, teachers reserved a "nigger seat" for white students, to punish them for stupidity. Sambo posed as ceramic figurines on dining-room tables or in living rooms, stood elegantly on front lawns as iron jockeys, was a backdrop for food and kitchen products, appeared attired in service-oriented dress on posters and wooden figures, and raised his smiling head atop men's canes. The material culture was full of him: place mats, wooden coins, whisky pourers, kitchen reminders, trays, shoehorns, belt buckles, tea sets, goblets, pillows, and countless bric-a-brac. Sambo's happy, grinning countenance lit up restaurants, stores, hotels, businesses, universities, and even churches. It was a testament to his ubiquitous talents that no part of the culture went untouched.

Sambo came to signify what Alan Gowans has labeled "Low Art," an ideational art concerned with perpetuating "the basic values and beliefs of society through symbols collectively inspired, anonymously executed, everywhere and immediately understood." Although Sambo figures were occasionally rendered by known illustrators, their images reflected folk sentiment of considerable depth and vitality. Moreover, as Gowans observed of the use of low art, not only is it found among the basic forms of art but, once established, it remains as "vigorous as ever—shifting in forms, as Low Arts always do; unchanging in function, as Low Arts always are."[8]

This relationship to art partly explains Sambo's longevity. As one of the earliest minority images to be translated into a cultural form, Sambo had become a multipublic figure by the eighteenth century, appealing across the social landscape. When, in the mid-nineteenth century, the figure was presented in the minstrel theatre, its long passage into the other levels of culture was virtually assured. The continuing presence of Sambo in the electronic media was made possible by this connection to the public art.

Sambo's relationship to the popular culture must be viewed within the context of stereotype. Sambo's wide range—as image and artifact and in the theatre—over an extended period confirmed the stereotype and made it credible. "To be sure," wrote Walter Lippmann, "a stereotype may be so consistently and authoritatively transmitted in each generation from parent to child that it seems almost a biological fact."[9]

At the same time, this pervasiveness in the culture often made it seem to be a singular entity—but this was far from the reality. Sambo was, rather, a figure consisting of different parts. Donald Bogle, in an important study, separated out the various sides of Sambo and labeled them "Tom," "Coon," "Mulatto," "Manny," and "Buck." There were lesser sides as well, but certainly these comprised the essential types.[10] Taken together, what often appeared was the image portrayed by Ralph Ellison in *Invisible Man,* in the last defiant act of Clifton as he hawks a jangling, grinning orange-and-black tissue doll before being shot down by a white policeman:

> "Shake it up! Shake it up!
> He's Sambo, the dancing doll, ladies and gentlemen.
> Shake him, stretch by the neck and set him down,
> —He'll do the rest. Yes!
> He'll make you laugh, he'll make you sigh, si—igh.
> He'll make you want to dance, and dance—

Here you are, ladies and gentlemen, Sambo,
The dancing doll.
—Buy one for your baby. Take him to your girl friend and
    she'll love you, loove you!
He'll keep you entertained. He'll make you weep sweet—
Tears from laughing.
Shake him, shake him, you cannot break him
For he's Sambo, the dancing, Sambo, the prancing,
Sambo, the entrancing, Sambo Boogie Woogie paper doll.
And all for twenty-five cents, the quarter part of a dollar . . .
Ladies and gentlemen, he'll bring you joy, step up and meet
    him,
Sambo, the—"[11]

The jangling, performing doll danced, pranced, and grinned.
The grin was crucial to its play. "We like to picture the Negro as
grinning to us," Bernard Wolfe cogently surmised in his assess-
ment of Uncle Remus, "and always the image of the Negro—as
we create it—signifies some bounty for us. Eternally the Negro
gives—but (as they say in the theater) *really gives*—grinning from
ear to ear."[12] The grin beguiled the culture and obscured the reality; but it was an art form in itself.

The entertaining grin was just one aspect of a large notion, the
presumption that Sambo was an overgrown child at heart. And as
children are given to impetuous play, humorous antics, docile
energies, and uninhibited expressiveness, so too one could locate
in Sambo identical traits. Thus, the American national jester was
a childlike figure whose enticing abilities centered on working *and*
entertaining, producing *and* laughing, servicing *and* grinning.

On occasion, there appeared a female Sambo. For a variety of
reasons, not the least of which was the refusal of men to allow in
women the ability to create humor, the black woman only was
occasionally fit into the mold. Men posed a far more complex and
trying challenge. To effect power over males was to control their
women and children.

Sambo was an extraordinary type of social control, at once
extremely subtle, devious, and encompassing. To exercise a high

degree of control meant also to be able to manipulate the full range of humor; to create, ultimately, an insidious type of buffoon. To make the black male into an object of laughter, and, conversely, to force him to devise laughter, was to strip him of masculinity, dignity, and self-possession. Sambo was, then, an illustration of humor as a device of oppression, and one of the most potent in American popular culture. The ultimate objective for whites was to effect mastery: to render the black male powerless as a potential warrior, as a sexual competitor, as an economic adversary.

As an art form in the popular culture, Sambo had virtually no peers and few challengers. There were, to be sure, serious questions regarding the stereotype's authenticity. Over the centuries there were those who railed against the image and its acceptance by a majority of the populace. Yet their energies were not enough to prevent the figure from assuming iconical proportions.

In the twentieth century, Sambo came under the careful scrutiny of social scientists who wrestled with the problem of his authenticity and characteristics—but mainly in relation to the plantation system. Stanley Elkins first posed the psychological problem of assessing the connection between the system and black personality in *Slavery: A Problem in American Institutional and Intellectual Life*.[13] His conclusion, which wavered between childishness and dependency as the dominant response, brought the issue into sharp focus. Elkins's work had an impact beyond the scholars' domain. William Styron's novel *The Confessions of Nat Turner*,[14] awarded the Pulitzer Prize for Literature, drew heavily upon Elkins's thoughts.

Many other social scientists, however, extracted different Afro-American responses from the plantation culture. David B. Davis aptly noted in *The Problem of Slavery in Western Culture*[15] that slave societies often equated their slaves with children or animals. In Eugene Genovese's pertinent works, particularly *Roll, Jordan, Roll: The World the Slaves Made*,[16] religion became the organizing force for blacks as they grappled with the problem of accommodation and resistance. More pointed was John Blassingame's *The Slave*

Community,[17] which trenchantly argued that Sambo was a necessary survivalist tool in circumstances of entrapment, a clever, complicated form of behavior. A consequence of this action was to make it appear that Sambo was, in effect, the essence of the black male. Nevertheless, many southern whites and blacks understood that a terribly serious game, a game with defined roles, was being conducted for the maintenance of a system of complex relationships. Finally, George M. Frederickson, in his incisive study *The Black Image in the White Mind,*[18] argued that white inventiveness in forestalling an egalitarian biracial society brought an insistence on both Sambo and "savage" images, so that the elimination of one would immediately trigger the other.

Little attention has been directed to the extensive role of the image and its fact and form throughout the culture and its connection to stereotyping. Fewer still have wrangled with the intricacies of humor in this instance and its relationship to an American iconical type. Sambo's reach was extraordinary, affected other minority images, and to a degree still lingers in the contemporary period. There were times when Sambo was more dignified and elegant, even intelligent, witty, and shrewd, but he was always Sambo. There is no doubt, moreover, that the image changed over the decades, that the gross caricature of the nineteenth century gave way to the more natural look of the present period, that the buffoonish names and funny dialect mostly disappeared because of a sensitivity brought about by Afro-American pressure and the generational revolt of the 1960s. Yet there should be little doubt that aspects of Sambo live on in the white mind and show through the crevices of American culture in subtle and sophisticated ways. For the uniqueness of the situation was that the black male was regarded as worker *and* entertainer, producer *and* performer, regardless of region or class. Black women, too, were aspects of this same stereotyping process, but their image in the culture was far more complex. Whites were unwilling to totally negate their role as the matrix of family structure. A serious and respectable mien accompanied the image of black women, thus limiting their humorous roles.

The creation of Sambo was ultimately intended to subordinate a minority group. The longer it persisted, the more believable the image became, and the more easily it was transmitted to succeeding generations. The history of the Afro-American as Sambo—and Sambo as the national jester—bespeaks the incredibly powerful function of imagery.

2

As His Name Is, So Is He

He that filches from me my good name
Robs me of that which not enriches him,
And leaves me poor indeed.
　　　　　　　—Shakespeare, *Othello*

I would like to point out . . . that I wasn't born
Malcolm Little. Little is the name of the slave master
who owned one of my grandparents during slavery, a white man,
and the name Little has handed down to my grandfather,
to my father, and to me. But after hearing the teaching
of the Honorable Elijah Muhammad, and realizing that I'm not
an Englishman, I gave the Englishman back his name; and
since my own had been stripped from me, hidden from me,
and I don't know it, I use X. . . .
　　　　　　　　　　—Malcolm X

Sambo was initially a name among names.

Names reflect a mixture of converging forces, among them symbolic connections, religious convictions, and projective references. Since they are frequently associated with status or standing, special care in their selection has frequently been counseled. "A good name is better than precious ointment" is the counsel of *Ecclesiastes* 7:1. Through the centuries philosophers have spoken to their import. "The beginning of all instruction," wrote Antithenes in the fifth century B.C., "is the study of names." And Confucius said that the "rectification of names" is the primary function of the state: "If names are not correct, language will not be in accordance with the truth of things."

The extraordinary function of naming another being is ubiquitous and possesses secular and magical implications. To the ancient Egyptians, one of the eight parts that made up a person was his name, without which the individual and his afterlife would be destroyed. Native American tribes, and various culture groups in Tibet, believed that sickness was the consequence of an improper name, reflecting George Herbert's maxim in 1640 that "an ill wound is cured, not an ill name." To the Tibetans and the tribes the cure hinged upon the designation of a more befitting name.

In the early Christian church, cognomen change was one of the most risky and symbolic of individual acts. To announce their conversion, the early Christians assumed a new name at the baptismal ceremony. The Church recognized the mystical bond of a name by declaring that only the names of martyrs and saints were acceptable at the baptismal rite. Certain names were forbidden to the Christians. At the Nicene Council in A.D. 325, the Church declared that taking the names of heathen gods was prohibited. Centuries later, the Church of England also forbade naming children after those of heathen origin. And Hebrews disallow the names of living relatives for an infant's appellation.

A particular aspect of the naming practice also explains its acute concern: it is usually a singular act. Only infrequently do people rename themselves, and even less frequently can they name another outside the familial group. Women have generally been an exception to the rule, in that until the late twentieth century they assumed a new surname upon marriage; like newborns, they were in no position to challenge the choice of their new designation. All this points up the initial power adults possess over children: they establish their earliest identity.

Yet, in the history of naming, perhaps the least practiced act, one fraught with extraordinary meaning, is the naming or renaming of an *adult*. And what might be said of the naming or renaming of millions of adults? That it is an act of magnitude indicating unique circumstances is quite clear. What has not been so clear, however, is the impact of such an occurrence in psychological terms. The most recent and instructive example was the vast renaming that occurred in the contacts between Western Europeans and Africans during the slave trade, when one group was able to establish its hegemony over the other and in the process attempted to re-create designations in its own image.

African names and geographical locations were not unfamiliar to European traders of the pre-slave-trade period. The shippers and merchants who plied the west coast ports were generally knowledgeable in the various African dialects and had conducted limited diplomatic relations. With the development of the slave trade, the diplomatic interactions swiftly increased, and some African chieftains were feted at European royal courts, which employed linguists to work out the complex transactions necessary in the trade. "There was a person then present," wrote captain William Snelgrave in his dealings with the king of Dahomey in 1727, " . . . whose name was Zunglar, a cunning fellow, who had formerly been the King's agent for several years at Whidaw; where I had seen him in my former voyages."[1]

Moreover, the knowledge of African naming procedures was considerable. John Atkins in his *Voyage to Guinea, Brasil, and the West Indies* gave a detailed accounting of Cape Corso naming practices. "They give Names by their Children," he accurately noted, "mostly by the days of the Week born on, Quashee, Yeday, Cunjo, that is Sunday, Monday, Tuesday, etc. and at Manhood, change it to something expressive of their Disposition: Aquerro, Occu, Yocatee, Tittwee, like a Parrot, Lion, Wolf, etc."[2]

In their dealings with Africans, Europeans recognized and recorded given names and titles. The Royal African Company records contain numerous legal documents in which African names are duly noted, even disputes between slaves. A complaint brought before an official in 1703, for example, identifies "Quashoo a black carpenter one of the Company's slaves" who had illegally sold his wife's son, Braboo, a charge that was upheld.[3]

Europeans were not only familiar with African nomenclature

but at times rather amused by the African inability to comprehend the Western style of surnames. Captain Theodore Canot, a slaver, was piqued when an African prince with whom he was doing business named him "Powder," which the tribe spontaneously changed to "Storee" as they gazed into his warehouse:

> It is a pleasant fancy of the natives, who find our surnames rather difficult of pronounciation, while they know very little of the Christian calender, to baptize a newcomer with some title, for which any chattel or merchandise that strikes their fancy is apt to stand godfather. My exploit with the prince christened me "Powder" on the spot; but when they saw my magnificent establishment, beheld the wealth of my warehouse, and heard the name of "store," I was forthwith whitewashed into "Storee."[4]

Despite the knowledge relating to African tongues and practices, however, records kept during the slave trade generally omitted given African names. Whether it was the vast numbers, disparate dialects, shortage of interpreters, or underlying prejudices that made it difficult to list specific names, the slavers chose not to include them in the accounts. Yet since maritime regulations, as well as the demand for accurate bookkeeping, necessitated detailed listings, the traders opted for either religious or practical solutions to the problem of record keeping. What resulted was the renaming of millions of Africans, an initial step in the rejection of African culture and the reidentification of the African along Western lines. Thus, an integral aspect of personal identity quickly faded at the moment of capture, a loss made more permanent with sale and resale. Many captured Africans underwent several renaming procedures in these transactions.

In the absence of extensive naming, the accountants listed Africans as articles of merchandise under a variation of the racial term "Negro"—"Negroes," "Negrose," "Negors," "Neigors," "Negros," "Neggars"—but also as "Slaves" and "Blacks." Phrases such as "Cargo of Slaves" or "Import of Slaves" became commonplace descriptions in business correspondence and ship manifests. Instructions to captain Marmaduke Goodhand in 1685, for instance, directed him to receive payment for a "Freight of the

Negroes." Occasionally merely the continental designation "Africa" was employed.[5]

Shipping companies maintained accurate files of African tribal ancestry, merchants who transacted sales, date of expected payment, type of currency, and loss of monies due to death—but again no names. The only designations were of those Europeans involved in the trade.

While African anonymity prevailed throughout the slave process, sickness and death aboard the ships in midpassage were duly recorded. "A stout man slave leaped overboard and drowned himself," wrote captain Peter Blake. "This day died one Negro man: some more wee have sick . . . " was Captain Doegood's description. Moreover, the causes of illness and death were specifically identified: "dropsy," "flux," "Wasting," "wasted to Nothing and soe died," "Consumption and Wormes," "dyed of a feavour," "Departed this Life Suddenly," "Departed this life of Convulsion Fitts." Most ship captains logged deaths in their manifests in a commonly used phrase of unintended symbolic meaning: ". . . a neagerman dep'ted this life whoe died suddenly. . . ."[6]

Even compassionate descriptions of conditions aboard the slave ships were made within the context of namelessness. Captain John Newton, in his *Journal of a Slave Trader,* wrote movingly of the space allotted for the slaves. "Let it be observed, that the poor creatures, thus cramped for want of room, are likewise in irons, for the most part both hands and feet, and two together, which makes it difficult for them to turn or move, to attempt either to rise or to lie down, without hurting themselves, or each other. . . . Dire is the tossing, deep the groans."[7]

Contact aboard the slave ships often required communication between the crew and the Africans. Stuck with this situation, Europeans hastily devised ways of addressing the slaves. "I suppose they all had names in their own dialect," wrote Edward Manning, a young seaman on the *Thomas Watson* in 1860, "but the effort required to pronounce them was too much for us, so we picked out our favorites and dubbed them 'Mainstay,' 'Cat-head,' 'Bull's-eye,' 'Rope-yearn,' and various other sea phrases."[8] At times a sardonic attitude motivated crew members. James Arnold, the surgeon aboard the slaver *The Ruby,* wrote in 1787:

> The first slave that was traded for, after the brig anchored at the Island of Bimbo, was a girl about fifteen who was promptly named Eve, for it was usual on slave ships to give the names of Adam and Eve to the first man and woman brought on board.[9]

Prior to their entry as permanent slaves in the colonies, then, to the Europeans many Africans were nameless. "The word nameless, especially in poetry and in much prose," novelist William Saroyan noted, "signifies an alien, unknown, and almost always unwelcome condition, as when, for instance, a writer speaks of 'a nameless sorrow.'"[10]

Not all Africans arrived nameless in the New World. The Spaniards went to considerable effort to baptize their slaves aboard ship and present them with Christian names. However, unless the Africans came from the West Indies, permanent naming in the southern colonies usually commenced with their arrival and permanent settlement. At this juncture, as Saroyan observed, "the fact of being named at all, however meaningless," was thereby "lifted out of an area of mystery, doubt, or undesirably into an area in which belonging to everyone else is taken for granted. . . ."[10]

Being lifted out of an aura of mystery was not so simple for the Africans. The English and Spanish slave systems had a significant impact on names. Of the initial group of Africans brought to Jamestown in 1619, only eleven of the names were known, and these indicate antecedent Spanish baptism. These included "Anthony," "Frances," "Fernando," "Madelina," "Bastiaen," "Paulo," and "Isabella." Over half of the first Africans to disembark in Virginia had already undergone a significant name change, indicating that the practice was widespread in the slave trade. One historian has suggested that there exists a "strong possibility that the majority of slaves brought into the Colonies prior to 1700 had Spanish names."[11] This may be an exaggeration, for many Africans went unnamed in the official censuses, and others were simply overlooked.

In any case, the Spanish was often replaced by English appellations: Juan became John and Maria became Mary. Those Africans who had entered the colonies with Spanish or Portuguese names in the early decades of the seventeenth century did not extend the practice to their children. Anthony and Isabella, both of African extraction, named their child "William." This distinction between the first two generations is striking in the inventory of 1644. The records list "one negroe man called Anthonio. . . . One negroe woman called Mitcahell (Michaela). . . . One negroe woman, Couchazella. . . . One negroe woman, Palassa. . . . One negro girle Mary 4 years old. . . . One negro called Eliz: 3 years old."[12] The adults' names apparently derived from the Spanish, the children's from the English.

In an apparent attempt to create an African in their image, the early English settlers clearly altered the Spanish cognomens. Among the first boatload of Africans were two Johns and a William, Edward, and Margarett, which in all probability had been Anglicized from Juan, Guillen, Eduardo, and Margarita. Several names were binational, as illustrated by an African called "John Pedro." What emerges is an extraordinary reluctance on the part of the English, in the earliest interactions with the Africans, to accommodate to Spanish and African names.

Two censuses taken in Virginia in the 1620s further demonstrate the denial of African name identities. The census of 1624 lists twenty-two living blacks in the colony and one as having died in the previous year. "What is most striking about the appearance of these blacks in the census is that although most of them had been in America for five years, none is accorded a last name and almost half are recorded with no name at all," observed Alden Vaughan in "Blacks in Virginia: A Note on the First Decade." In the census Africans were listed as "one negar," "A Negors Woman," or just "negors," A comparison with Caucasians in that census is instructive: few of the whites had incomplete names, and where parts were omitted other vital information was provided, such as "Symon, an Italien."

The following year a more exacting and complete tabulation of the colony was undertaken. Twenty-three blacks were enumerated, but again the information was scanty in contrast with whites. Several given names are listed, and only one black possessed a full name, a "John Pedro, a Negar aged 30." Equally significant in both censuses were the data preceding the names. Conspicuously missing from the rolls of the blacks was such important information as age, arrival date, ship of passage, possessions, and food staples—information that appeared alongside white names. Despite their having been in the colony for six years, moreover, none of the Africans was mentioned as being free. All were placed under the heading of "servants." That blacks were placed at the end of the lists of servants, occasionally with a Native American, suggests a distinct status of inferiority.[13]

The general omission of family names for Africans in the censuses of the 1620s was a common practice that was continued throughout the period, and that eventually would affect the Sambo image. Only a handful of blacks were accorded surnames: Andrew Morroe, Philip Gowen, Robert Traynes, John Phillip, Bostian Ken, Zippora Potter, and several others whose names were totally Anglicized. Not all blacks, however, remained single-named. In Virginia, at least, the small group of free blacks in the latter decades of the seventeenth century were able to call themselves by both given and family names, which demonstrated the relationship between status and name identification. The names were a composite of English and Spanish origins.[14]

But the majority of Africans were designated by their skin color, status, or relation to owner. Court records were full of such phrases: in 1672 a suit was brought against "Betty Negro" for insulting a white male and his mother; "Wonn Negro" testified in a witchcraft case in 1679; "Mary Black" was tried, convicted, and imprisoned for witchcraft in 1692 (she petitioned and was released the following year).

More often a single name, sometimes followed by a description was used to identify the person. Thus, "Hannah" was convicted (and later acquitted) of stealing (1679); "Jugg" was whipped for fornication (1660), as were "Grace" and "Juniper" (1674); "A Mulatta named Manuel" was listed in another case. "Mingo the Negro" was a witness in a suit involving warehouse arson in 1680.

There was the case of John Barnes's "negar maide servant" (1653). Another situation brought "Will" into court in 1673: "Whereas Will, a runaway Negroe Suspected to have Lett out of Prison a Negroe Condemend the last Court and Confesseth that he did See the Negroe breake Loose out of irons. . . . " "Angell a negro servant" sued for her freedom in 1673. Occasionally there were full designations, such as "a negro named John Punch," who in 1649 was ordered by the court "to serve his said master or his assigns for the time of his natural life here or elsewhere."[15]

Spanish and English appellations, then, took the place of African names. In all of the inventories of the era, only a handful of names suggesting an African past appeared: "Samba," "Mookinga," "Quash," and "Palassa." Absent from the records, at least, was any hint that a portion of the population was of African origin. Absent as well was any special status the Africans possessed in their own societies. And by the latter half of the seventeenth century the legal term "slave" would come to define the African in Virginia and Maryland.

Nor did the African fare much better in the northern territories. The black names survived with a distinctly English flavor. On occasion, though, recorders listed cognomens that were unmistakably African. "Quesaba," "Quash," "Quaco," "Sambo" were some of the names in censuses in New York City and Charlestown, Massachusetts, prior to 1800. Dutch names in New York City also reflect the widespread practice of name alteration. Africans were recorded as "Piet," "Saar," "Dien," and similar Dutch names.[16]

What is important about the renaming practices is not only that Africans were given European appellations but particularly that they were denied the Christian custom of surnames. In the New York Conspiracy Trial of 1741, for example, 20 whites, more than 150 blacks, and a Native American were charged with insurrection. *All* of the whites but only *one* of the blacks had a family name. Intriguingly, the sole black with a full name was easily identifiable: he was known as "Curaçao Dick." Although the white defendants were listed according to occupation, the blacks were filed under masters or owners, without reference to work skills or position.[17]

In smaller communities in the North the situation was not much different. George Sheldon's history of Deerfield, Massachusetts, notes that five adult slaves were baptized in 1735, of whom three were eventually admitted to church in full communion. The event was recorded in the church documents:

> Aug. 29, 1736 Pompey Negro and Rebecca his wife
> Feb. 27, 1736–7 Cesar, servant to Ebenezer Wells

Antisocial behavior was a primary subject of churchly concern, and acts were recorded for divine evaluation as well as for communal demerits. Blacks in Deerfield who were reproached for their disruptive character were listed by their given names, preceded by the names of their owners.

But not all blacks received partial names. The first known slave in Deerfield was Robert Tigo. Little is known of Tigo except that he was "a Negro servant to Mr. John Williams" and died on May 11, 1695. Tigo, however, was an anomaly. When two other servants of John Williams were "joyned in Marriage by Reverend John Williams" on June 4, 1700, their names were entered merely as "Frank and Parthena."

From the late seventeenth century to the mid-eighteenth century, blacks in Deerfield were largely addressed without family designations. Estate records provide a contrast with public documents. At his death in 1732, captain John Sheldon left seven slaves, who were appraised as part of his estate:

Coffee his wife and child	£130
Boy George	80
Boy Coffee	80
Boy Robin	70
Girl Sue	60[18]

In their earliest and subsequent encounters with Africans, the English made little attempt to learn the names of their captives and workers and thus severely restricted the Africans' sense of identity and their own understanding. It can be argued that captives, by their very servile and demeaned position, lose a considerable portion of their identity in the overall process of being passed from one party to another. But in the tight quarters of the seaside communities in the seventeenth century, many Africans must have told the English their names. That many settlers largely refused to heed this basic sense of self attests to their denigration of the African. Although this type of denial was not unique to the English, failure to view the Africans in their own context seriously affected the Africans' ultimate standing in the community.

By contrast, the English were relatively open to, if not intrigued by, various aspects of North American Indian culture and made concerted attempts to comprehend Native American designations, titles, and names. They were, after all, outsiders in a strange and hostile setting. Survival depended upon quickly learning all of the pitfalls as well as the advantages of the terrain. Yet the interaction occurred for other cogent reasons as well, not the least of which was the English recognition of Native American strength and power. As James Axtell understood, "The shifting frontier between wilderness and civilization seems an unlikely place for a school, but the cultures that meet there never fail to educate each other."[19]

In reports, diaries, and letters the English spelled and translated Native American names, places, tribes, crops, and more. The spellings of these words varied according to the scribe—John Rolfe listed his wife's name as "Pokahuntas"—but the important fact is that Native American languages were acknowledged, sometimes adopted, and communicated to others by the English. Native American leaders' names—as "Powhatan" or "Pohatan," "Opechancanough," and others—appear with regularity in the dispatches of John Smith and other Englishmen. Smith writes of the rivers "Wichcocomoco" and "Kusharawaocke." Difficult tribe names are registered in the *Records of the Virginia Company:* "Quiyoughquohanocks," "Chickokonini"; and by Smith in his records: "Soraphanigh," "Nause," "Arsek," and "Nautaquake." Ralph Hamor, secretary to the Virginia Colony, wrote in 1615, in *A True Discourse of the Present State of Virginia,* of meeting with a group of Native Americans "who walked up and down to us and amongst us, the best of them inquiring for our Weroance or king. . . . "[20]

For good reason, Native American geography was carefully

mapped and detailed. Over three hundred years later, Massachusetts maps direct residents to such coastal inlets as Waquoit Bay and to the beaches at Sippewisset, Mananhant, and Wingaersheek. If the English made similar serious efforts to learn and record African designations, the documents do not show them. At the same time, African onomastic survivals occurred despite the conscious or indifferent actions of the English to deny them. As J. L. Dillard has significantly noted, "there is evidence of the way in which white influence reshaped the surface of black onomastics without affecting the underlying structure in the translations of the day-names" of West Africans.[21]

That the Africans attempted to retain continuity with the past, however, is quite clear; and their efforts were partially successful. The use of many West African day-names abounded in various guises in the seventeenth and eighteenth centuries, though often beyond English awareness of their meaning or signification. Ayuba Suleiman Ibrahima Diallo of Bondu, a merchant who served as a slave for two years in Maryland in the 1730s but eventually made his way back to Africa after being emancipated and brought to England, was given the name of "Simon." He discarded this name in favor of "Job Ben Solomon," the Biblical title being the English equivalent of "Ayuba."[22]

Many slaves fought against the recasting of their original names. Lorenzo Dow Turner, in his study of slaves from Benin who worked in the coastal region between Georgetown, South Carolina, and Jacksonville, Florida, noted that a majority of "littoral" blacks possessed two personal names. One, a Christian name of European derivation, was reserved for whites; the other was of African origin and expressed a personal preference.[23]

The frustration of the slaveowners was evident in this connection as they attempted to recapture runaway slaves. "Run away," said an announcement in the *Georgia Gazette*, June 3, 1767:

TWO NEW NEGROE YOUNG FELLOWS:
one of them . . . computed eighteen years of age, of the Fallah country; slim made, and calls himself Golaga, the name given here *Abel;* the other a black fellow . . . computed seventeen years

of age, of the Suroga country, calls himself Abbrom, the name
given here Bennet.[24]

Personal struggles were unceasing. Paul Cuffee, the dynamic
shipping merchant of early nineteenth-century Massachusetts, was
one of the few blacks who managed to replace his surname, "Slo-
cum," which derived from his former owner. In 1778 he selected
the name "Cuffee," after his father's day-name, which in West
Africa means "male born on Friday." Day-names were an African
practice, and "Cuffee" was perhaps one of the most common of
the day-names.[25]

Alex Haley's "furtherest-back-person"—his Kunte clan blood
relation who was captured while chopping wood near his village in
West Africa in 1767 and enslaved in Virginia—was another poi-
gnant example of attempted name retention. Given the name
"Toby" by his owner, he constantly protested when the other
slaves referred to him in this manner. Repeating over and again
that his name was "Kin-tay," he was attempting to maintain tribal
roots. In fact, his name was "Kunta," and he was descended from
the Kunte clan in the Gambian region. Undeterred by efforts to
eliminate his past, Kunta repeated not only his name but also vital
facts of his background to "Kizzy," his daughter:

> As she grew up her African daddy often showed her different
> things, telling her what they were in his native tongue. Pointing
> at a banjo, for example, the African uttered "ko"; or pointing at
> a river near the plantation, he would way, "Kamby Bolong."
> Many of the strange words started with a "k" sound, and the
> little, growing Kizzy learned gradually that they identified differ-
> ent things.[26]

In many ways, some overt but others purposefully hidden,
blacks managed to retain certain African cognomen styles.
Because of poor bookkeeping practices, as well as ignorance of
African ways, it is highly probable, as J. L. Dillard has surmised,
that "there were many more West African names which went unre-
corded than there were ever put on paper."[27]

Once they had the opportunity, free southern blacks moved
quickly to alter their names. "Free Negroes," wrote Ira Berlin in

Slaves Without Masters, "commonly celebrated emancipation by taking a new name." Ex-slaves not only eliminated their classical or comical given names but further added a surname.[28]

So did many plantation slaves. Slaves undertook to make themselves more respectable by taking their masters' names, but, as Eugene Genovese has noted, in one region at least slaves assumed the names of another slaveholding family held in high repute. The places where slave surnames prevailed were essentially those of greater community stability. Upon emancipation, during and immediately following the Civil War, freed men and women either maintained and legalized names already assumed or proceeded to rename themselves.[29]

An undergirding sense of awareness and anger propelled many Africans in their quest of name retention; yet it was not enough to prevent changes of major proportions throughout the colonies. Stripped of status and unable to defend their culture, much less to communicate its intricate and subtle ways, the Africans found themselves in an extremely vulnerable position. Their weakness was a consequence not only of a captive situation but of the character of their captivity. Previous titles, places, family background, and African skills meant little in an economy that demanded brawn and durability. Sometimes the name was ironic against the backdrop of slavery. Olaudah Equiano, who was kidnapped as a boy in the 1750s, bought his freedom, wrote his memoirs, and was active in the British antislavery movement, noted the significance of his name: "I was named Olaudah, which in our language signifies vicissitude, or fortune also; one favoured, and having a loud voice, and well spoken."[30]

It is possible to garner from the renamed Africans the expectations and projections the English and colonists had for their subordinate class, not only in the selections themselves but also in the manner in which they were recorded. Slave and free blacks, for instance, were accorded different status, the former frequently being incorporated with the family pets and animals. In fact, it was often difficult to distinguish between the slave and animal names in probate records—but by their appraised values it was possible to know them.

Regardless of place, however, certain definable patterns merge in the naming process. To fulfill their religious mandate, and to instill a sense of newly acquired importance, the English essentially turned to Biblical sources for their names. Peter, John, James, Daniel, Abram, Abraham, Jacob, Samuel, Thomas, and Joseph were highly favored male names. For females, it was Mary, Hannah, Sarah, Dorcas, and Tabitha that prevailed. But a classical and literary style also flourished. More blacks were whimsically dubbed Caesar than perhaps any other classical name. Also popular were Cato, Pompey, Jupiter, and Nero. Females were called Diana, Dido, Phoebe, and Venus.

When unconcerned about the past, whites turned to reference points closer to home. Here geographical sites and locations served as the basis for many names. Towns, boroughs, cities, rivers, ports, islands, and other geographical names came into extensive use; blacks were named Baltimore, Boston, Bridgewater, Bristoll, Cambridge, Carolina, Dallas, Essex, Lancaster, Limehouse, Marlborough, New Port, Oxford, Portsmouth, Richmond, Salisbury, Warwick, Willoughby, and Isle of Wright *(sic)*. A not uncommon practice was to name slaves after the colony or state in which they suddenly found themselves; many were called Georgia, Carolina, Verginia, Misourie, Missouria, Indiana, Lousianna, Jersey, Tennessee.

Occasionally the locale of the slave was retained, as in the descriptive names of blacks who were indicted for participating in the New York Slave Conspiracy: "Curaçao Dick," "Cuba, a wench," "Cajoe alias Africa," and "Jamaica"; one slave, "Congo Pomp," hanged himself on Cape Cod after escaping from his master in the 1660s.[31]

In Africa it was a practice to name someone after an unusual or spontaneous event. In the colonies, the names suggest a less serious intent. One slave was named "Last Night" because of his master's arousal from sleep by the announcement of Clementine's having given birth the previous evening. Another was "Fed" after having been breastfed.[32] Spontaneous responses on the part of owners formed the basis of a variety of names: "Notice," "Smart," "Tomboy," "Seas," "Holiday," "Fayerweather," "Lies," "Loos," "Present," "Obey," "Obedient." Others were more directly related to occupation or skill: "Boatswain," "Baker," "Dyer," "Gardener," "Miller," "Sowers," "Tooler."

Titular and eminent names were less frequently invoked. For humorous reasons, or because the person possessed an aura of dignity, slaves were sometimes called "Prince," "Duke," "Esquire," "Earl," "Gouvenour," "Coloniel," "General." Names of prominent colonists were downplayed, but there was an occasional English politician, such as Cromwell, after whom an African was named. On the other hand, popular Revolutionary leaders, especially Washington and Jefferson, had their names liberally bestowed.

While whites did not complain of slaves taking their surnames, the adoption was not always received with pride. Cotton Mather, the sensitive Puritan leader, was quite vexed when he learned that a slave had been named after him. "A Lieutenant of a Man of War whom I am a Stranger to, designing to putt an indignity upon me, has called *Negro-Slave* by the Name of COTTON-MATHER," he complained.[33]

Names were thus culled from a myriad of sources, some suggesting a serious attitude, others a frivolous. Regardless of intent, renaming millions of grown beings could not but have an impact upon the process of subjugation. Nowhere was this better seen than in the degree of aggressive humor that motivated the renamers. Even when surnames were appended, a considerable proportion of black names throughout the colonies were strikingly comical or suggested ridicule. Some were outright ludicrous. Black males were dubbed "Fiscal," "Apollo," "Black Fat," "General Washington," "Nausea," "Limmerick," "Polite," "Valentine," "Wisdom," "Fortune," "Lemon Peel," "Sham," "Ventured," "Pomp Liberty," "Caesar," "Cupid," "Fodder," "Such," and "Cow." Similarly, females were termed "Fiscal Fanny," "Lies," "Gabby," "Paddle," "Present," "Mooning," "Peachy,"

"Loos," "Nutty," "Prosper," "Spice," "Grief," "Chatt," "Icy," "Marvel," "Ails," "Means," "Moaning," "Frolic," "Gamesome," and "Strumpet." Exaggerated titles, such as "Prince" and "Princess," "King" and "Queen," "Squire" and "Dutchess," were utilized for their buffoonish effect. Names derived from English authors were employed in this way; Africans became known as "Shakespeare," "Marlowe," and "Milton." Even age added to the comic style. The descriptions "big" and "little" often referred to age rather than physical stature and led to such appellations as "Big Patience" and "Little Patience."[34]

The list of ludicrous names was expanded in the nineteenth century as men and women were called "Bituminous," "Snowrilla," "Vanilla," "Precious Pullins," "Jeremiah Chronicles," "Magnolia Zenobia Pope," and, a play on the fruit lemon, "Lemon Brown," "Lemon Freeze," "Lemon Custer." A factor in the determination of names apparently centered on personal peculiarities. Nicknames abounded throughout the country: "Baldy," "Bellow," "Bold," "Boney," "Brag," "Crip," "Grizzy," "Hardtimes," "Fly-up-de-Creek," "Junior," "Mangy," "Muss," "Racket," "Senior," "Short," "Tarter," "Bitsey," "Happy," "Mourning," "Peachy," and, finally, "After Dark," who was so named "because he was so black that 'you can' shu'um fo' dayclean.'"[35]

It is difficult to assess what proportion of slave names, or nonslave to a lesser extent, were comical or purposefully buffoonish. There were many blacks who were given what was regarded as a proper, Christian name for the period, but derogated by a nickname or affected moniker. It was not uncommon for whites to address blacks whom they did not know by a whimsical or funny tag, as in the use of "Uncle" and "Auntie." Later, as we shall see, certain stereotypically comical names became commonplace throughout the culture. What can be said is that blacks were vulnerable to white naming practices, yet also struggled to maintain African consciousness. Black name retention, as Herbert Gutman has indicated (*The Black Family in Slavery and Freedom, 1750–1925,* 1976,) was more tenacious and accomplished than previously had been assumed. But there is no question that one of the most insidious aspects of slavery was its oppressive humorous effects, names being just one link in a larger design.

Such name affectations were observed by outsiders. European travelers in the nineteenth century commented about their comedic tone. Typical was the diary entry by captain Frederick Marryat in 1839. "I have often been amused," he wrote of black servants attending both masters and mistresses in Virginia, "not only here, but during my residences in Kentucky, at the high-sounding Christian names which have been given to them. 'Byron, tell Ada to come here directly.' 'Now, *Telemachus,* if you don't leave *Calypso* alone, you'll get a taste of the *cow-hide.*' "[36]

Of the various comic names and titles, several had become highly popular by the nineteenth century. The winnowing process appears to have singled out the male names of "John," "George," "Pompey," "Sam," "Rastus," and "Sambo"; and those associated with hierarchical family position, namely, "Uncle," as in "Uncle Tom" and "Uncle Remus." Likewise, certain female names became fashionable: "Diana," "Mandy," "Dark Mear," "Brown Sugar"; and the family designation of "Auntie," including "Aunt Diana," "Aunt Mandy," and "Aunt Jemima." There would be regional difference, and particular names were more popular at different periods—"Rastus" was a special favorite of whites—but the one that became indelibly fixed as the male stereotype was "Sambo." Although "Sambo" winged his way in the popular culture in the early decades of the nineteenth century and remained until the post–World War II period, his antics could be seen as early as the Revolutionary period.

The roots of the name Sambo were both African and Hispanic; but the English may have had an important part in transposing it because of the name's easy pronunciation and natural ring. One source derived from the naming practices of at least three West African cultures:

Hausa sam bo   "name given the second son in a family";
            "name given to anyone called Muhammadu";
            "name of a spirit"

Mende sambo   "to disgrace"; "to be shameful"
Vai sam bo   "to disgrace"[37]

Moreover, the name also appears to have been used in other tribes; in some West African communities it was the name of one in power. Ayuba Suleiman Diallo of Bondu was a friend and schoolmate of King Sambo of Futa. Ayuba's memoirs of his capture and experiences as a slave, published in England in 1734, may have contributed to the name's familiarity in the colonies. In any case, the fact that he called his third child Sambo was at least indicative of the name as conveying a sense of dignity and meaning.[38] At the same time, as the Mende and Vai tribal uses clearly suggest, Sambo was also a term of derision.

As a proper name, Sambo was listed in the late-seventeenth-century enumerations of Africans in the colonies. An appraisement of Negroes taken aboard the ship *Margarett* in 1692–93, which unloaded its cargo in St. Mary's County, Maryland, included "2 Negrose Sambo and Jack."[39] Thereafter the name appears with some regularity throughout the eighteenth century. John Atkins wrote enigmatically of a black man who may have been in debt for drinking: "*Sambo* is gone, he never cares to treat with dry Lips, and as the Expence is in *English* Spirits of two Shillings a Gallon, brought partly for that purpose. . . . "[40] The name appeared several times in mid-century in separate regions. The New York census of 1755 lists a slave with that name as belonging to Issac Sibring in Kings County.[41] Several hundred miles away there was an announcement of three runaway slaves from an ironworks in Virginia, "all new Negroes who had not been above 8 months in the Country," one of whom was Sambo, a smallish thirty-year old man who could speak English "so as to be understood."[42] Toward the end of the century another call of a runaway slave appeared in the *South Carolina Gazette and General Advertiser*, "a negroe named Sambo, of the Guinea country, five feet four inches high, twenty-five years of age, pitted a little with the small pox. . . . "[43]

The name cropped up on numerous occasions in the early decades of the nineteenth century. In 1808, a play was published bearing his name, *Sambo and Toney: A Dialogue in Three Parts*. In the drama, an obedient and zealous Sambo chastises his close friend Toney for poor working habits, wayward behavior, and an irresponsible attitude.[44] A work circulated by a British author in the 1820s was entitled *Samboe: or, the African Boy*.[45] In her memoirs of plantation life, Mrs. Henry Rowe Schoolcraft mentioned the activities of "Nigger Sambo" who planned "to spend the morning catching fish."[46] A white Mississippi colonel overheard blacks use the name in a folk-rhyming session:

> "Is dat you, Sambo?" "No, dis am Cin."
> "You'se pooty good lookin', but you can't come in."[47]

On the surface, then, Sambo was not an uncommon name. At the same time, however, there was clearly a comical aspect attached to it. In the late eighteenth century, the name surfaced in humorous ways. Among the characters in English dramas playing in New York and Boston—Issac Jackman's *The Divorce* (1781) and J. Murdock's *Triumphs of Love* (1795)—were two actors dubbed Sambo, both of whom were used in comical fashion. No doubt the theatre was of English origin and the name Sambo had already become a white expression, for John Davis, a young Englishman in his early twenties, a sailor with a literary bent who traversed the seas and the country before Ohio was a state, generically referred to blacks in the South as "Sambo" and "Cuffy."[48]

By far the clearest exposition of the name in comical form, however, had appeared earlier, in the waning days of the Revolutionary War. Entering Richmond in 1781, British regulars captured several slaves from Thomas Jefferson's plantation. One was Issac, Jefferson's valet, who later recounted his experiences with the British officers. For inexplicable reasons, he told his interviewer in the 1840s, "one of the officers give Issac name Sambo," and then ordered him to perform, "all the time feedin him." They draped outlandish clothing on him, he recalled,

> put on a cocked hat on his head & a red coat on him & all laughed. coat a monstrous great big thing; when Issac was in it it couldn't see nothin of it but the sleeves dangling down.[49]

The English connection between name and comical form was certainly extensively used in the colonies in the decades preceding the nineteenth century. Whether the colonists themselves adopted this form in similar fashion at this time is somewhat unclear. It would be surprising if they had not imitated their overseas kin. That Americans did make name synonymous with form, and form with image, shortly thereafter there can be no doubt, and by the 1830s the name rolled off white lips with ease. "There Sambo led his steeds up the sides of a high bank, when lo!, the whole party came tumbling down, like so many hogsheads of tobacco rolled from a storehouse to the banks of the Ohio," wrote naturalist and painter John James Audubon on one of his many journeys in the Midwest. Shrugging off many white epithets, however, "Sambo . . . leaped on the naked back of one [horse], and, shewing his teeth, laughed at his master's curses."[50] The stereotypical configuration of the black male as a "Sambo" had preceded its specific labeling, but by the mid-nineteenth century the name and image were conjoined in a stereotypical marriage that was to last well into the mid-twentieth century.

This comical connection began to appear in music, in titles and in lyrics, in folk sayings and literature, and in thousands of artifacts. "Yah, yah, Sambo" was a popular phrase used in the minstrels, an expression that no doubt helped spread the name. Sheet music made the rounds of the country bearing such titles as "The Jolly Sambo" in the 1840s, "Sambo's Invitation" in the 1860s, "Sambo and His Banjo" in the 1890s—there was even *The Sambo Girl*, a musical in 1905. Children's games displayed the name Sambo prominently underneath a grinning child; stereoscopic slides featured men called Sambo; posters highlighted Sambo in script; postcards showed a smiling man dubbed Sambo; joke books featured Sambo on their covers and in the contents; and a children's book title became a trademark of the name. Helen Bannerman's *The Story of Little Black Sambo*, written in 1898, was not, in fact, in the "Sambo" tradition. Its title has misled many a reader. The Indian youth is no buffoon; on the contrary, he uses his wits to defeat the tigers. But the wording of the title, as well as the illustrations in several editions, was in keeping with the stereotypical pose.

Despite its popularity as the whites' symbol of the comic, there appears to be something amiss in explaining its transition from ordinary name to kinetic image. Surely there must be an additional factor, a word or phrase, an event perhaps, that initiated and/or buttressed the humorous content of the name.

Several historical inputs could have contributed to its comic preeminency, one English, the other Hispanic. It must be noted that "Sam" has traditionally been used in humorous fashion in English popular culture, a practice that carried over to American society. Throughout the slave period and beyond, Sam was one of the names whites applied to someone they thought comical. Sam and Sambo were obviously too close for the transition not to have occurred.

A more likely source, however, is a Hispanic word. In all probability the comic aspect of the name Sambo was extrapolated from the sixteenth-century word "zambo," which even in contemporary Hispanic cultures refers to a person who is bowlegged or knock-kneed. In short, a "zambo" is a type of monkey. Intriguingly, the term conveyed an almost identical meaning in another slave-trading country, Portugal.

The pejorative connection between animal and human, especially between monkey and African, has a historical etymology. It is a bias that has been maintained into the contemporary period. When anthropologist Pierre van den Berghe traveled to the Belgian Congo in the post–World War II years, he observed that the Belgians referred to the Congolese as "macaques," the word for rhesus monkeys.[51] It is conceivable that the Spanish and Portuguese slavers mocked the Africans by calling them "zamboes." It is not going too far to suggest that that English translated "zambo" into "sambo." In fact, it is possible that the West Indian slave traders had already begun the practice.

An 1883 folklore compilation, *Folk-Etymology: A Dictionary of . . .* , using language typical of the period, assumed this very transition. The author defined the name as being "The ordinary nickname for a negro, often mistaken as a pet name formed from 'Sam,' 'Samuel,' just as Chloe is almost a generic name for a female nigger, is really borrowed from his Spanish appellation 'zambo,' originally meaning bandy-legged, from Lat. 'scambus,' bow-legged, Greek 'skambos.' . . . "[52] Literal definitions of the name, in addition, reveal that it was used in racial contexts. In various Latin American societies, the terms "zambo" and "sambo" denoted a light-skinned person of mixed ancestry, either Negro and Indian, Negro and European, or Negro and Negro. The word was applied in this manner in the 1748 edition of *Earthquake Peru:* "Sambo de Mulatto, sprung from Negroes and Mulattoes; Sambo de Indian, sprung from Negroes and Indians. Giveros, the Offspring of Sambo Mulatto and Sambo Indians."[53]

The use of the name to signify mixed ancestry appears in various writings in the late eighteenth and nineteenth centuries. Captain John Stedman in his *Expedition to Surinam* (1796), an account of his trip to Guinea to subdue a revolt, wrote a member of his force, "One of the unhappy deserters, a samboe* [*a *sambo* is between a mulatto and a negro.]"[54] An 1831 *Webster's Dictionary* defined the term as "The offspring of a black person and a mulatto."[55]

But the name was not merely descriptive; it also conveyed a degraded place within society. Captain Frederick Marryat in the novel *Peter Simple* (1834) observed that "The pride of color is very great in the West Indies . . . ; a quadroon looks down upon a Sambo, that is half mulatto half negro, while Sambo looks in his turn looks down upon a nigger."[56] In his famous *Dictionary of the English Language* (1806) Samuel Johnson, though not pointedly employing the Sambo name, nevertheless defined the term "Mulatto" in a pejorative manner: "One begot between a white and a black, as a mule between different species of animals."[57] Similarly, the 1873 edition of the *Encyclopaedia Britannica* listed "Zambo" as "Any *half-breed,* but mostly the issue of Negro and Indian parents. . . . "[58]

Twentieth-century works have largely adhered to the definition of the name as meaning a person of mixed ancestry, but continued its derogatory sense as well. Gertrude Jobes, in the *Dictionary of Mythology, Folklore and Symbols,* wrote that Sambo was "A *pet* name given to the male offspring of a Negro and a Mulatto."[59] The 1953 Funk and Wagnalls *New Standard Dictionary of the English Language* laconically defined the name as "the offspring of a negro and a mulatto" and "a widely used nickname."[60] On the other hand, the third edition of Roget's *International Thesaurus,* in 1962, included the name under two categories; the first applied to a mixture, a mulatto, the second as a slang expression synynomous with "darky" and "pickaninny."[61]

Between the 1880s and 1920s, Sambo was the most widely used of all black male comic names, its closest rivals being Rastus and Uncle Remus. The rivalry was in name only, for its imagic form was hard-cast. The name appears to have lost some popularity in the twenties and was replaced by a more respectable-sounding nonblack one. Mark Sullivan, an important chronicler of the era, noted that "negroes had ceased to be called 'Sambo' and were coming to be addressed generically as 'George'; after Aunt Dinah, illiterate and happy in the kitchen. . . ."[62]

As observant as this statement was, however, it was not entirely accurate. Neither stereotypes nor their appellations are easily transformed or eliminated. Sambo in name made his appearance as a clown in a number of silent film subjects and was even the title of a series of all-black comedies produced in Philadelphia. The generic Sambo, in fact, was accorded considerable stature by one of the most prestigious of American historians. Samuel Eliot Morison, in his 1930 text, *The Growth of the American Republic,* a work that later expanded into several volumes which quickly became required reading in a substantial number of universities over the next decades, applied the name to blacks in his interpretation of slavery. Although he employed other racist terms to describe men and women, all in the lower case, Sambo was his major designation: "As for Sambo, whose wrongs moved the abolitionists to tears, there is some reason to believe that he suffered less than any other class in the South from its peculiar institution."[63]

Other names were adopted by whites in the following period,

the visually descriptive "Stepin Fetchit" ranking high because of the movies featuring the antics of Lincoln Perry Monroe. Sambo hung on, however. That a restaurant bearing the name appeared in California in the post–World War II period, a pancake house that managed to franchise throughout the country amid growing protests, attested to its attraction and acceptance in white culture. The crowning figure atop the restaurant was a lad in an Indian turban, but his facial features were in the typical exaggerated Sambo style.

Not until the fierce demands of Black Power in the 1960s and early '70s was the name finally eliminated from the popular culture. By that time, Afro-Americans, in alliance with frightened librarians, had managed to purloin or force the removal of *The Story of Little Black Sambo* from the shelves, along with other Sambo-type books. Even the Sambo figure above the restaurants that bore his name was altered to resemble an Indian youth.

Sambo in name was laid to rest.

Sambo the image could be found stomping around in the cultural cellar.

3

Ladies and Gentlemen: Your Attention, Please. Would You Welcome The First Truly American Entertainer, SAMBO!!

ACT ONE

In the South: The Entertaining Slave

> Then there is your plantation nigger . . . [who] is too an oddity
> and sometimes possesses some whit and humor, which are most
> usually exhibited in his songs. . . . They seem a happy race of
> beings & if you did not know it you would never imagine they
> were slaves. The loud laugh, the clear dancing eye, the cheerful
> face show that in this sad world of sin & sorrow they know but
> very few.—Henry Benjamin Whipple, *Bishop Whipple's Southern
> Diary, 1834–1844*

The cultural fusion that begat Sambo was as tangled and peculiar
as any in history. Sambo the performer was a major event in the
long course of entertainment, whose unfolding requires—as do
twentieth-century visual media—a high degree of suspended
disbelief. Image and reality were often theatrically interwoven. In
this particular instance, the theatricality was compounded by the
fact that what the audience often saw was not only an actual performance but at times their own imaginations projected and
enacted. When there was more of a reality, more of an actuality,
than the imagined is difficult to ascertain. At this distance, and

with these cultural eyes, it is sometimes hard to distinguish when Sambo was present in the flesh and when his image conjured up the flesh.

There is no precise date, but Sambo was apparently conceived in the minds of Western Europeans in their early interactions with Africans in the fifteenth and early sixteenth centuries and was born during the early period of the slave trade. Long before traders began to pull bodies out of the African Gold Coast, Westerners viewed those bodies with a mixture of fascination and disgust. Europeans evinced a deep and curious interest in certain African customs, particularly music and dance. Hundreds of travel accounts, oral reports, and diaries circulated throughout Western countries over the centuries, detailing African musical customs, their unusual instruments, intense rhythmical-sexual dance movements, and secular and religious ceremonies. "Their dances are commonly in a round," wrote the experienced captain John Barbot in the early 1700s of a Nigerian dance, "singing the next thing that occurs, whether sense or nonsense." In the following century, slave captain Theodore Canot was treated to "a whirling circle of half-stripped girls," as he wrote in his log, who "danced to the monotonous beat of a tom-tom." Like many whites, Canot was intrigued by the variations of the dancing. "Presently, the formal ring was broken and each female stepped out singly, danced according to her individual fancy. Some were wild, some were soft, some were tame, and some were fiery." Barbot observed that when both sexes danced, "both sides always made abundance of lascivious gestures," heightened by an occasional "draught of palmwine."

Knowledge of African musical practices was skillfully applied once bodies became a highly profitable commodity. Written late in the slave trade, Canot's observations suggested that musical techniques for controlling the Africans had been in use for some time. He watched newly caught Africans, guided by troops, perform in the barracoons. "I have often seen seven hundred slaves, guided by half-dozen musketeers, singing, drumming, and dancing, after their meal."[1]

Aboard ships, slavers utilized entertainment as a means of exerting strict control, ensuring stamina, and warding off depressed spirits. "Dancing the slaves" became a commonplace ritual. Occasionally a musician was specifically employed for the purpose of keeping the captured constantly on the move. A drum, upturned kettle, African banjo, bagpipe, harp, fiddle—any instrument or thing that could be used to serve up music was employed. On some ships instruments were provided to the Africans. On Barbot's ship, tambourines were passed out, "which some of the younger darkies fought for regularly, and every evening we enjoyed the novelty of African war songs and ring dances, fore and aft. . . ." As Barbot's description reveals, practical necessity was not the only reason for providing instruments to the slaves. Boredom on the long voyage and voyeurism were not incidental motives. Europeans were clearly drawn to and equally repelled by African musical styles. After a trip to the West Indies in the 1790s, George Pinckard, a London physician interested in conditions aboard the slavers, was "pleased to observe an air of cheerfulness and contentment" that prevailed among the Africans. He was particularly impressed with the antics of the young. Boys were inclined to be "playful" and exhibited "youthful tricks." Some of the girls' behavior, on the other hand, was sorely disturbing. "Unchecked by the reserve of education," they "occasionally glanced an expressive look or displayed a significant gesture." Pinckard scrutinized the movements of the young as they "threw about their bodies into a multitude of disgusting and indecent attitudes. Their song was a wild savage yell, devoid of all softness and harmony, and loudly chanted in harsh monotony."[2]

African entertainments "often made us pastime," logged captain Barbot in reference to a group of Nigerians on one of his innumerable trips. Seeing them dancing, singing, and "sporting in their manner," Barbot was highly satisfied that their activity also "pleased them highly." The captors were always comforted when Africans displayed a cheerful or playful attitude and comported themselves in musical fashion. When the slaves were "a good natured lot," as one captain wrote, it meant that Africans were faithful to their customs, that hostility and the possibility of uprisings were diminished, and that more bodies might survive the excruciating midpassage. For these reasons, it was common practice to force Africans to the upper deck to jump, sing, dance, and generally move about as often as the weather permitted.

Although many of the slavers pointedly recognized the melancholy and despair that afflicted the slaves—more than one captain and sailor wrote about the fate of being wrenched from familial surroundings—these remarks stood in contradistinction to those on playfulness and general merriment. Whites were often surprised that people so oppressed could sing and dance. They knew further, therefore, that they could be goaded into these activities when circumstances required it.

Captor and captive thus worked, each from his own vantage point, to ease the circumstance in which both were bound. "The fate of master and slave was intertwined," Eugene Genovese incisively noted, "and formed part of a single social process; each in his own way struggled for autonomy—struggled to end his dependence upon the other—but neither could ever wholly succeed."[3]

Because of the intense psychological demands slavery made on the shippers and the owners of humans, as well as those who became its victims, a language was gradually worked out to permit social interaction within clearly defined bounds. Over time, as those interactions during the slave trade indicated, entertainment became one of the primary modes of communication, the means by which relations could be conducted with minimal energies, if required. The language of entertainment affected all areas of engagement, from the workplace to leisure activities, and acted as a salving lubricant and conflict reducer. Entertainment provided both owners and their slaves with a system of signals that could be conveyed with relative ease and enable each to understand expectations as well as deal with petty annoyances.

Consequently, contact between whites and blacks during the long period of slavery almost always involved intricate forms of performing. Lessons accumulated during the slave trade were extended and refined within the plantation system, regardless of region or territory. Entertainment became not only an acceptable way of relating but, for whites, a necessary conduit of imagery.

On the plantations, it was expected that one of the slaves' primary tasks was to entertain their whites. "Slaves were expected to sing as well as to work," Frederick Douglass pointedly noted in his autobiography. "A silent slave was not liked, either by masters or overseers." Whites wanted their workers to "make a noise." Because of this constant exhortation, plus the "natural disposition of the Negro to make a noise in the world," there was "singing among the teamsters at all times."[4]

Moreover, the music was to be light and cheery, the words gay and frivolous. Frances Anne Kemble, who visited rice and cotton plantations in Georgia in 1838–39, noted rules to this effect. "I have heard that many of the masters and overseers on these plantations prohibit melancholy tunes or words, and encourage nothing but cheerful music and senseless words. . . ." What this accomplished, she continued, was to reduce "the effect of sadder strains upon the slaves, whose peculiar musical sensibility might be expected to make them especially excitable by any songs of a plaintive character, and having any reference to their particular hardships." To Kemble, as to the majority of whites, most lyrics were indeed nonsensical and meaningless, although Kemble did, occasionally, learn of a hidden connection in at least one of the songs. "To one, an extremely pretty, plaintive and original air, there was but one line, which was repeated with a sort of wailing chorus— "Oh! my massa told me, there's no grass in Georgia." Although Kemble does not indicate her source, she was told that it was a lamentation of a slave from Virginia or Carolina, where the labor of hoeing the weeds, or grass, was not so severe as in the rice or cotton lands of Georgia. Despite this revelation, Kemble exclaimed, "I have never heard the negroes on Mr. ————'s plantation sing any words that could be said to have any sense."[5]

Wherever whites went, they frequently heard the singing voices of working slaves. White diaries and oral reports happily recorded the innumerable occasions. These experiences were corroborated by outsiders. Frances Trollope, who resided in the South in the

1840s, recalled the joyous sentiments of her traveling group, who "were much pleased by the chant with which the Negro boatman regulate and beguile their labour on the river; it consists but of very few notes, but they are sweetly harmonious, and the Negro is almost always rich and powerful."[6] Traveling through the region in the next decade, northern urban architect Frederick Law Olmsted similarly encountered a working party and feverishly tried to capture their song. As his steamer rounded a bend, "a dozen of the negro boat-hands, standing on the freight, piled up on the low forecastle, began to sing, waving hats and handkerchiefs, and shirts lashed to poles, towards the people who stood on the sterns of the steamboats at the levee." After missing a few lines, Olmsted picked up the rhythm and words:

> Ye see dem boat way dah ahead
> > Chorus.—Oahoiohieu
> De San Charles is arter'em, dey mus go behine
> > Cho.—Oahoiohieu
> So stir up dah, my livelies, stir her up;
> > (pointing to the furnaces).
> > Cho.—Oahoiohieu

Olmsted was deeply impressed by their musical abilities. "The love of music which characterizes the negro, the readiness with which he acquires skill in the art, his power of memorizing and improvising music is most marked and constant." These talents caused him to question the prevailing notion of the blacks' limited intellectual capacities. "The common plantation negroes, or deckhands of the steamboats—whose minds are so little cultivated that they cannot count twenty—will often, in rolling cotton-bales, or carrying wood on board the boat, fall to singing, each taking a different part," and perform with such spirit and independence, and in such perfect harmony, "as I have never heard singers, who had not been considerably educated, at the North."[7]

Although Kemble referred to "this accursed system of slavery" and wrestled with the problem of blacks' intellect, she was also taken with their styles. The "peculiar characteristics of this veritable negro minstrelsy—how they all sing in unison, having never, it appears, attempted or heard anything like part-singing," indicated something "quite wonderful" on their part. For "such truth of intonation and accent would make almost any music agreeable." Her praises of and wonderment at the rowing teams' and field hands' chanting as they worked filled her accounts of labor in the South.[8]

Because cheerful slaves implied so much, whites demanded to see blacks in this state. "Marster lak to see his slaves happy and singin' bout de place. If he ever heard any of them quarrelin' wid each other, he would holler at them and say: 'Sing! Us ain't got no more time to fuss on dis place. . . .'"[9]

The line separating workplace from private place was often nonexistent, as blacks were constantly called into the master's house to provide entertainment for any and all occasions. "Whenever there was a big party," recalled one ex-slave, "we had to jump about." After one feast had finished, "the slaves would be up to dance and sing." On this occasion, the song that the whites wanted played was the "Arkansas Traveler," a particular favorite, and it led to "some dancing done." Whenever this occurred, "Usually we slaves sat around on the fence and boxes or stumps and watched them dance."[10]

Some owners wanted their slaves to frolic only on special holidays. They were concerned that dancing drained energies. "We never was allowed to have no parties nor dances, only from Christmas Day to New Year's eve," remembered a former South Carolina slave. It was a remark many others made as well. Despite this prohibition, slaves frequently met at night to celebrate. "I 'members one time I slip off from de missus and to a dance," he continued, "and when I come back, de dog in de yard didn't seem to know me and he bark and wake de missus up and she whip me something awful. I sho didn't go to no more dance widout asking her."[11] On the other hand, the accounts fully indicate the frustration that beset many masters at their inability to prevent the slaves from frolicking.

Yet one wonders about the degree of frustration. Surface protest often masked much deeper desires. Whites wanted to see their blacks perform not only because it conveyed a sense of content-edness but because they were entranced at the black style. "After dinner Ol' Marster would give us a little tap wid de switch. He say he was settling our dinner. Den he'd let us play and he'd set on de big porch and watch." Whites constantly *watched*. "Ef de fiel wuk wuz up, us didn't wuk Saddy ebenin," recounted a former Ala-bama slave, "en we could hab er banjo dance nearly ebery Saddy night. Lots er times, Ole Mistis en her company come ter our dances en looked on, en when er brash nigger boy cut some su'is steps, de men would trow him dimes, en dey would all laugh fit ter kill." Many an ex-slave recalled similar situations:

> Our Mistress would cum down sometime, early ter watch us dance.

> Marse Bennett would call all us little niggers up to de big house to dance for him, and us sho would cut de pigeon wing, den us would sing "reels" for him.

> Miss Jane Massingale wud cum to de slave quarters wid her young com'ny an' j'ine in wid de slaves.[12]

The dancing slave was a ubiquitous sight throughout the South. At slave auctions, as Solomon Northrup, a free black who was kid-napped and enslaved for twelve years, wrote in his account of his first sale, "After being fed, in the afternoon, we were again paraded and made to dance." Musical abilities in general were often a major selling point at the auctions. Northrup immediately grasped the significance of the image and became what whites wanted, an expert fiddler. Throughout his stay in the South, Northrup tuned up: "Alas! had it not been for my beloved violin, I scarcely can conceive how I could have endured the long years of bondage. It introduced me to great houses [and] supplied me with conveniences for my cabin—with pipes and tobacco, an extra pair of shoes, and oftentimes led me away from the presence of a hard master, to witness scenes of jollity and mirth."[13]

Whites rewarded those who amused them. At times, manipulat-ing the situation for their own use, slaves performed when they knew it would have an impact upon their owners. "When we reach near de big house," said a South Carolina slave who was returning with a group from a church "freedom o' spirit" meeting very late in the evening, "us soften down to a deep hum dat de missus like!" When the master's wife opened the window, as they had hoped she would, she requested that they sing "Swing Low, Sweet Chariot." "Dat all us want to hear," the slave declared. "Us open us and de niggers near de big house dat hadn't been to church would wake up and come out to de cabin door and jine in de refrain. From dat we'd swing on into all de old spirituals dat us love so well and dat us knowed how to sing."[14]

Windows were open and doors ajar for the watching whites. And the watching extended to black culture as well. Funerals, church services, Saturday night, holiday frolicking, and sports activities became theatre for whites. Northern and European travelers, in addition to Southerners, frequently recounted black dancing and revelry. Frederick Douglass maintained that white interest in holiday merrymaking was "among the most effective means in the hands of slaveholders of keeping down the spirit of insurrection among the slaves."[15] No doubt. Yet it was further evidence of the need of whites to maintain their image of blacks as natural performers—whose style was enticingly different from their own.

On the plantations, slaves performed not only spontaneously on demand but for special occasions. Mrs. Henry Rowe Schoolcraft wrote in *Plantation Life,* "the negroes Sambo, Robert, and Jack, who were enthusiastic and talented performers on the fiddle, should come in, with their violin, and tambourine, and banjo, and strike up electrifying music for their young master's guests to indulge us in terpsichorean exercises during the whole jubilant season between the 25th of December and the first day of the new year."[16]

In part, slave entertainment provided escape from boredom and the awkward rhythms of agrarian life. Bennet H. Barrow, "finding no cotton to trash out" in early 1846 on his plantation in West Feliciana, Louisiana, "sent out for the Fiddle and made them Dance from 12 till dark, others from the Quarter soon joined for the frollic and became quite lively to the close. . . ."[17] At times whites initiated the songfests. "I recalls de days befo' de war when us niggers sat out in back of de big house in de moonlight an' young massa played his fiddle an' us'd sing."[18] And there were occasions when field slaves, particularly children, were called to the big house. After dinner, wrote William Russell on a trip in the South, "as we sat on the steps, the children were sent for to sing for us. They came very shyly, and by degrees. . . . With much difficulty the elder children were dressed into line; then they began to shuffle their feet, to clap their hands . . . ," after which they were rewarded with lumps of sugar.[19]

One South Carolina slaveowner, desiring to reciprocate a kindness from Michigan friends in 1860, invited them to stop by and spend a week or two with him and "see my negroes, that I want them to see them dance and make merry over the dance and if they do come, tell the negroes Christmas time will come with them—that is, I want the negroes to dress up and dance for them."[20]

And many were regaled, especially Northerners and Western Europeans who, like English geologist Charles Lyell, were "surprised" to find slaves in South Carolina and Georgia in the 1840s "so remarkably cheerful and light-hearted." Lyell observed the accent on music in black culture. "Of dancing and music the negroes are passionately fond." Nor was this passion due to external influence: " . . . it is notorious that the slaves were not given to drink or intemperance in their merry-makings."[21] Olmsted was not alone in his sentiments on a black funeral: "The music was wild and barbarous, but not without a plaintive melody"; "I have never in my life, however, heard such ludicrous language"; "singing a wild kind of chant."[22] The remarks of Timothy Flint, a clergyman sent out by the Missionary Society of Connecticut to assist in building the Presbyterian Church on the frontier in the early decades of the nineteenth century, were not untypical in their comparative impressions of Afro-Americans and Native Americans. Although the cultures, Flint declared, were of two extremes, "the negro is easily excitable, and in the highest degree susceptible of all the passions." Once pain and hunger were removed, the natural state of blacks was one of "enjoyment." For as soon as burdens were lifted and working suspended, "he sings, he seizes his fiddle, he dances."[23]

The performing slave, however, was not limited to singing and dancing roles before white audiences or to the merrymaking emanating from the quarters, but took a place in other activities as well. Blacks could be found in sporting events as boxers, wrestlers, foot racers, whiskey guzzlers, and in countless contests. Count Francesco dal Verme, in letters to his father in Italy in 1783, noted that in horse racing in North Carolina there were "Negroes in early teens" who "rode bareback" as the jockeys.[24]

Betting on blacks with particular sports agility was invariably part of the action. One former South Carolina slave proudly recounted his ability in outracing horses on the plantation. A horse apparently owned by another slave and others owned by whites brought bets against him. Whites sometimes gave him "some of de bettin money" when he beat the slave's horse, an action that brought laughter from the other slaves.[25]

Slave dance contests were also contrived by whites. Plantation owners placed bets against each other: "Old Massa Day and Massa Bryant, dey used to put dey niggers together and have de prize dancers. Massa Day allus lose, 'cause us allus beat de niggers at dancin'." On many a plantation, whites intruded themselves on black parties and selected winners: "Sometimes de slave owners come to dese parties 'cause dey enjoyed watchin' de dance, and dey 'cided who danced de best."[26]

Plainly, whites enjoyed watching blacks. Douglass was of the opinion that most slaveholders promoted amusements in order to maintain the system within its emotional framework. "Everything like rational enjoyment was frowned upon, and only those wild and low sports peculiar to semicivilized people were encouraged." The freedom allowed on holidays "appeared to have no other object than to disgust the slaves with their temporary freedom, and to make them as glad to return to their work as they had been to leave it."[27]

Arguably, however, there were other subconscious reasons, not the least of which was the rigid image of blacks as natural creatures. They performed because it was in their nature to do so. More than one slaveholder would complain, as did a Virginia plantation owner to Olmsted one day, that "his negroes never worked so hard as to tire themselves—always were lively, and ready to go off on a frolic at night." They never did half a fair day's work, he continued, in a refrain that chorused from masters and overseers across the South, and they could not be made to work hard—they conserved energies for other matters. Olmsted was almost convinced of the accuracy of this complaint. "This is just what I thought when I have seen slaves at work—they seem to go through the motions of labor without putting strength into them. They keep their powers in reserve for their own use at night, perhaps."[28]

Blacks giving themselves to the moment, to frolic when their status was the most demeaned, both angered and intrigued whites. That slaves, or even poor free blacks, for that matter, were not depressed and sullen but extremely lively and merry confused whites. Describing a black holiday in New Orleans, Timothy Flint, with some astonishment, observed that "they dance, and their streamers fly, and the bells they have hung about them tinkle. Never will you see gayer countenances, demonstrations of more forgetfulness of the past and the future, and more entire abandonment to the joyous existence of the present moment."[29]

What was more, they always appeared to be laughing among themselves. Singing and dancing made sense to whites, who could interpret this behavior in terms of tribal customs and primitive rites. Laughter, however, demanded a different or at least a wider interpretation. Slave accounts contain many references to the vibrancy of their frolicking: "You could hear 'em laughin' and talkin' a smile," exclaimed one ex-slave of such a scene.[30] It was the laugh, the raucous laugh, and the energy that propelled it, that most jolted whites. Of all the slave's characteristics, this appears to have been the most perplexing—and extremely grating.

"The peculiar hearty negro guffaw" was but one of Olmsted's many references to this black trait. On a tour through South Carolina in the 1850s, Olmsted was suddenly awakened "by loud laughter" from nearby slave cabins. Peering out from his railway car, Olmsted spotted a group of workers seated around a campfire enjoying "a right merry repast." Then one worker spoke out, and

> raised such a sound as I never heard before; a long, loud, musical shout, rising, and falling, and breaking into falsetto, his voice ringing through the woods in the clear, frosty night air, like a bugle-call. As he finished, the melody was caught up by another, and then, another, and then, by several in chorus. When there was silence again, one of them cried out, as if bursting with amusement: "Did yer see de dog?— when I began echoing, he turn 'round an' look me straight into der face; ha! ha! ha!" and the whole party broke into the loudest peals of laughter, as if it was the very best joke they had ever heard.[31]

Such laughter was clearly at variance with their dire situation: how could people play and laugh when their position was so downtrodden, so entrapped? The incongruity of play against circumstance propelled whites toward a conception of personality that explained the contradiction and simplified their future behavior toward the black male. It was a conception that attempted to encompass all the facets of blacks' playfulness: their cheerful and lighthearted manner, penchant for frivolity, rhythmical movements, unusual mannerisms, even their patter of language. It was an image whose elements were viewed both as a blessing and a curse, one that whites were convinced would serve them well in dealing with blacks in any environment or circumstance.

It was a conception of the African-American as an embodiment of humor, whose nature was inherently triggered by comical forces. Thomas R. R. Cobb, in his influential defense of the peculiar institution in the 1850s, *An Inquiry into the Law of Negro Slavery,* summed up what had become an essential prop in white thinking, the idea that blacks were "mirthful by nature."[32] Being "mirthful" meant the full gamut of humor, the ability to contrive and to be an object of laughter. Thus, the entertainment blacks provided was not limited to performing but encompassed humor itself—not the humor of the child, despite the heavy use of this word by contemporaries and later scholars, but of the fool.

Consequently, jokes about black behavior became a main staple of white laughter over the centuries. All types of stories and anecdotes traversed the country relating the antics of those naturally funny black people. A comicality enveloped their every action, a comicality deeply tied to the numbskull tradition. Even an anti-slave individual such as Frances Anne Kemble thought of African-Americans in this vein. Upon returning to a plantation, Kemble's group met "a most extraordinary creature of the negro kind" who in a series of quick movements bowed low before the group till his hands almost touched the ground, exclaiming, "Massa ————, your most obedient." And with a flourish he moved over to permit them to pass. This act, which could be interpreted as comically hostile, instantly produced "shouting with laughter" among the whites. Their laughter "broke out again every time we looked at each other and stopped to take a breath: so sudden, grotesque, uncouth, and yet dexterous a gambado never came into the brain or out of the limbs of any thing but a 'niggar.'"

Presumed to be intrinsically comical, black actions became a vast source of white humor. Joking about their behavior became, in time, one of the most important elements in American humor. The antics of slaves were such a source of merriment that Harriet Martineau zeroed in on its psychological significance to the system. In New Orleans in the 1830s, Martineau daily heard the slave stories from women on their early-morning social calls. "I heard so many anecdotes . . . that I began to suspect that one of the use of slaves is to furnish topics for the amusement of their owners." Martineau's illustration presented the problem—black cleverness was misunderstood by white, either by conscious design or by stereotypical entrapment:

> Sam was sadly apt to get drunk, and had been often reprieved by his master on that account. One day his master found him intoxicated, and cried out, "What, drunk again, Sam? I scolded you for being drunk last night, and here you are drunk again." "No, massa, same drunk, massa; same drunk."[34]

What further surprised Martineau was white insensitivity to the presence of their slaves while they related such jokes. At a dinner party, a high-ranking public official of the American Theatre in New Orleans regaled the guests with "a facetious story" of a couple from the "Green Island," Pat and Nancy,

> who had settled on the Mississippi, and, in course of time (to use the language of the region), "acquired six children and nine negroes." Pat had a mind to better his fortunes, and to go unencumbered higher up the river; and he therefore explained his plans to Nancy, finishing with, "and so, my darlin', I'll lave you; but I'll do my best for you; I'll lave you the six dear, nate, pretty little childer, and I'll take the nine nasty dirty negroes."

Waiting on the tables were three black servants. Everyone at the table "laughed without control," except for one slaveowner who glanced up at the blacks and made a determined effort not to engage in the collective action.[35]

The laughing space was constantly filled with stories of the foolish black. Many former slaves narrated accounts in which the laugh was on them. In the woods with his master one day when they came across a slippery elm tree, a slave was prodded to say "right fast" an alliterative sentence: "Long, slim, slick saplin' and when I say long, slim, sick slaplin', him 'most kill hisself laughin'." Another, as a little boy, was often asked by his master "what the rooster said, what the cow said, what the pig said," and when the master heard the sounds he "used to get a great deal of amusement."[36] As previously noted, many a slave's nickname was conceived in laughter. One slave, told to quickly retrieve an item, recalled that "ah wuz so slow dat he done breck out in er great beeg laugh at me . . . and den he say yew is sho is slow and ah's gwinter call yer aftah der fasses thing awn earf . . . and datz Lightnin.'"[37] When he was a young boy, another male remembered, "All de white folks at de table joke me so bout bein' so lazy," "I soon stop dat foolishness," he exclaimed, angered about being the butt.[38]

Black speech patterns were particularly bewildering. As African dialects underwent changes from their traditional structure to that of English, many whites were quick, at least when selling their slaves, to pointedly note that the blacks had achieved some "clarity" and "fluency" in their speech habits.[39] Yet it is equally clear that their phrasing and the need to communicate beyond the understanding of their owners made for an odd mixture indeed. Consequently, unusual phrases and mispronunciations were picked up by whites and used as examples of the fool. "It is certainly assumed," Max Eastman cogently observed in his work on laughter, "that when we smile at a misused language, what amuses us is the ignorance, or pretended ignorance, of the character using it."[40] Whites did not presume intentional ignorance— although it would be incorrect to state that all whites were so beguiled by black speech, for many understood the patter and the use to which it was put—but rather saw it as an aspect of black comicality.

White amusement extended to both genders. "White folks would sit on the gallery and laugh," declared a former Alabama slave about the antics of her childhood friends. Another suffered from constant laughter because of a misguided notion regarding her birth. She had taken seriously her mother's humorous story of her birth, which involved a railroad train rather than the stork— until "white folks laugh me out of it!"[41] Kidding with blacks was an approved form of play among whites. At a trial, a 108-year-old Alabama black woman was asked to testify because of the reputation of her memory. The judge, however, amused himself and the courtroom audience with a series of jiving questions:

> "Aunt Letitia, you have such a wonderful memory you ought to remember before you were born!"
> The jury and spectators in the court room roared with laughter.
> "Yes, sur, Judge, I 'members General George Washing when I was a little girl, he shook mah han', and he say, 'Tishe, yo' sartinly can polish de silver,'" answered Aunt Letitia.
> The court room again roared with laughter.
> "Well, tell me," said the Judge, "do you remember the fall of the Roman Empire?"
> "Yes, sur, Judge, I 'members something drop jus' 'bout dat time," answered Aunt Letitia with all earnestness.
> Again, laughter ran through the courtroom. . . .[42]

Humor, however, is a force of intricate dimensions. Fully cognizant of the white image, blacks played the humor theme as well, and with considerable energy and deftness. "Them smart-alec nig-gers'd make the white folks yell wit' laughin' at their crazy antics. You know a nigger is jest a born show-off."[43]

The consequences were ambiguous at best. On the one hand, blacks' sly use of play at times secured what they desired; on the other hand, their antics became another tale in the storehouse of numbskull humor. At the same time, though, humor was a means by which social distance could be narrowed. Frances Anne Kemble related a situation between a master and his servant in which humor served both parties. "Doctor ———— told us today of a comical application which his negro man had made to him for the coat he was then wearing." Kemble was uncertain whether the ser-vant wanted the coat on loan or as an outright gift. "But his argu-ment was (it might have been an Irishman's) that he knew his mas-ter intended to give it to him by-and-by, and that he thought he might as well let him have it at once as keep him waiting any longer for it." Kemble noted that the doctor related the story "with great glee," and felt that it furnished a very good illustration of what Southerners were fond of exhibiting, "the degree of license to which they capriciously permit their favorite slaves occasionally to carry their familiarity."[44]

In his seminal analysis of joking, Sigmund Freud observed that humor is wholly a social process wherein the shared experiences of the participants enable them to aggress and/or regress together. It is clear that within the encapsulated system of slavery, humorous interchanges came to serve a vital role: they provided a psychological place within which each group could operate for certain ingroup advantages, and a political place within which each could inflict punishment on the other. Whites were in the domi-nant position of setting the parameters of the exchanges, but blacks were able to develop a repertoire of retaliatory humor to partially offset their situation. Thus, humor lessened the chance of further violence in a system already determined by violence.

Humor provided maneuverability in such a way as to disguise, if either party so desired, outright hostility; yet at the same time it conspired to perpetuate the image of blacks as fools. "Buck he never was uppity but he could say things to his white folks and they'd think it wuz funny," an ex-slave recalled. "Like one time a lady asked Buck would he eat his Chrismus dinner in her kitchen. Buck he say: 'Is you gonna have turkey?' And the lady she say: 'No, Buck, but we gonna have a mighty good dinner with plenty of fixin's.' But Buck he say: 'If you ain't got turkey den please don't look for me, ma'am.'"[45]

A more revealing circumstance involved J. F. D. Smyth, an English traveler to Virginia in the 1780s. Smyth had purchased "Richmond," whose job it was to transport him down the Roanoke River in a canoe. His newly acquired slave was directed to meet him at a designated spot, but when Smyth arrived there no one was in sight. Calling out "as loud as I could vociferate," and receiving no reply, Smyth set out along the river, assuming that his slave "might be asleep, which all negroes are extremely addicted to." The riverbank was treacherous, and Smyth was forced inland for miles, where he encountered impenetrable briars and swarms of insects. Every quarter of a mile he hollered loudly for his servant. Traveling through the countryside all day and into the evening, Smyth ultimately arrived in wretched condition back at the very spot from which he had departed—and there he found Richmond fast asleep in the canoe. Smyth was about to administer severe punishment when the slave pleaded his case:

> Kay massa (says he), you just leave me, me sit here, great fish jump up into de canoe; here he be, massa, fine fish, massa; me den very grad; den me sit very still, until another great fish jump into de canoe; but me fall asleep, massa, and no wake till you come: now, massa, me know me deserve flogging, cause if great fish did jump into de canoe, he see me asleep, den he jump out again, and I no catch him; so massa, me willing now take good flogging.—

Smyth immediately "understood" poor Richmond's predicament: "I laughed heartily at the poor fellow's ignorance, and extreme simplicity, in waiting there for more fishes to jump into his canoe, because one had happened to do so; and therefore forgave his crime."[46]

A situation in which a slave was actually caught in an act of contrivance was received in an identical way. Harriet Martineau accompanied her hostess to dine at a neighbor's estate. The carriage to transport them back to the plantation was ordered for eight o'clock. Promptly at six the driver, a slave, arrived and informed them that his master had sent him. They should go home directly, he "begged." This they did, and upon arriving there was met by the host, who was "very much surprised to see us home." Martineau explained: "The message was a fiction of the slave's, who wanted to get his horses put up, that he might enjoy his Sunday evening." The response? "His master and mistress laughed, and took no further notice." And yet another story was added to the trove.[47]

Even when blacks outwitted them, however—so long as it did not occur too often and interfere with the black role as entertainer—whites permitted a degree of sassiness. Being a "smart aleck" was one thing—to be humorously superior was quite another.

Although humor was a weapon of no mean importance for blacks, nevertheless their surface jocularity worked against them. Whites assumed that their performing and laughing were clear and definite signs of their natural and inherent natures. "Fortunate it is indeed for them, that they are blessed with this easy, satisfied disposition of mind . . . for they indeed seem to be the happiest inhabitants in America, notwithstanding the hardness of their fare, the severity of their labour, and the unkindness, ignominy, and often barbarity of their treatment," concluded Smyth.[48]

These sentiments were echoed throughout the countryside. In his celebrated *Sketches of Eighteenth Century America*, Crèvecoeur commented on the black disposition: "You may see them at particular places as happy and merry as if they were freemen and freeholders. The sight of their happiness always increases mine. . . ."[49] Describing a group of black oarsmen, Mrs. Henry Rowe Schoolcraft noted that "their eyes glistened with fun. . . ."[50]

The most extensive comments about Afro-American humor came from John Bernard, a brilliant English comedian who was one of the earliest of American theatre managers. Bernard made his first American appearance in 1797 in Greenwich Village and performed and stage-managed in cities along the seaboard for the next two decades. Like other whites, Bernard extolled the black for his humorous constitution. "My fingers have long been itching to touch upon a bright subject—blacks—the great humorists of the Union, and notwithstanding all that has been said of their debasement and wretchedness, one of the happiest races of people I have ever seen." Bernard compared blacks to the Irish. "I have termed the negroes the greatest humorists of the Union, and in many respects I have thought them like the lower Irish; with the same confusion of ideas and difficulty of clear expression, pouring words out of their mouths on the high tide of natural drollery, as broad as it is rapid." Even the Irish, however, were unable to compete with a "profound simplicity" that lowered "the most dignified subjects into ludicrous lights" and elevated "the most trivial into importance. . . ." Black humor was but "Nature's spontaneous product in full bloom" and similar to gold, "that scarce, previous commodity"; it constituted a "black loam."

With an effusive sweep, Bernard further termed this loam "Samboisms" and served up numerous illustrations of his chosen humorous people. One of the "heartiest specimens of fun" was a black youth who was on duty with a fan to keep flies from disturbing his master's rest. Spotting a persevering bluebottle fly alight on his owner's "flaming promontory," then fly off, the slave declared, "Aha, um berry grad o' dat, *oo burn oo foot at last,* massa fly!" A more pointed slave's rejoinder was in response to his master's death. The slave went to communicate the news of his owner's sudden demise to a close neighbor. The neighbor after recovering from the initial shock, declared with a sigh of resignation, "Well, Cicero, there's one thing to console us; your poor master had a d——d bad gout, and he's gone to happiness." "Iss masa, bum berry sorry he hadn't gone to heb'n," responded Cicero, to the surprise of the neighbor. "Not gone to heaven, you black rascal! Why?" "Cause, massa, he tell a me he should never be comfortable anywhere he wasn't berry warm!"

Responding to his task of presenting blacks as simplicity personified, Bernard offered the quip of an exhilarated fiddler who, coming home from a dance one dark night, fell over some rubbish in the road. Regaining his footing, the fiddler remarked to his companion, "Now Caesar, tell a me iss—why de debil do a sun shine all day when nobody want um, and nebber shine a night, when it's so berry dark gentlum can't see his way?"

The anecdote that most amused Bernard involved an act of physical retaliation. Three men—a businessman from New Jersey, a Georgia planter, and the planter's slave—were conducting a survey, and it became necessary for them to seek shelter in the overseer's hut for the night. The two white men slept in the hammocks, the slave on the floor. When the planter and his slave were asleep, the Jersey man, responding to some slight he had suffered from the servant, smacked him with his whip on an exposed and sensitive part.

> Agamemmon bounded up as with a galvanic impulse, and the Jerseyman threw himself back, but not before his motion had betrayed him. The sufferer, fearful of disturbing his master, could only apply friction to the irritation, and lie down again. The next day past in the neighborhood, at night they repaired again to the hut, where our hero expressed a strong wish to repose outside. This led to a disclosure, upon which the Jerseyman said, in his defence, "If I struck you, Aggy, it must have been in my sleep; a man may do many things in his sleep which he can't remember next morning." Such an explanation satisfied the planter, and perforce his property, but it conveyed no conviction to the latter, nor was it the unction he required for his skin. It was the Jerseyman's fate this night to go off first and give his victim the pleasure of watching him. Rising softly on his legs, Aggy approached his hammock, and taking down the brandy-keg suspended by his side, emptied its contents. The loss was discovered the first thing next morning, and Aggy was collared and charged with the offence, when, eyeing the tyrant significantly, he replied, "Well, massa, if I did drink um, it must hab been in my sleep; a man may do many ting in his sleep he can't remember next mornin."

This act, concluded Bernard, "tickled the planter as much as it dumbfounded his guest." Again, a story about the "funny darkies" made the rounds of the white community.[51]

As with much humor, the stories were embellished and twisted to fit the imagination. Thus, Calvin Jones in 1817, in a brief note in his diary, recorded what he regarded as a comic scene between two plantation slaves—one of whom was, interestingly, named Sambo:

> Called at Mrs. Kirkpatricks for Dinner—out in the piazza an old negro on his knees clearing the way before the door a strapping negro girl ran out of the house and went right over him. He grumbled out that "Clara was a damned bitch." "Misse," says Clara, "Sambo call me dam bitch." "No Misse," says Sambo, "I no say so, I only tink so and she hear um."[52]

With that line Sambo probably avoided being punished or beaten for uttering a blasphemy. Thus, those natural humorists—singing, frolicking, and laughing during and after work—were enabled by a gift of nature to cope with, even overcome their enslaved condition. Whites were obviously buoyed by this particular image because it assuaged whatever guilt might have burdened them. Further, it narrowed the contradiction between slavery and the tenets of democracy, permitted a dialogue devoid of rational substance, undercut the frightening possibility of the hostile black male, and created a "bond" of affection and sentimentality. Once the stereotype became lodged in the inner reaches of the white mind, moreover, once the conception of the black male as the fool became the primary focus of white imagery, it assumed a centripetal energy of its own, as stereotypes often do. It was for this reason that owners adopted the practice of "humouring" their slaves. Harriet Martineau had sharp comments about white behavior in this regard. "As long as the slave remains ignorant, docile, and contented, he is often taken good care of, humoured. . . ." On the other hand, "from the moment he exhibits the attributes of a rational being—from the moment his intellect seems likely to come into the most distinct competition with that of whites, the most deadly hatred springs up;—not in the black but in his oppressors."[53] For whites, humor was the antithesis of rationality. Sambo thus became a fixture in southern culture, a figure whose role as humorist was central to the theatre of racism. It was a role joyously created and maintained by whites, and would be disturbed only by slave uprisings and rumors of impending violence. But once the danger was past and anxieties had been repressed, Sambo would pop up, laughing and frolicking and full of jargon. Whites would again breathe a sigh of deliverance and welcome their humorist back with a smile and a story or joke to tell the folks in the neighborhood, who could be heard laughing "fit ter kill."

4

And Performing Today at Balls, Circuses, Theatres, Picnics, Churches, Schools, and Prisons: The Indomitable, Spirited, Laughing... JIM CROW, ESQUIRE!!

ACT TWO
In the North: The Blackface Minstrel Man

> The negro is a bundle of oddities, of strange conceits and sin-
> gular notions, and among them all not the least singular is his
> love of high flown words and his aping the manner of whites.
> Some of the funniest beings I have ever seen are of the negro
> dandy species—so much gas and wind and smoke with a little
> charcoal is seldom seen. They are decidedly *bloods* as may be seen
> by the dashy dress and foppish air.—Henry Benjamin Whipple,
> *Bishop Whipple's Diary, 1834–1844*

> Officer Krupke, we're down on our knees
> Nobody wants a fellow with a social disease.
> —Leonard Bernstein and Stephen Sondheim, *West Side Story*

Racial laughter resounded throughout the North. Blacks laughed
at themselves and, out of earshot, at whites. Whites could be seen
laughing at blacks in their presence. The content of black laughter
was rarely heard in the white community. The content of white
laughter was almost invariably heard in both communities.

The humorous characteristics attributed to the Afro-Americans in the South were similar to the images held by their northern counterparts. "Under a thick skin," English comedian and performer John Bernard observed after seven years in the colonies at the turn of the nineteenth century, "the negro seems to be endued with very sensitive nerves; climate, music, and kind treatment act upon him like electricity, and with all the ignorance of the child he possesses its disposition for enjoyment."[1] *Enjoyment* personified the white view of black behavior, regardless of region.

Uppermost in the image of black amusement was the laugh. The passionate guffaw was a marvel and an annoyance. Its range and power produced many comments, as illustrated by Washington Irving's concise remark in *Knickerbocker's History of New York* (1809). On a clear, still summer evening, Irving noted, could be heard "from the Battery of New York, the obstreperous peals of the broad-mouthed laughter of the Dutch Negroes at Communipaw [a small village located on the Jersey shore overlooking New York harbor] who, like most other negroes, are famous for their risible powers." On Sunday evening they were heard to "laugh loudest" because, as one resident explained, "of their having their holiday clothes on."[2]

Such laughter was unnerving—as expressive laughter often can be to outsiders. In this instance, the black laugh appeared to whites too vigorous, too unrestrained, and connoted frivolity and immediacy. Novelist James Fenimore Cooper, describing Pinckster Day in New York City in 1757—the name deriving from the Dutch term for the Pentecost—wrote disparagingly of the occasion as "the great Saturnalia of New York blacks," when the majority of blacks in and around the city "were collected in thousands of those fields, beating banjoes, singing African songs, drinking, and worst of all, laughing in a way that seemed to set their very hearts rattling within their ribs. . . ."[3]

This attraction to—and anxiety about—the laugh was, as in the South, but an aspect of a larger concern regarding black diversion and pleasure-taking. The terminology used to describe Afro-Americans in the latter decades of the eighteenth century and into the nineteenth—"unabetted vigor," "passionately animated,"

"animated the whole body," "amusing antics," "as they became more excited, they became more expressive," and the like—suggested the personae of the performer.

Northerners, with an eagerness that surpassed southerners', seized upon the image of the performer, which took root in white consciousness in the pre-Revolutionary period. The performer became the conception by which whites regarded and perused black culture. Black talent was subsequently sought, nurtured, and energetically employed. Throughout the colonies, blacks could be seen fiddling, drumming, strumming, dancing, storytelling, prancing, and generally frolicking at white social functions and on special occasions. So desirable were those traits that numerous advertisements of slaves referred to their special musical abilities, and a number of blacks developed regional reputations. Caesar, for instance, owned by the Reverend Jonathan Todd of Connecticut, was frequently called upon to play for the dancing youth in the area. In New York City there was "Old King Charlie," a legendary character who performed on Pinckster Day. Though nearly seventy years old, "Old King Charlie," so named because of his royal birthmark, danced "to the delight and wonderment of the surrounding crowd, and which, as frequently, kept the faces of this joyous multitude broadly expanded in boisterous mirth and jollity."[4]

Commentary about their special endowments as "exquisite performers" abounded in the North. Irving was even moved to cite a unique ability as whistlers. Not a horse or an ox "will budge a foot until he hears the well-known whistle of his black driver and companion."[5] In New York, during the Dutch reign, blacks introduced dance steps and songs at Catherine Market, an important trading place and center for jockeys and boxers, and openly danced for whites in the streets during spring festivals. At Catherine Market and similar places, blacks engaged in contests and regularly performed for paying bystanders. Dancers usually brought along shingles—wooden planks about five or six feet in length—which were held by companions, who provided the beat by thumping out rhythms with their hands, or sometimes on a tom-tom.[6] Blacks paraded around circus rings as early as the Revolutionary period and, dressed as clowns, rode on horses.[7] In Baltimore in the 1790s, blacks applied for entertainment licenses. One male was granted permission to "Exhibit on the Slack Rope, Tumbling, &c.," another performed as a "Negro Rope Dancer," and a third was permitted to turn "White As A Show."[8] Still others developed reputations as storytellers. A widely known raconteur was Senegambia of Narragansett, whose style was reportedly reminiscent of Aesop.[9]

Listening and watching, northern whites were both fascinated and repelled by other aspects of black styles. Particularly intriguing were speech and dress patterns. That these mannerisms were having an effect on whites, especially children, could be seen in the counsel of no less a figure than Josiah Quincy, Jr., who likened black speech to a social disease. The young, he observed, "are early impressed with infamous and destructive ideas, and become extremely vitiated in their manners; they contract a negroish kind of accent, pronounciation and dialect, as well as ridiculous kind of behavior." Not only children, but "even many of the grown people, and especially the women, are vastly infected with the same disorder." Quincy's advice was that "Parents instead of talking to their very young children in the unmeaning way with us, converse to them as though they were speaking to a new imported African."[10]

What the attraction-repulsion further focused on—especially in contrast to the English tradition of public reserve and decorum—were the vibrantly expressive black mannerisms: their playful quality, rhythmical gait, high decibel levels, and quixotic mixing of English and African cultures, much of which bordered on the ridiculous to them. When whites attempted to convey these characteristics, to describe and translate them onto the printed page in the most scrupulous way, they often emphasized their humorous aspects. Stories of blacks' physical swivelings, dialect patter, and boisterous habits made their way into newspapers, diaries, and almanacs. In short, black behavior became humor fodder for the white community.

For an image to persist and take permanent hold of the social consciousness, however, more is required than its reportage in print and/or in the oral culture. It is essential that it develop a niche, a definable place, in the popular arts and culture. In the South, this place became the plantation house and the institutions that reflected its power and structure. The entertaining slave was enshrined as the performer throughout the region, whether he played at the master's house or in churches, at fairs, horse races, balls, or wherever the dominant class dressed up. In the North, in the absence of a narrow agrarian upper class, the counterpart of the entertaining slave eventually trooped to the theatrical stage as the minstrel man.

Although born of a single conception, the two regional figures were unequal in a curious way. So long as slavery defined the legal place of the African, whites anointed him as their official humorist in a direct and visible manner. The figure who performed was of black flesh. Once slavery was abolished in the North, however, a significant difference developed. In the beginnings of minstrelsy, and for several decades thereafter, the black minstrel man was white. Even though black minstrels would eventually claim part of the stage in the post–Civil War period, the blackface white figure became permanently etched in the popular culture. There he would remain for a full century, taking his stage antics to film and radio until the civil rights movement yanked him into the wings. Strangely, then, the image of the black man as a natural humorist was convoluted by its adoption by the white minstrel man, who sustained the initial image.

It was Alexis de Tocqueville, that incisive French observer who toured the country in the 1830s, who explained why the differences developed: "In the South, where slavery still exists, the Negroes are less carefully kept apart; they sometimes share the labors and the recreations of the whites. . . . In the North the white no longer distinctly perceives the barrier that separates him from the degraded race, and he shuns the Negro with the more pertinacity since he fears lest they should some day be confounded together."[11] There were other reasons for the rise of minstrelsy as the first indigenous American theatre, but once it became the dominant form of entertainment, it made possible a social distance between whites and blacks. Through the minstrel man and the theatrical apparatus, moreover, whites were able to control and certify the image that served them so well, and to ensure its longevity in the popular media.

Minstrelsy built its imagery, as we have seen, on folk and community expressions that extended as far back as the Revolutionary period. Blacks' presence as comics and performers expanded in the early decades of the next century as they cavorted in various guises in circuses, roamed the city streets fiddling and dancing, plied their skills for money before markets, saloons, and other popular places. Stage audiences also found them occasionally playing comics in dramas—but theatre audiences much oftener saw whites mimicking blacks.

Blackfacing as a device for injecting comic relief in dramas is traceable to ancient Greek theatre, but it came into high practice during the Elizabethan period. The blackening effect was heightened through the use of color-contrasting gloves, stockings, and face masks. In the latter part of the eighteenth century, the blackface character could be found in at least five plays in colonial and English dramas. In three of these productions, Africans were depicted as servants, and of all the various characters, they alone lacked Christian names.

In the first native musical work, *The Disappointment* (1767)— advertised as "a new Comic Opera"—the comic black, "Raccoon," is described as "an old debauchee." Mumbling in a thick dialect, a practice that would become stock minstrel formula, Raccoon displays vanity, greed, cowardice, and a fear of spirits and ghosts.[12]

As revolutionary fervor pitched toward confrontation, another English production, *The Candidate: or, The Humours of Virginia Election* (1775), presented a black character, "Ralpho," in Sambo fashion. Besides being foppish and vain, Ralpho spoke in a thick West Indian accent and hankered for watermelon: "Ahse gwine down to de sprink house 'n' ead me some waddemellon."[13] Blacks as fools make their appearance in John Leacock's *The Fall of Brit-*

ish Tyranny or, American Liberty Triumphant (1776), a romanticized version of the struggle between the Tories and revolutionists. "Cudjo" presents himself to Lord Kidnapper, who is eager to enlist blacks in the British army and has offered freedom as a reward for service. Kidnapper asks the name of the man who has run away:

CUDJO: Me massa cawra me Cudjo.

KIDNAPPER: Cudjo?—very good—was you ever christened, Cudjo?

CUDJO: No massa, me no crissen.

KIDNAPPER: Well, then I'll christen you—you shall be called Major Cudjo Thompson, and if you behave well, I'll soon make you a better man than your master, and if I find the rest of you behave well, I'll make you all officers, and after you have serv'd . . . a while, you shall have money in your pockets, good clothes on your backs, and be as free as them white men there. [Pointing forward to a parcel of Tories]

CUDJO: Tankee massa, gaw bresse, massa Kidnap.

SAILOR: [Aside.] What a damn'd big mouth that Cudjo has—as large as our main hatch-way—

COOK: [Aside.] Aye, he's come to a wrong place to make good use of it—it might stand some little chance at a Lord Mayor's feast.

Colonial theatres were sometimes rudimentary arrangements. Before funds could be procured for a permanent edifice in Boston in the early 1790s, for instance, a wooden shed of rude construction was built in an alley. There, amidst mud and livery stables, young men (no women were allowed) witnessed farces and pantomimes. One melodrama, *House,* required the action of several wild beasts, played by young boys hired for the occasion. As they cavorted, the audience participated by firing guns indirectly at the animals. Among the players was "a negro boy belonging to Doctor Jarvis," who took the part of a black bear. "Cuffy, equipt in a shaggy costume of Bruin, danced and hugged to admiration in a contest with a hunter. . . ." Unfortunately, a newcomer to the theatre took direct aim at the bear. He "died" a theatrical death to a "thunder of applause," but Cuffy had been severely wounded.

"These gaucheries occurred often," the author callously wrote, "and were not to be wondered at among a people in an incipient stage of playhouse amusement."[14]

The first production in which a black role was woven into the action was J. Robinson's *The New York Strategum; or, Banana's Wedding* (1792). Written for a New York audience, the play involves a black resident who disguises himself as a rural Yankee in order to woo a West Indian heiress. Although the black was an integral part of the plot rather than a momentary comic character, the comedy touched on class and racial pretensions. Banana is an ignorant West Indian whose status-driven mother wants him to marry a white woman of wealth.

Similarly, John Murdock's *The Triumph of Love; or, Happy Reconciliation* (1795) explored contemporary social customs by using a comic black. The main character, "Sambo" (played by white comedian William Bates), is a servant with a West Indian dialect who sings and dances, and seeks equality with whites. In the latter half of the play, Sambo is freed by his Quaker master—an act that has been cited as one of the earliest examples of abolitionist politics—but is clearly unable to cope with this new responsibility. Once released from bondage, Sambo proceeds to get drunk and wobbles off to bed loudly singing "liberty and quality forever." To himself he declares, "Sambo what a gal call a pretty fellow. Dis wool of mine curl so Sambo tinks himself handsome. He very 'complished, too. He sing well, he dance well; can't tink so pretty well."[15] Murdock's next drama, *The Politician* (1798), dealt with the political reaction to Jay's Treaty (1794). Four figures, "Pompey," "Sambo," "Cato," and "Caesar," perform a comic dialogue on the merits of the nations involved in the negotiations. Each discourses on the foreign events of the day, presenting not their own thoughts but those of their masters or former masters. Caesar encounters Pompey on the street:

CAESAR: Citizen, Pompey, how you do today, Sir?

POMPEY: Tank you, citizen Caesar, berry well; I hope you and you lady, enjoy good health.

CAESAR: Berry good, I gib you tank Sir.

POMPEY: Here cum citizen Sambo, twig he pig cu. Since he go free, how he wag his tail.

SAMBO: Gemmen, it gib me extreme pleasure to see you bote: I hope you are bote well, citizens. . . . Any ting new today, gemmen?

POMPEY: Trong talke French War.

CAESAR: Dam French.

POMPEY: Dam English.

CAESAR: Whay you dam English, for?

POMPEY: What debil you dam French, for?

CAESAR: Cause I don't like 'em.

POMPEY: Why you no like'em?

CAESAR: Cause massa no like'em.

POMPEY: My massa no like English—I hate'em too—drom proud—so conceit coxcomb—look like ebery body trunk in e nose . . . who you dor Sambo?

SAMBO: I go we massa, too. . . .[16]

That four black men could engage in a prolonged conversation about a current and complex subject indicated that the Sambo image was not rigid. At the same time, it was not open-ended, either. Rather, as the minstrels would later demonstrate, it suggests that Sambo could talk on relevant matters, from politics to religion, so long as he remained within the limits of the image.

Nor should it be overlooked that the narrow humorists' image was challenged on several fronts during this period. Blacks responded to their entrapment by presenting their own comedians and legitimate theatre. In the mid-1790s, a group of black comedians performed in Boston, only to encounter considerable opposition from the community. Antagonisms to the establishment of a theatre were equally intense. At the African Grove in Greenwich Village in the 1820s, blacks staged their own Shakespearean productions. Among the players was Ira Aldridge, who would achieve renown as a Shakespearean actor in Europe. So persistent were the physical assaults that the theatre was forced to close.

Because the colonial stage was dominated by the British, the voice inflection of black comedy was essentially in the West Indian mode in the late eighteenth and early nineteenth centuries. The patriotic fervor engendered by the War of 1812 changed that style in a way that would allow for greater American authenticity—or what passed as authentic in the white mind. In Albany, New York, a "Negro" sailor celebrated the victory over the British on Lake Champlain in the song "The Siege of Plattsburgh." The actor used the accepted form of blackface, but he accentuated an American black rather than a West Indian dialect. The song became highly popular—it could be heard into the late 1830s—and it influenced other songs such as "The Guinea Boy" (1816) and "Massa George Washington and Massa Lafayette" (1822).

By the early 1820s, songs and dances by white actors along the eastern seaboard expanded the character of the black. Wearing "black" clothing and imitating "black" dialogue, whites pranced in a jolly and comic style. In a popular tune, "The Bonja Song" (1818–1821), whites sang of black joys:

> Me sing all day, me sleep all night
> Me have no care, me sleep is light
> Me tink, no what tomorrow bring
> Me happy so me sing.[17]

A broadside circulated throughout Boston in the early 1820s celebrated the anniversary of the abolition of the slave trade. The circular parodied the event in the newly accepted black-voiced mode. A toast to the occasion highlighted "De day, one of does great nashumnal hepox which will call fort de sensumbility and de herhaw of good feelum of ebery son and daughter of Africa in dis world, and good many udder place beside, which you find tell of in de jography. . . ."[18]

By the late 1820s, the background props that had been slipping into place were finally assembled and the curtain opened on an indigenous form that would fix the Sambo image. To an extent, the minstrel show had its beginning in 1827, when George Washington Dixon and others smeared on blackface and donned exaggerated attire and sang "Coal Black Rose" and "My Long Tailed Blue." The significance of these two songs lay in the presentation of two specific comic black types, the flip sides of one coin that would become the currency of the minstrel theatre and the white jokes thereafter: the plantation "darky" and the city "dandy."

With the stage primed for a new type of theatre, all that was necessary was an especially catchy song coupled with a spritely dance and structured format to bring it to fruition. That came with Thomas D. Rice's performance in 1828 of a tune called "Jim Crow," a popular English ditty done in the African-American style. Rice, who eventually became known as "Jim Crow" or "Daddy" Rice, entertained audiences with a little jig and words to match:

> Wheel about, turn about,
>   Do jis so,
> An' ebery time I wheel about
>   I jump Jim Crow

Donning tattered clothing, applying blackface, singing in "darky" dialect slightly tempered by New York background, Rice jumped to "Jim Crow" thousands of times and was eventually dubbed by his fellow actors "the first and best knight of the burnt-cork."

Rice was quickly joined by other performers, all northerners, most of whom had had little or no contact with southern culture or slavery. Some were immigrants who had only recently settled in the North. The close similarity of the minstrel airs and English and German songs made it possible for immigrants to adopt and extend the style. The mélange of these differing dialects and inflections attempting to mimic and convey African-American music, dance, language, and comedy must have been peculiar, if not weird. For not only did the performers present diverse geographical and cultural views, they spiced their acts with personal experience. As a result, the minstrel was also a conveyor of mid-nineteenth-century immigrant messages. The potpourri became even thicker when immigrants from Eastern Europe added to the theatre at the end of the century.

Once established, the minstrel show became the most popular fare throughout the country, the extender of Sambo in both high and low culture. Shuffling and drawling, crackling and dancing, wisecracking and high-stepping, the white minstrel men welded the image of the black male to the material culture, laid the foundation for its entry into the electronic media of the following century, and carried it to audiences on three continents.

Minstrelsy's reach was vast, its acceptance instantaneous. At least thirty full-time companies performed the show at its height, in the decades immediately preceding and following the Civil War, before blacks themselves challenged it, improved it, and changed its style. Blackface players strutted before groups representing all levels of society and traveled to all sections of the country. Ralph Keller, an aspiring young white player who spent three years on the road, later wrote that "we steamed thousands of miles on the Western and Southern rivers. We went, for instance, the entire navigable lengths of the Cumberland and Tennessee. The *Palace* and *Raymond* would sometimes run their noses upon the banks of some of these rivers where there was not a habitation in view, and by the hour of the exhibition the boats and shore would, be thronged with people."[19] Such was the international drawing power of minstrelsy that its troupers reversed the direction of the Atlantic theatrical trade and made their imprint on English and French stages.

Minstrelsy was not limited strictly to the professional troupes. Having been involved with low culture in its development, it naturally continued its practice, but with the newly devised big stage formats. Amateur groups quickly were organized in the cities and countrysides, establishing a tradition that would continue well into the post–World War II period. The national identity of the minstrelsy as *the* American stage form made possible its extension. Prior to the signing of the trade treaty with Japan in 1854, in the ceremonial change of presents and rituals, American sailors aboard the *Commodore Matthew C. Perry* offered a shipboard minstrel show. (The Japanese had presented a demonstration of the ancient ritual of sumo wrestling and ceremonial dancing.) The minstrel program stated that the players would appear first as "colored Gemmen of the North" and then as "niggas of the

South," maintaining the bipolar unity of the "dandy" and "darky." "Yah-yah-Sambo," intoned Bones to Tamborine, "how you be?" as the players shuffled and guffawed before their Japanese audience, who "laughed heartily at the costumes and antics of the performers."

Did the Japanese comprehend the language and the meaning of blackface? A member of the delegation, fascinated by the performance, sketched the affair—and "Sambo" became part of Japanese language and customs. A hundred years later, advertisements for toothpaste and other products used a grinning blackface man attired in top hat and tails.[20]

The heyday of minstrelsy went on for several decades, but its theme and format—especially its use of blackface—extended beyond the years. At the time of its heaviest influence, the debate over slavery was polarizing the country, the earliest attempts were being made to assimilate thousands of blacks in the North, and laws and practices were hammering out civil rights. The popularity of the show reflected the peculiarities of white attitudes. On the one hand, as Robert Toll has argued, the minstrels portrayed blacks as "invariably inept fools or absurd imitations of the worst in whites"; yet on the other, as William Stowe and David Grimsted have amply countersuggested, the complexity of comic portrayal and the variety of the theatrical mode were most impressive: "the black was allowed a much more varied theatrical life than many of the other stage ethnic or regional stereotypes. Wit and buffoonery, music sentimental and comic, dancing stately and grotesque, pretension and simplicity, pathos and farce, all were stressed and held together by a consistently shrewd simplicity and naturalness."[21]

At the very least, as Constance Rourke declared in her seminal work, *American Humor: A Study of the National Character* (1931), the rise of minstrelsy signified a change of the Afro-American's position in northern society. Jim Crow appeared as *The Liberator* issued its militant call for the abolition of slavery—and minstrelsy's dissemination of black culture heightened the struggle for emancipation. For what minstrelsy did was connect black comedy to the mainstream of American humor. "The Negro minstrel joined with the Yankee and the backwoodsman to make a comic trio, appearing in the same era, with the same intensity."[22]

While "joined" has a harmonious ring to it, the comic trio was hardly of equal proportions. Two became personifications of individualism, whereas the other served in the role of national jester. The fact that the minstrel opened a window into black culture should not distract from the format in which he functioned. Northern whites, like Southerners, could now watch *their* blacks perform. And *watching*, in and of itself, defused the threat to white culture.

The minstrel, then, expanded the white view of black culture and comedy not previously possible, but did so within a preconceived formula. That formula, built on an imagic foundation, was buttressed by a brassy and exciting theatrical format. Wherever the minstrel went, the show was preceded by a street parade announcing its arrival and advertising its attractions; blackface actors in tattered dress danced to music and blaring noise. Once inside the theatre, audiences focused their gaze on a backdrop of slave cabins surrounded by cotton fields. Instantly the action began, with the interlocutor engaging the end men in swift, comical repartee followed by acts of minstrel choruses and dancing. "The effect was exotic and strange," Rourke noted, "with the swaying figures and black faces of the minstrels lighted by guttering gas flames of candlelight on small country stages, or even in the larger theatres."[23]

The substance of minstrel materials ran the gamut from the enlightening and witty to the derogatory and mean. Within this range, the language was exaggerated, the blackface characters were exciting and pretentious, the costumes were a mélange of colors, and the action was upbeat and lively. In their treatment of race relations, whites could be cruel and brutal, but could also be fooled and mocked. Skits occasionally reflected on the black plight and social inequities. Yet a theme that coursed through the lyrics was the intrinsic difference between blacks and whites:

> Niggers hair am berry short,
> White folks hair am longer,
> White folks dey smell very strong,
> Niggers dey smell stronger.[24]

Minstrelsy's attraction extended beyond the stage and was reflected in print media. Newspapers, pamphlets, comic books, broadsides, handbills, posters, and sheet music covers reproduced the humor, monologue, stump speeches, and images of the dancing minstrel. A series of newspaper sketches appeared in 1855: *Black Diamonds: or, Humor, Satire and Sentiment, Treated Scientifically by Professor Julius Caesar Hanibal in a Series of Burlesque Lectures Darkly Colored.* In an example of dialect most demeaning, an anonymous blackface lecturer pretentiously regales his audience with a discourse:

> I hab come, as you all know, from 'way down in ole Warginna, whar I studded edicashun and siance all for myself, to gib a corse of lectures on siance gineraly, an events promiscuously, as dey time to time occur. De letter ob invite I receibed from de komitee from dis unlitened city, was full ob flattery as a gemman ob my great disernment, edication, definement, and research could wish.[25]

It was during this period that the names Tambo and Sambo became more closely associated with the comic. Tambo was often the name of one of the minstrel end men. Sambo made his appearance in song titles and jokes and skits. The plantation figure was popularized in such musical pieces as "Sambo's Lamentation or Dinah Mae" (1852), "Sambo's Right to Be Kilt" (1864), and "Sambo's Invitation" (1869). The urban dandy came alive in "Sambos 'Dress to be Bred 'run," in which a well-dressed black in cutaway tails lectured to a black audience, all of whom were thick-lipped, toothy, wide-eyed, and animated.

Known as authentic black comedy, minstrelsy had a pronounced effect on amusement formats. Steamships, railroads, and canalboats featured entertainment for passengers, and black comedy immediately became part of the popular fare. A Norwegian lawyer and jurist, sent by his government to study the American jury system in the 1840s, was treated to performances by bands aboard public conveyances. On one trip he found the band "none too good," but "it won general approval by presenting comical Negro songs, accompanied by the guitar. . . ."[26]

It is a matter of speculation whether for the majority of whites the theatre of minstrelsy was a valid presentation of black culture. Yet the question of its authenticity is important in attempting to assess minstrelsy's impact on contemporary white attitudes and images. For one thing, the extent to which minstrel materials were based on direct contact with blacks, North or South, derived from black culture via osmosis, or added by blacks themselves, is uncertain. Constance Rourke maintained that the "songs and to a large extent the dances show Negro origins," although she further observed that "they were often claimed by white composers."[27] Rourke contended that white actors had close contact with Afro-Americans. "Many minstrels had lived in the South and West and knew the Negro at first hand." One minstrel man had "mastered his lingo, cries, snatches of song, as well as his odd manner" by following and watching "an old peddler of watermelons with a donkey cart in a Georgia town." Performers such as Daniel Emmett, who wrote "Ole Dan Tucker" and "Dixie," had "close contact with the Negro," and Stephen Foster "haunted Negro camp meetings for rhymes and melodies." Such experiences, "freshly caught," made their performances "whole and rich."[28]

Rourke's examples suggest a high degree of contact on the part of several popular minstrel men. Yet it would appear that she was subliminally influenced by the stereotype itself. Rourke argued that traits of the Afro-American made him susceptible to imitation. In a revealing passage, she exclaimed that "Burlesque appeared, but burlesque was *natural* to the Negro."[29]

Other scholars also suggest a high degree of familiarity with the plantation and black life. Hans Nathan, in *Dan Emmett and the Rise of Early Negro Minstrelsy,* held that several of the early impersonators were "close to life."[30] John Pendleton Gaines asserted in *The Southern Plantation* that there were some early tunes with roots in black reality, such as "Old Dan Tucker" (1841).[31] Robert Toll added a different cultural factor. Unbeknown to whites, he asserted, elements of black culture infiltrated white practices and consciousness. "Since cultural interaction between blacks and whites was common in Southern frontier areas, minstrels probably unwittingly included elements of black culture in some of what they thought was white frontier lore," he surmised in *Blacking Up*. Its impact upon the entertainment industry was but another positive aspect of minstrelsy. "Besides confirming the folk origins of American popular entertainment, minstrelsy's borrowing of Afro-American culture is of great significance because it was the first indication of the powerful influence Afro-American culture would have on the performing arts in America."[32]

Despite these inputs, however, Toll viewed the minstrel as a dehumanizing portrayal of the black. William Stowe and David Grimsted, in an analysis of "White-Black Humor," shrewdly noted that minstrel publications of the nineteenth century make it difficult to ascertain minstrelsy's racial origins. The minstrel should be seen, they argued, as expressing the strength and willingness of the underclasses. Though reinforcing social exclusion, the minstrel also allowed "a complexity in comic portrayal," a variety of theatrical forms that stressed the blacks' own mode, and, even more significant, "a mask which allowed deep expressiveness of emotions of loss and longing, as well as ridicule of social and intellectual platitudes and the discrepancies between American dreams and American realities." Rather than obscuring reality, the blackface mask actually "distanced things enough so that truths could be expressed which would have been profoundly troubling or socially dangerous if presented or taken in serious form."[33]

Certainly, in the long run minstrelsy's widespread acceptance and charm paved the way for ragtime's popular development at the turn of the century, thereby enabling black musicians to present their own compositions to audiences already partly educated in nuances of black music.[34] In a curious way, then, the Caucasian *feel* for black styles was enormously enhanced and widened by the minstrel's complex utilization of the black experience. At the same time, however, the minstrel sustained the image of black as possessing a unique connection to happiness. Kenneth Lynn put it bluntly when he stated that the minstrels created "a white imitation of a black imitation of a contented slave."[35]

Many white songwriters and performers of the early minstrel period prided themselves on their ability to emulate the black style. One composer even offered a fifty-dollar reward to anyone who could prove that he was not the author of some forty-odd popular "Negro" songs.[36] The most famous practitioner, Dan Emmett, spent hours perfecting black speech mannerisms and gait and was praised by whites for this special talent. "His understanding and rendering of the Negro dialect was perfect," wrote a reporter in 1895, in Emmett's declining days; he was "thoroughly trained to the sweet tone of the melodious Negro's voice"; and despite his age, "a few old Negro expressions and songs from him showed that he had not lost his old-time understanding of them." Minstrelsy had undergone considerable changes, the reporter added, in a boastful nod to Caucasian cleverness, but the minstrels of Emmett's day "did nothing but what the Negro could and did do."[37]

The personae of the black minstrel came in for some contemporary criticism. An occasional white, North and South, and for different reasons, objected to the malapropisms and caricatures of the blackface figures. A particularly scathing indictment came from an anonymous southerner in the mid-1850s whose intent, he explained, was to accord minstrelsy a literary status while rectifying the erroneous view of plantation life. Hardly a song had been produced since "Ole Dan Tucker," he charged, "which does not present the most glaring of blackfaced impudent imposition." There were "vile parodies, sentimental love songs, dirges for dead wenches who are generally sleeping under the willow on the bank of some stream, and melancholy reminiscenses of negroic childhood," which had replaced the grand ballads of a former period. There were not more than ten songs "which bear any trace of the cotton-field afflatus, and these ten, with only one exception, have been so patched and dressed up for drawing-room inspection, that they look like a bumpkin who has suddenly come into possession of a fortune." What the anonymous southerner desired was realism—and a recognition of the essence of black humor. "No hardships or troubles can destroy, or even check [Negro] happiness and levity. As I pen these words, the grinning image of the boy Quash rises up before me like a type of his race."[38]

No matter, for in the decades before the Civil War such criticisms were drowned out by the din of minstrel sounds to thunderous applause. An evening at the theatre produced memorial praise and sentimentality. Wrote a New York editor ecstatically after attending a minstrel show in 1840: "Entering the theatre, we found it crammed from pit to dome, and the best representative of our American Negro that we ever saw was stretching every mouth in the house to its utmost tension. Such a natural gait!—such a laugh!—and such a twitching-up of arm and shoulder! It was *the* Negro par excellence. Long live James Crow, Esquire."[39]

Mark Twain's enthusiasm was no less restrained. It was "the real nigger show—the genuine nigger show—the extravagant nigger show." It was theatre that had "no peer." In later life, Twain exclaimed that minstrels still had no peer to rival his early experience. He saw his first "negro musical show" in Hannibal in the 1840s. It "burst upon us as a glad and stunning surprise." He was enamored of the extravagant burlesque, colorful attire, carnival tone, and full makeup, with lips "thickened and lengthened with bright red paint to such a degree that their mouths resembled slices cut in a ripe watermelon." What made the minstrel "delightfully and satisfyingly funny," Twain wrote in his *Autobiography*, was the opening exchange between the end men. It was a faithful representation of a piece of Negro life. "Sometimes the quarrel would last five minutes, the two contestants shouting deadly threats in each other's faces with the noses not six inches apart, the house shrieking with laughter all the while at this happy and accurate initiation of the usual and familiar negro quarrel."[40]

Analogous praise came from the other side of the Atlantic. Minstrelsy had a powerful tradition in England, and when Rice made his first appearance on the English stage he was called back for twenty encores. In England and Scotland, minstrel-song collections were sold in large numbers, troupes were organized, and songs were performed in blackface on stages and in pubs. Novelist William Thackeray visited a minstrel show and wrote gushily of his authentic Negro experience: "I heard a humorous balladist not long ago, a minstrel with wool on his head and an ultra-Ethopian complexion, who performed a negro ballad that I confess moistened these spectacles in a most unexpected manner."[41]

Neither time nor appearance diminished the equation of the minstrel with the black idiom. In certain ways, both strengthened it. When blacks managed to reclaim their own heritage, it was often, though not always, within the white mold. Several black troupes functioned before the Civil War, but they had trouble securing bookings and were forced into prevailing standards. A shortage of actors during the war enabled blacks to appear in white minstrel shows—ironically, in blackface. An observer of the scene in the 1860s wrote whimsically: "Soon the opera glasses revealed the amusing fact, that, although every minstrel was by nature as black as black could be, yet all the performers have given their faces a coating of burnt-cork, in order that their resemblence to Yankee minstrels might be in every respect complete."[42] Changes occurred after the war, when black groups performed *au naturel*, in their own style, and deepened the character of the format. As invigorating as the black input was, its effect on white attitudes and images remains unknown.

The minstrel style fed into other forms but also remained highly popular in low culture. It altered the way in which clowns performed—for instance, adding splits, jumps, and cabrioles, and blackface makeup as well—and a new and different clown emerged. Competition from these other forms forced minstrelsy to adjust to changes, and changes occurred not in the format but in the material. As newer immigrants poured into the cities, dialects from the Eastern European countries filled the songs with specialized humor and added to the black image. There was a decrease in the use of blackface and an increase in the number of black actors, troupes, and influence.

Yet the problem that had confronted blacks in the mid-nine-teenth century continued to plague them. Bert Williams, one of the finest dancers and comedians in the *Ziegfeld Follies,* was forced to hide his light complexion—and many of his special talents as well—under dark makeup. "Theatre-goers who saw him in his blackface did not know what he actually looked like."[43] In his act Williams was the slouching Jonah man, the careless, unlucky black for whom everything went awry. Williams ached to convey both sides of the "shiftless darky—the pathos as well as the fun." It was not to be. "White America gave him no choice. He was damned to be a 'funny nigger.'"[44]

For black performers and black culture at large, the later min-strel theatre offered ambivalent choices. On the one hand, there were many more black minstrels introducing such innovations as the jig, buck-and-wing, Virginia "essence," soft shoe, and stop-time dance; black songwriters were originating new tunes and approaches. Yet many of these styles were generally controlled by a white power structure, and black troupes became popular by performing before white audiences in the traditional minstrel guise. The "creole show," a highly creative format devised by blacks in the 1890s, reached only a small white audience. Black songs were frequently popularized by white actors. And in the 1870s and 1880s the themes of songs and acts written by whites expressed a yearning for the plantation past. Sambo lived on in these productions, the skits resounding with a familiar patter: "Well, Sambo, how is you feeling dis splendiferous evening?" intoned Bones in *The Boys of New York* (1890s). "Oh, I'se feelin' good—sorter twilightly as it was. . . ." "Did you know I was mar-ried, Pomp?" "You married?" "I am—are you?" inquired Sambo. "—No—I—I—escaped," Pomp sputtered.[45]

By the turn of the century practically every city, town, and rural community had amateur minstrel groups, aided by the publication of hundreds of low-cost minstrel books containing full produc-tions. All occasions and social levels were included. *The Darkey & Comic Drama,* for example, contained instructions for fraternal organizations in "The Masonic Lodge," and a complete show for adolescents, literally entitled *Unchanging Voices for Boys and Girls of the Upper Grammar and Junior High Schools,* appeared in a compilation, *The Newsboys and Bootblacks Minstrel Show.*[46]

Minstrelsy's drawing power remained surprisingly strong throughout the country but particularly in small towns and rural areas in the early decades of the twentieth century. A narrowed variation of the minstrel, the "Uncle Tom show," became extremely popular in the South and the West. It probably reached more "amusement starved people," than any other entertainment, wrote J. C. Furnas in *Goodbye to Uncle Tom,* because "pious folk— for whom other kinds of shows were sinful—could be persuaded that Uncle Tom was different."[47] By the mid-1920s there were more than a dozen Toms operating in small towns and cities.

And in such unexpected places as prisons. Prison officials sanctioned blackface theatre in both men's and women's institutions. Some shows were unusual indeed. At the Federal Industrial Institution for Women in Alderson, West Virginia (the first federally authorized prison for females, built in 1923), minstrel acts were performed throughout the 1920s and '30s. Directed by the authorities, the inmates enacted such shows as *Wotta Night* (1933) and *Down in Haiti* (1935)—the "Emperor Jones" was the central role here. "A clever minstrel was staged and arranged by Miss Cook . . . ," lauded a report of one typical performance, "and the colored girls gave their customary good entertainment."[48]

Minstrel songs in the decades before World War II commemorated the halcyon days of minstrelsy and chorused for its resurrection. "Bring back, bring back those minstrel days—" went a 1926 song ("Those Minstrel Days"), "Bring back those old faces in black, Features we all love so— . . . Altho' they've gone to rest their memory stays—Bring back those minstrel days."[49]

"Down at the Old Minstrel Show!" was no less sentimental:

> Where, tell me, where are the old minstrel shows,
> That I saw years ago with my dad?
> Where, tell me, where are those sweet melodies,
> That have clung to my heart since a lad?

Gone are the days of those old minstrel men.
Oh, why can't we bring them back again?

Chorus
I'd love to hear them play—the songs of yesterday,
DOWN AT THE OLD MINSTREL SHOW

Songs that brought the tears, and lingered on for years,
DOWN AT THE OLD MINSTREL SHOW

Old fashioned jokes, for old fashioned folks,
Old fashioned songs of long ago. . . .[50]

So powerful was the blackface style and dialect humor that the curtain kept going up—and up. Among the federal government's efforts to lift downcast spirits during the wrenching depression of the 1930s were minstrel shows sponsored by the Works Progress Administration. The Federal Theatre Project not only produced minstrel shows around the country, it also distributed minstrel publications for local use. *56 Minstrels* (1938), for instance, contained a repertoire for juvenile groups: Boy Scouts, schoolchildren, club associations, and similar community outfits. The work contained such arrangements as "The Coon-Town Thirteen Club," "The Darktown Follies," "Watermelon Minstrel," and "Plantation Days with the Snowflake Family." Instructions indicated whether blackface or whiteface was to apply. The shows were smaller versions of the large extravaganzas of the past but were faithful to their thrust: dialect, shuffling, buffoonery, and low comedy.[51]

During the socially conscious days of the 1930s, audiences were treated to polished but also insensitive minstrel fare. Serious topics were often undermined by crude humor. *The Chain Gang Minstrel* was a typical defusing of an issue made highly public in the print and movie media. In the show, six prisoners—Agony, Bozo, Crawfish, Drumstick, Eggnog, and Funnybone—were the end men. The spoofing began with the opening line from the interlocutor: "Gentlemen, be seated. Well, Mr. Crawfish, how are you?"

CRAWFISH: [Looks about himself with disconsolate expression]
I's all in.

INTER: Yes, I guess you are all in for ten years. How about you, Mr. Drumstick? Are you having a good time?

DRUMSTICK: *Havin'* a good time? Man, I's *doin'* a good time.

INTER: Mr. Bozo, you look as snappy as a firecracker.

BOZO: An' not so long 'go I was a snappy safecracker.

INTER: It appears to me that you are quite a wise cracker.

BOZO: No, sah, boss. If I'd been a wise cracker, I'd nevah got ketched safe-crackin'. Trouble am with safe-crackin' 'taint safe 'nough crackin' safes.

INTER: What are you thinking of, Mr. Eggnog, that makes you so blue?

EGGNOG: Lawsy! Is I lookin' blue? If I isn't black, I's sho' colorblind.[52]

The WPA also produced minstrel shows in the puppet tradition. In the northern cities, the *Marionette Vaudeville* had stringed dolls jumping to minstrel tunes and skits. Among the different types of shows was a version of Helen Bannerman's *Little Black Sambo,* one of the most popular of the nation's children's stories. It featured a young black couple with a son, depicting them in the mode: the mother was attired in a servant's outfit, with a long skirt and multicolored bandanna, the father in a multicolored shirt and panama hat, and son Sambo was only partially clad, in overalls. Being puppets, they wore perpetual grins against coal-black faces with wide eyes and thick red lips.[53]

Forms of minstrelsy played right through the years of the Second World War. Undeterred by democratic ideology, the blackface minstrel pranced and sang for both the military and civilian populations. As it had in 1917–1918, the federal government utilized the entertainment industry as a means of creating a unified and militant populance and easing its personal tragedies. Shortly after the beginning of hostilities, the Writers War Board under the United Services Organization (USO) was set up, one section of which dealt with supplying comedy and entertainment materials to special service units in military facilities. The overall aim was to have the military develop its own productions with the aid of established writers, composers, and producers.

Within the USO, the Writers and Materials Committee, headed by John Shubert, a member of the powerful theatrical family, published material for the military. The comedy division of the committee was headed by Mort Lewis, a radio and movie scriptwriter who had been with the *Amos 'n' Andy* and *Pic 'n' Pat* radio shows. Lewis's specialty during the war was writing minstrel and comedy shows for hospitals and other military institutions. In some of the productions, both white and black patients participated on makeshift stages, drawling and moving to a minstrel beat.[54]

At least six volumes containing hundreds of minstrel and comedy acts were distributed to military bases around the world under the aegis of USO–Camp shows. "Minstrelsy is the one form of American entertainment which is purely our own," the introduction to the materials patriotically intoned. "It delighted our great-grandfathers and has survived through the years because it offers an audience a full evening of entertainment, complete with comedy, singing and various 'specialties.'" Using blackface, it explained, was not entirely necessary for the full production, but it recommended that the end men "do so to give the traditional atmosphere of the minstrel show."

The "magic realm of minstrelsy" was the theme offered by the committee. In a typical production, the end men were directed in their Sambo roles: "Euphus" was a small, meek, nervous type whose behavior was characterized by occasional stuttering and stammering, a slight quivering of the lower lip, and rolling of the eyeballs and trembling of the body when frightened by spooks; "Asbestos," patterned after Brother Crawford of the *Amos 'n' Andy* show, articulated very rapidly in an extremely high-pitched voice, and moved in quick and jerky movements.[55] Two other end men encounter each other in *The Dance:*

> JANUARY: Say Molasses, do you know what happened to your gal, Ducky Pew?
>
> MOLASSES: Ah, dear old Ducky. The last time I seen Ducky, she tossed me a rose between her teeth.
>
> JANUARY: Is that so? What did you do?
>
> MOLASSES: I threw back her teeth.

JANUARY: Well, you'll be interested to know that the new hostess
here at camp is none other than Ducky Pew.

MOLASSES: Ducky? (Enter DUCKY PEW in slinky gown). Here she is,
Ducky!

DUCKY: Hello, small, dark and repulsive. Are you glad to see me?

MOLASSES: I should smother to congeal.[56]

The stage minstrel show had its parallel in the Paramount movie
Dixie (1943), a hackneyed version of the life of Daniel Emmett,
the song's composer. Bing Crosby, featured in the lead role, performed in blackface; Willie Best, one of the outstanding film
"Sambo" practitioners, provided the comedy. In the opening
scene, a paddle steamer plies the Ohio River. "Negro" workers are
heard singing on the banks. Aboard the freight deck, sprawled out
on the cotton bales, are "husky negro stevedores and roustabouts.
They are singing a rousting spiritual." On the passenger deck, puff-
ing his pipe and viewing the scene, is Dan Emmett. On impulse,
he joins in the group performance. Black eyes pierce upward; then
the men grin, and continue the song with him. It is a comfortable
if not a contented scene. Mechanical trouble, however, occurs in
the boiler room. Emmett assists four "big negroes" shoveling coal
and inquires, "How far is it to New Orleans?" "'Bout fo' million
shovelfuls, boss," answers one of them. The major minstrel scene
is an extravaganza of color and exaggerated costumes; a full stage-
wide curtain in the form of an extended, grinning, toothy, red-
lipped mouth with kinky hair; southern drawls à la Hollywood
Boulevard; animated dancing and a formulaic plot.[57]

Life magazine ran a four-page article on the film, showing pictures from old-time minstrel shows intermixed with movie stills.
Ironically, a nine-page article in the same issue, "Race War in
Detroit," subtitled "Americans Maul and Murder Each Other as
Hitler Wins a Battle in the Nation's Most Explosive City," brought
no editorial comment on the juxtaposition of the two seemingly
most disparate events of the year.[58]

In sharp contrast to a series of socially conscious films of the
immediate postwar period—*Home of the Brave, Pinky, Lost Bound-*

aries, Intruder in the Dust, and *No Way Out*—the blackface minstrel demonstrated his vast continuing appeal in *The Jolson Story* (1946). The film was a remake of the first, partly "talking" Warner Brothers production of *The Jazz Singer* (1927), which, in a general way, mirrored the life of the popular singer Al Jolson, who starred in the movie as well. In the second version, the voice and songs of Jolson were dubbed into the miming body of Larry Parks, another white actor, who had previously appeared in lackluster parts. So rewarding were the box office returns that a sequel was made several years later, *Jolson Sings Again* (1949). Eddie Cantor, the singer-dancer who had achieved stardom by donning blackface and rolling his saucer eyes in the *Ziegfeld Follies* and later in films, advertised his praise in blackface in the *Hollywood Reporter*. "Al" was mawkishly congratulated for having his life story "enacted by such a great cast, listening to those heart-warming songs and looking at familiar scenes . . . even if you think I'm a sissy I want you to know that I cried a little. . . ."[59] A fourth film appeared in the early 1980s, starring Neil Diamond, a soft-rock singer, sans blackface.

The initial movie, *The Jazz Singer,* and to an extent the films that followed over the decades, cast insight into the influential role blackface performing assumed in white culture. Moreover, it demonstrates how the cinema industry, by promoting and uplifting the self-effacing Jolson, furthered the field of entertainment as a desirable, if not preferred, profession.

The only son of an immigrant Russian Jew, an orthodox cantor from a continuous line of cantors, eschews his father's urging to maintain the heritage and opts for the musical stage. He desperately wants to become a jazz singer, or, as the movie states, "a raggety-time" singer, meaning one who performs black songs in blackface. The father is appalled and the son is adamant. In a progression of wrenching scenes, father and son are constantly torn apart by their opposite drives, both representing conflicts in American society at that historical moment: between first- and second-generation immigrants, tradition and opportunity, the individual and the family, and the altar and the stage.

After years of separation and struggle on the vaudeville circuit, the son has an opportunity to achieve stardom, a chance to appear in a Broadway show. That opportunity, though, coincides with another significant event. The father suffers an illness on the eve of Yom Kippur, one of the holiest of Jewish holidays, and cannot officiate; the synagogue is without a cantor to perform the service. Symbolically, both the religious occasion and the opening of the show occur at the exact same time. His mother and the family's closest friend go to the theatre to plead with the jazz singer to take his father's, indeed, *his* place on the altar. The son is anguished. To leave the show on opening night, as the producer angrily explains to him, is to ruin his opportunity. Yet to perform in the cantor's role is to honor his dying father's wish and maintain historical continuity. Which will be sacrificed, the European past or the American future? "No man has the right to make that decision," the jazz man cries out.

On the eventful night, the jazz singer is seen in the synagogue, delivering the melodious prayers. The decision has been made; he has connected with his past. Or has he? The film does not end with the synagogue but with the stage. His absence has not damaged his chance. On the contrary, in the closing scene he performs, in the movie's sole blackface act, to a packed house. The jazz singer, the raggety-time singer, he of Russian-Jewish ancestry, belts out "Mammy," a sentimental ballad to his mother, whose tears stream down her beatific face.

The admixture of the scene is revealing. Although the film has it both ways—both father and son are fulfilled—it is the blackface entertainer who prevails. Not the European cantor but the American minstrel man is the role that has eminency. The black as performer—or, rather, the blackface white performer representing the black—is the one destined for celebrity status.

On the national level, the Jolson films marked the end of a century of burnt cork and blackface grease on the white circuit. The minstrel show and blackface theatrics virtually disappeared on the urban stages and in the electronic media. The Jolsons and the Cantors were gone. In Philadelphia in the 1960s, bowing to pressure from civil rights groups and adverse publicity, the customary blackface of the Shriners in their Annual Mummers Parade on New Year's Day was discarded in favor of goldface.

The minstrel image, however, was tenacious. Gone from the national stage, minstrelsy continued to flourish in high schools and colleges, in the small cities, towns, and villages. As late as the mid-1970s—in Traverse City, Michigan, for instance—the annual Rotary Minstrel Show was a mainstay in the town's affairs. Every spring the Rotarians organized a two-day event consisting of comedy skits, specialty acts, and a blackface chorus with vocal solos. Describing it as "a wholesome, end-of-winter laugh at ourselves," the president of the local college sold tickets to the faculty and applied blackface for his part in the chorus. Similar shows were performed in nearby communities. In Ballaire, Michigan, the Lions presented an annual minstrel show to coincide with a screening of *Jolson Sings Again* at the school gym.[60] On the East Coast, in Lowell and Chelmsford, Massachusetts, minstrel shows were regular events.

These events, though, were hidden from the national view. The generations of the post-1960s, reared in an entertainment culture controlled by film and television industries sensitive to minority groups, only rarely came into contact with the white blackface performer, or with the main elements of minstrelsy. Minstrelsy as a force, as an aspect of white perceptions, swiftly receded in the national consciousness.

Minstrelsy's legacy was as complex as it was devious. Without doubt, the minstrel disseminated the image of the black man as the natural performer, the comedian par excellence. Once wedded to the stage, minstrelsy made the plantation slave and urban dandy into institutionalized images locked into the national culture. That image was often assaulted, especially by blacks when they had the power to do so, but it remained fast in white society, which resisted attempts to have it overturned.

Within its humorous confines, whites could peer into black culture without much anxiety, subject their stereotypes to some skepticism, cope with ambivalent racial feelings, and appreciate the nuances of the black experience. Early minstrelsy was especially crucial in allowing blacks and whites the opportunity to work out complicated living arrangements in the face of violent situations.

Still, the black-and-red grinning face of Sambo, his laughable malapropisms and pretensions, his energetic manner of movement and exaggerated clothing styles, conveyed the jester. They especially connoted a being with limited intelligence. As minstrelsy declined, it gave way to a crudity that reinforced the viciousness of unrestrained racism. At the zenith of Jim Crow, minstrelsy was but another aspect of the popular culture that featured a stereotype which was wholly demeaning.

Sheet music cover, 1829

Joke book cover, in the minstrel tradition (1850s-1880s)

A medicinal product hawked by an "Uncle Remus" type— 1880s' trade card

A "dandy" couple in an 1880s' trade card advertisement

An exaggerated pose of a
turn-of-the-century chef
in a magazine advertisement

Advertisement from the turn of the century

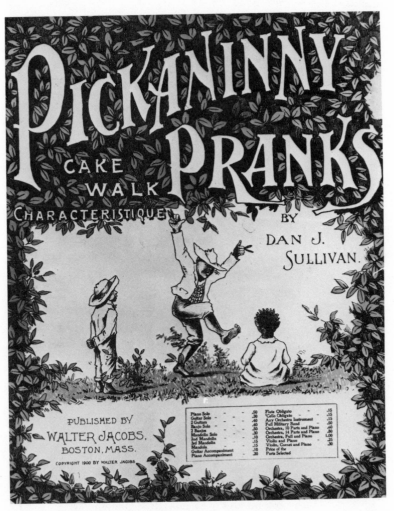

1900 "darky" sheet music cover

Early postcard, this one mailed from Ohio in 1908

The stolen prize is a watermelon
on this 1920s' postcard

A New Year's greeting card, 1910-1920s

A Familiar Figure
on the "Campus"
Do you recognize Him?

Deliveryman on a postcard, 1930s

5

Impressions in Boldface

He is extravagantly imitative. The older negroes here have—
with some spice of comic mixture in it—that formal,
grave and ostentatious style of manners, which belonged
to the gentlemen of former days; they are profuse of bows and
compliments, and very aristocratic in their way. The
younger ones are equally to be remarked for aping the style
of the present time, and especially for such tags of
dandyism in dress as come within their reach. Their
fondness for music and dancing is a predominant passion. . . .
Their gayety of heart is coinstitutional and perennial, and
when they are together they are as voluble and noisy as so
many blackbirds. In short, I think them the most good-
natured, careless, light-hearted, and happily-constructed
human beings I have ever seen.
>   —John Pendleton Kennedy, *Swallow Barn, or a Sojourn*
>   *in the Old Dominion* (1832)

I've never forgotten the colored elevator operator in the
Birmingham hotel who called each stop in the usual manner:
    "Eleventh floor."
    "Sixth floor."
    "Fourth floor."
    But at the lobby level he threw open the elevator door with a flour-
ish and proudly announced: "Birmingham."
>   "Life in These United States," *Reader's Digest*
>   (February 1944)

The print Sambo existed contemporaneously with his blackface
counterpart. Ubiquitous in the print culture of the nineteenth and
twentieth centuries was the grinning contour of the black male. In

pamphlets, magazines, sermons, novels, short stories, children's books, manuals, joke collections, political articles, and school texts appeared a familiar comic form. At the very moment when white blackface actors were coming into vogue and performing white black-songs, white writers were describing the blacks as natural servants and joyous workers, childlike and easily prone to laughter and frivolity.

This literary expression was already in vogue by the early decades of the nineteenth century as black characters emerged in the print culture. As personalities, regardless of skill or position, they were usually posited as performers, in either plantation or urban dress, their behavior for the most part highly predictable, although on occasion an accomplished writer saw them as individuated.

Happy black servants made their appearances in Washington Irving's *Salmagundi* (1807) and James Fenimore Cooper's *The Spy* (1821). "Caesar," in Irving's work, is affectionate, garrulous, irresponsible, and highly loyal. A comic character with the same exalted name played a brief but prominent part in Cooper's novel. Despite Cooper's sensitivity to the black's slave predicament, his Caesar was utilized for comic relief. Old, faithful, superstitious, easily delighted with gaudy colors, Caesar is unnerved by "Spooks": "Best nebber tempt a Satan," he declares as the whites of his rolling eyes reveal the glare of a fire. Cooper had other black servants with similar characteristics. "Agamemnon" in *The Pioneers* (1823) and "Jaap" in the *Littlepage Manuscripts* (1845–46) adversely contrast with the beauty and intelligence of Caucasians and Native Americans—although it should be noted that the latter perform jokester roles as well. Nonetheless, a white man confuses Agamemnon with his dog at one point. Cooper's black servants become more complex in those stories where they depart land for sea voyages—yet they remain in servile positions.

Edgar Allan Poe turned to a black figure to undercut his heavy mystery in "The Gold Bug" (1843). "Jupiter" is gregarious, woefully ignorant, and superstitious, and in his initial appearance grins "from ear to ear" as he prepares dinner. He becomes totally absorbed in "dat deuced bug." On one occasion he questions the eyes of the skull: "Is de lef' eye ob de skull 'pon de same side as de lef' hand ob de skull too?—cause de skull aint got not a bit ob a hand at all. . . . "[1]

By the 1830s a fully discernible and lovable figure had been woven into novels and stories. Shuffling forth in dozens of literary works, as Kenneth Lynn has amply noted—reflecting, according to Lynn, the profits from the slave system and the volume of abolitionist propaganda—was "a white-toothed, dehumanized buffoon, impervious to pain, incapable of anger—a harmless, empty-headed figure of fun who wouldn't have the sense to revolt even if he cared to, which he didn't."[2]

Lynn further characterized this outpouring of Sambo literature as a soothing, guilt-ridding national massage. If so, the tendency to release such emotions had begun long before. At the time John Pendleton Kennedy brought out his *Swallow Barn* (1832), he was already writing for an audience highly conversant with the comic type. In this novel, the Virginia squires of the Old Dominion, endowed with "an overwhelming hospitality which knows no ebb," view their black wards paternalistically and with comical bemusement. Kennedy's portrayal contributed generously to the image of the African-American as the proverbial child. "I am quite sure," Kennedy wrote of the southern blacks, that they "never could become a happier people than I find them here." Among the laboring peoples of the earth, they embraced more "enjoyment" than any other he was acquainted with.[3]

In the same decade that Kennedy extolled the sunny disposition of slaves, a spate of novels about the Old South saw them in a variety of comic roles. William Gilmore Simms published a romance of Indian warfare, *The Yemassee*, that went through three printings in its first year of publication and was reprinted in 1898, 1911, 1937, and 1961. In many of the early novels, as William R. Taylor noted of plantation literature, "no point is more emphasized than the dependence and helplessness of the slave—except perhaps his unquestionable happiness."[4] Simms's black was just one of many of this type. "Hector" is "the very prince of body servants," exclaims his master, a ship captain, "and he loves me, I verily believe, as I do my mistress." Hector, who is described as "so obtuse," has a tenacious loyalty and also timidity; his world totally revolves around his superior. When master suddenly disappears, there is Hector scurrying around. "Speck he is in berry much trouble," Hector mumbles anxiously as he begins his search despite the possible presence of Indians. To the captain's woman, he declares, "I can't help it, missues—I must go. I hab hand and foot—I hab knife—I hab eye for see—I hab too for bite—I 'trong, missues, and I must go look for maussa. God! missus, if anyting happen to maussa, what Hector for do? where he guine— who be he new maussa?" No matter his fate, Hector wants it known that he is consummately loyal. "I scalp—I drown—I dead—ebery ting happen to me—but I no runway."[5]

The black servant was not always portrayed in such simple, comedic terms. Among the literature of the antebellum decades, Herman Melville's novella *Benito Cereno* (1855) and Harriet Beecher Stowe's *Uncle Tom's Cabin* (1852) were intricate works in which the black figures were often complex and operated at complicated levels. Yet permutations of the comic were a constant subtheme. *Benito Cereno* utilizes a slave insurrection to probe human violence, and black savagery in particular. Nevertheless, Don Benito's servant, "Babo," has "the great gift of good-humor." Good humor, Melville explained, did not mean the mere grin or laugh. Rather, it was a certain "easy cheerfulness, harmonious in every glance and gesture, as though God had set the whole negro to some pleasant tune." To a considerable extent, this very harmony of comedic spirit made the black male dangerous for Melville— for how then was it possible to explain outbursts of black violence? It was the identical question whites had anxiously posed regarding the contradiction between the pious history of Nat Turner and his subsequent violent revolt. Likewise, the character "Sambo" in Stowe's novel moves in a merry but at times devious way. Despite being "of great size," Sambo is "very lively, voluble, and full of trick and grimmace."[6]

There is in many of these black characters the gait of the performer. The disparity between their outer play and questionable inner motivations led to the observation that blacks had the ability to easily hide their feelings and could act out whatever might be necessary for the moment. After the white man has left the ware-house where the slaves are working in *Uncle Tom's Cabin,* Sambo pokes Tom facetiously in the side and inquires " 'What you doin' here? . . . Mediatin', eh?' 'I am to be sold at the auction to-mor-row!' said Tom, quietly. 'Sold at auction,—how! how! boys, an't this yer fun! I wish't I was gwine that ar way!—tell ye, wouldn't I make 'em laugh? . . . ' "[7]

The black comic's gait became common reading material in the popular almanacs of the period. Countless jokes and anecdotes reported the antics, verbal as well as physical, of the American jester. Intriguingly, the tone of the humor was not at all harsh, in the way that other minority groups, such as the Irish, were lam-pooned. Viewed as being dangerous religious and economic rivals, the Irish were viciously ridiculed. The jokes directed toward the blacks were more of what Robert Frost called the humor of "good-natured triumph."[8] Blacks were clearly satirized, but they were also permitted a clever foolishness. They were, after all, control-lable, whereas the Irish could get downright nasty and posed the larger threat. Thus, in dialogue between a white and a black, the former was permitted to be duped—but any revengeful remark or action had built-in limitations. In the preface to a typical yarn, "Ingenuity of a Negro," which appeared in the *Hagerstown* (Mary-land) *Almanac* (1831), blacks were described as "a careless, laugh-ing race, faithful, subservient, impudent and affectionate; and under the pretense of being slaves, often took great liberties." In this particular anecdote, a white master and his slave are involved in a humorous power struggle. Two white friends, Drs. Cooper and Chauncy, both clergymen, and the latter's slave, Scipio, are the main characters in the comedy. An odd habit of Cooper's is his obsessive inquiry of any stranger who appeared in town dressed in black coat and tie, whether he would be willing to preach the following day. Armed with this small bit of knowledge, the slave Scipio "laid his scheme to obtain a particular object from his master."

Scipio goes into his master's study one morning to receive instructions for an errand—but he remains fixed after being directed to leave. Chauncy looks up from his writing and asks what his slave desires. Scipio replies that a new coat is his wish. Chauncy answers that he may have one, and tells Scipio to go to Mrs. Chauncy and acquire one of his old coats. Chauncy then returns to his work. Scipio, however, remains in the same position. The contest is on:

> After a while, the Doctor, turning his eyes that way, saw him again, as if for the first time, and said, "What do you want, Scip?" "I want a new coat, massa." "Well, go to my wife, and ask her to give you one of my old coats," and fell to writing once more. Scipio remained in the same posture. After a few minutes, the Doctor looked towards him, and repeated the question, "Scipio, what do you want?" "I want a new coat, massa." It now flashed over the doctor's mind that there was something of repetition in this dialogue. "Why, have I not told you before, to ask Mrs. Chauncy to give you a coat? get away." "Yes, massa, but I no want a black coat." "Not want a black coat! and why not?" "Why, massa, I 'fraid to tell you, but I don't want a black coat." "What is the reason you don't want a black coat? tell me directly." "O! massa, I am sure you be angry." "If I had my cane, you villain, I'd break your bones; will you tell me what you mean?" "I 'fraid to tell you, massa, I know you be angry." The doctor was now highly irritated, and Scipio perceiving by his glance at the tongs, that he might find a substitute for his cane, and that he was sufficiently excited, said, "Well, massa, you make me tell, but I know you be angry. I 'fraid, massa, if I wear another black coat, Dr. Cooper ask me to preach for him." This unexpected termination realized the negro's calculation. His irritated master burst into a laugh: "Go, you rascal, get my hat and cane, and tell Mrs. Chauncy she may give you a coat of any colour; a red one, if you choose." Away went the negro to his mistress, and the doctor to tell the story to his friend, Dr. Cooper.[9]

The comic black: clever but not dangerous, and always capable of performing.

With few exceptions, then, the print Sambo was not dissimilar in form or style to the blackface performer, a product of white writers whose contact with black culture had been minimal. In the latter decades of the nineteenth century, however, there appeared a literary figure of considerable authenticity. It came from the imagination of Joel Chandler Harris, one of the first to utilize the folktale as a literary device, and the character was the plantation slave "Uncle Remus." Harris's stories were instantly recognized as projecting an iconical type. During his lifetime, Harris came to be regarded as the primary force in establishing the folktale as a means of uncovering an American identity—in this case, a male slave whose personality was unmistakably Sambo-like. Kudos from other writers were heaped on Harris; he was visited by business-men and politicians, including Andrew Carnegie and Theodore Roosevelt. His Uncle Remus works were serialized, translated, reproduced, cinematically animated, and constantly reissued in one form or another. Uncle Remus may be a hazy figure in the post–Black Power generations, but from the latter decades of the nineteenth century until after World War II he was the most widely recognized of black fictional characters. His name even rivaled that of Sambo.

Harris was born in a county seat in Georgia thirteen years before the nation tore itself apart over the slave issue. His town, according to his friends, was "a simple, old-fashioned slave-hold-ing community."[10] From early childhood, Harris's friends and biographers state, he was on extraordinary intimate terms with plantation blacks.

Peers often found him "sitting quietly on the steps of a Negro cabin, listening intently to some old Negro man who was telling him a legendary tale of his race."[11] Minstrels played an important part in his developing years. When despondent, he would sud-denly jump up and exclaim, "Let's have some fun—let's play minstrels!"[12]

"Uncle Remus" was not fashioned from a specific individual. "He was not an invention of my own," Harris noted, "but a human syndicate, I might say, of three or four old darkies whom I had known. I just walloped them together into one person and called him 'Uncle Remus'. You must remember that *sometimes* the negro is a genuine and an original philosopher."[13]

To contemporary observers, Harris was remarkable for his abil-ity to think, speak, act, and perform in the "Negro dialect." Walter

Hines Page, the publisher, editor, and ambassador to England, after an interview with Harris in 1881, accepted Harris's personal estimate of his Negroid representations: "I have Mr. Harris's own word for it that he can *think* in the negro dialect. He could translate even Emerson, perhaps Bronson Alcott, in it, as well as he can tell the adventures of Br'er Rabbit." Laudatory comments came from Thomas Nelson Page, whose *In Ole Virginia* (1887) was a continuation of the Uncle Remus stories: "No man who has ever written has known one-tenth part about the negro that Mr. Harris knows." Page advised that anyone seeking insight into blacks would have to consult Harris: for "the real language of the negro of that section, and the habits of all American negroes of the old time, his works will prove the best thesaurus."[14] Similar assessments echoed far into the twentieth century. "He is, in general," wrote D. A. Walton in the mid-1960s, "the most reliable authority on the Negro tale during slavery."[15]

Harris himself declared that black dialect was his second language and that the line between his reality and fiction was virtually nonexistent. To his friends, Harris stated that he often carried on conversations with his various fictional characters. "His characters all became extraordinarily real to him," wrote journalist Ray Stannard Baker in 1904, "so that he carries on conversations with them as though they were living persons. And they keep clamoring for recognition with him."[16]

So enmeshed with his black storyteller did Harris become that in letters and newspaper articles, even in his personal contacts, he frequently referred to himself as "Uncle Remus." Inscribing a book to a friend—another work about blacks, *Daddy Jake*—Harris signed it in the name of his innermost friend. Later in life, Harris began editing a special publication, revealingly calling it *Uncle Remus's Magazine* instead of a title he had previously considered, *The Optimist.*

What was Harris's motivation for devising "Uncle Remus" as the prototype of the black male storyteller? How could Harris be unaware of the Sambo tradition, which by that time had become a fully acceptable cultural form clothed in the comic? Was he interested in viewing the black male in a light other than that of the natural humorist, the exceptional performer? Harris disclaimed these reasons for writing the stories. It was not, he emphatically stated, to portray his beloved Negroes as humorous foils. His intention was quite serious. He was disturbed by the buffoonish aspect of the image. Rather, what he wanted most of all was to present "the shrewd observations, the curious retorts, the homely thrusts, the quaint comments, and the humorous philosophy of the race of which Uncle Remus was the type." In this connection he was quite dismayed by the "intolerable misrepresentations of the minstrel stage." But he was also not unmindful that his own fiction might distort the Negro. In an intriguing passage, Harris sought to disarm his critics—and thereby exposed his own stereotypical impulses. If the language of Uncle Remus "fails to give vivid hints of the really poetic imagination of the negro," he wrote in the introduction to *Uncle Remus, His Songs and Sayings* (1880), the book that catapulted him into a central position as the disseminator of African-American folklore: "if it fails to embody the quaint and homely humor which was his most prominent characteristic; if it does not suggest a certain picturesque sensitiveness—a curious exaltation of mind and temperament not to be defined by words—then I have reproduced the form of the dialect merely, and not the essence, and my attempt may be accounted a failure."[17]

Taken out of historical context, the Br'er Rabbit and related stories are engrossing, contain amusing and exciting situations, and strongly project many homiletic virtues. Connected to the trickster motif in African folklore, wherein a physically weaker character overcomes his adversaries through guile and imagination, they further had the power of tradition and familiarity. And the parallel to the slave's situation could not have been clearer. The fox and bear, obsessed with trapping, carving, and devouring the rabbit, are symbolic forms that slaves comprehended only too well. Within *that* context, Harris's alertness to the slave's predicament and inner resources, his ability to convey the plantation cadence and subtleties, were indeed highly acute. There is wisdom and strength, and considerable dignity as well, in the stories. The stature of the black storyteller is impressive, his imagination powerful and uplifting, his tone self-assured. Harris's monologist contrasts with the gross exaggeration of the black male that appeared in many stories of the period.

In according Harris his literary merit, it is not unfair to assert that his contribution to the Sambo image was substantial. His Uncle Remus strengthened and reinforced the stereotype. Consider, first, the storyteller: a gentle, white-haired, cherub-faced man displaying no outward rancor or animosity as he spins stories before entranced youngsters on the niceties of plantation life and of the struggles of a weaker cunning animal against more vicious ones. The reader of the tales, argued a Harris biographer, "scarcely thinks of Uncle Remus as a slave," because he comes through as "an independent and realistic figure, revealing his humor and his knowledge of human nature." But he had indeed been a slave, and, even more, as the author noted, "If he had an instinctive desire to be free, he gave no outward indication of it, and his personal difficulties came upon him in freedom, not in slavery."[18] Little wonder. Harris summed up his storyteller's slave experiences in the introduction to the tales by declaring that Uncle Remus had "nothing but pleasant memories of the discipline of slavery."[19]

Fitting the teller is the plantation setting of the tales. Uncle Remus appeared in print during the latter decades of the nineteenth century, when segregation was being riveted into the social fabric by legal, extralegal, and violent means. The first civil rights movement had disintegrated in the face of overwhelming opposition to black freedom throughout the country. What was to be the Afro-American response to this ominous situation? The white hope expressed in print—and reflected at every level of the popular culture—was to create an idyllic setting: the lost horizon of the plantation past. Br'er Rabbit encountered enemies on the plantation, but he cunningly survived. Uncle Remus, by contrast, was having his decided difficulties living on the outside. Better that he, and by implication all blacks, should have remained in their former surroundings. After all, the purpose of the fables, according to Harris, was to demonstrate what was most characteristic of the Negro: "It is not virtue that triumphs, but helplessness; it is not malice, but mischievousness."[20]

"Mischievousness" can be read as one of the essential features Harris had in mind when he described Uncle Remus as the poetic representative of the Negro, as having a "quaint and homely humor which was his most prominent characteristic." Having immersed himself in his and the blacks' past and poured his insights into the folktale, is it surprising that Harris never thought very highly of black intellect? "It has been said," he wrote in a 1907 article that questioned the need of higher education for blacks, "that the negro race is not yet in a position to be benefited by higher education. This is true, of course. . . ."[21]

Perhaps, as Bernard Wolfe has insisted, "the Remus stories are a monument to the South's ambivalence." Like many whites, Harris sought the love of Negroes—hence the Remus grin—but also subconsciously sought their hate—hence the Rabbit's violence. There existed within Harris, Wolfe surmised, "an unconscious orgy of masochism—punishing himself, possibly for not being Negro, the unstinting giver." He noted that there appears to be a powerful implication of interchangeable colors in the stories that "whites are bleached Negroes and Negroes are dusky whites."[22]

What can be concluded about the black storyteller, his tales of African origin, is that he deviated not one whit from the essential image of the black male as an entertainer. The performing black now lived on in freedom well beyond the lost plantation, and he was just as beguiling, clever, and humorous as ever. Through no fault of Harris's, the Uncle Remus tales spawned a host of imitative literature of lesser quality. "Mr. Harris's genius," Thomas Nelson Page exulted, "blazed the way" for more stories based on folklore.[23]

Uncle Remus's counterpart showed up at the end of the century in Martha S. Gielow's *Mammy's Reminiscences and Other Sketches* (1898). Gleaned from "actual happenings related to me by my own black Mammy," wrote Gielow, the sketches were intended to offset the images of blacks in the minstrels and other works that made the slaves "almost unrecognizable by those who knew and loved them." Like Harris, the author acknowledged that slaves did indeed possess a "quaint humor" that reflected "their happy, simple natures."

Mammy's Reminiscences are set in the cabins of the Old Plantation. Some of the chapter headings provide instant recognition of their intent: "How Br'er Simon Got Erligion," "De Pianner Juett," and "Seein' Sperrits." Exclaims Mammy as she greets her white mistress and the latter's grandchild, "Well, Lawd, ef dar ain' Miss Ferrginia! I sholy is proud ter see you, Honey!" In the story on "sperrits" the main figure is Uncle Tom, a proud coachman stylized as the "Uncle Remus of Hazelwood," who does a twist on the chicken-stealing theme:

> One night I started ter cut across de orchid fer ter wisit er frien' on de jinin' plantation, an 'ef de Lawd'll fergibe me I nebber cross no orchid ergin uv er night.
>
> What I *seed?* You better ax what I hyeard! I seed *sperrits!* Dat what I seed, an' mo'en dat, I *hyeard ghos'es!* I had er bag er chicken under my arm—(some what er frien' gib me) an' er hat full er aigs in my han' . . . Well, jes' es I git ter de aige uv de orchid (hit was dark es pitch) I hyeard sum'n nu'r groan' "h—m!" I stop an' lis'en, hit groan ergin, "hu—m!"[24]

Mammy's Sketches was the printed version of stories delivered on the lecture circuit. Northern audiences were apparently beguiled by Gielow's rendering of "the plaintive Negro dialect" and the monologues, which were "fully the equal in their delicate humor and pathos of anything written by Thomas Nelson Page or Harris," wrote a *New York Herald* reviewer. A Boston admirer was quoted as saying that Gielow's illustrations of antebellum and southern life, her impressions of "the negro character, the 'Mammy,' the 'Sambo,' the 'pickaninny,' and the plantation preacher, had a verisimilitude of humor, of pathos, and of rollicking fun. . . . "[25] Compilations of folk stories from other black regions were refractions of the type. In *Annancy Stories* by Pamela Colman Smith, a young West Indian Negro woman, wearing a colorful bandanna and speaking in thick dialect, makes her debut. Page cited the stories as being "perhaps the most original contribution to negro folklore since the day when Uncle Remus gave us

his imperishable record of 'Brer Rabbit.'" The tales were indeed
reflective of Harris and Gielow, although their range is strangely
often unrelated to black culture. Tales of royalty, " 'giner flies,"
elfs and animals, and the "debil" filled the pages.[26]

Reinforcing the Uncle Remus focus during this period—the
nadir of race relations, as Rayford Logan put it—were hundreds
of short stories and vignettes published throughout the nation.
Prestigious journals, local magazines, and religious publications
lent their weight to segregationist policies by reporting on Sambo.
A typical anecdote in the *Chatterbox,* published in the 1880s in Boston, provides insight into the widespread dissemination of the
image. "Have you ever seen a negro in the street," began the story
titled "So Funny," "and thought how funny he looked, with his
thick lips, his sooty face, and his wholly black hair? I dare say you
have—and, perhaps, laughed out loud, too—and wondered why
some people are made of such very queer faces! Well, now, listen
to me," wrote the author, H.A.F., "and I will tell you a true story
that was told to me."

As the tale unfolds, a kind clergyman has brought home two
Africans, meaning to have them educated in England. The clergyman's first act is to introduce the two black youths, described as
being intelligent and well behaved, to a close friend. A morning
prayer is conducted, and the Africans sit with folded hands await-
ing the reading of the Scriptures.

> Suddenly, without apparent reason, a broad smile broke over the
> countenance of one darkey, followed by a titter from the other;
> and as their mirth could not be concealed the service was
> stopped, and the clergyman told them to state what it was
> amused them so much.
>
> "There! there!" cried both the lads at once, bursting into fits
> of laughter; "very much funny! Sambo must laugh!"
>
> And what do you think it was that amused them so much? The
> four little red-headed daughters of their host, who were sitting
> gravely opposite the negro lads. The Africans had never seen red
> hair before.

The author's conclusion: "I do not think it is necessary for me to
point out the moral of this anecdote."[27]

Magazine quality made little difference. In one way or another they all mirrored the racial *Zeitgeist* of the period. Wide-ranging literary journals—*Harper's, Atlantic Monthly, Scribner's Monthly, Century Monthly,* and *North American Review*—fed their readers constant morsels of comic imagery. "The magazines repeated derogatory epithets, inconsistent dialect, and stereotypes," wrote historian Rayford Logan. "They glorified the Plantation Tradition and condemned Reconstruction. . . . "[28]

Not surprisingly, the bulk of the stories were written by whites who identified their characters in variations of "nigger," "darkey," "aunt" and "uncle," "pickaninny," "coon," or "buck." Rarely capitalized was the term "Negro," and the dialect, regardless of social standing, was usually exaggerated. Blacks were invariably addicted to any one of several major habits—alcohol, gambling, stealing, superstition—and to a host of foods—watermelon, 'taters, possum, and fried chicken. Readers expected, and were rarely disappointed, to be brought into a comical situation or to be aroused by a laughable character. The stories in *Harper's* typified the fiction that appeared in the magazines from the 1870s to the 1920s. A minimum of two humorous incidents were printed in each issue, the number increasing in the early decades of the twentieth century. The comical effect was heightened by the continued ludicrous use of famous names or overblown titles. Representative designations included "Senator," "Colonel," "Sheriff," "Prince," and "Apollo"; derivations of familiar names such as "Abraham Lincum," and "Napoleon Boneyfidey Waterloo"; and unusual combinations, for example, "Prince Orang Outan," "Solomon Crow," "Nuttin 'Tal," "Wan-na-Mo," and "Had-a-Plenty."[29]

Adult literary racial forms were eventually transmitted—and thereby extended and prolonged—into the world of children's literature. Identical imagery appeared in thousands of children's stories and storybooks. Early works, such as Louise Clarke-Pyrnelle's *Diddie, Dumps and Tot* (1882), reprinted twenty times before the 1960s, were slave apologias in which the faithful and loyal blacks muse about the happy life of the plantation past.

Among the more popular of the children's works were *Epaminondas and His Auntie* (1907) by Sara Cone Bryant, illustrated by Inez Hogan, *Eneas Africanus* (1920) by Harry Stillwell Edwards, the multivolume *Nicodemus* series (1930s) by Inez Hogan, *Frawg* (1930) by Annie Vaughn Weaver, and, somewhat curiously, *The Story of Little Black Sambo* (1899) by Helen Bannerman. The last, probably the best-known book whose central character was a black lad (whose name, incidentally, became prominent on a restaurant pancake chain in the decades following the Second World War), was not actually in the Sambo mold. Save for the obvious fact of its name and its early illustrations—both mother and father, "Black Mumbo" and "Black Jumbo," as well as child Sambo, were dressed in flashy multicolored outfits and went barefoot, with grossly exaggerated features—the story itself was hardly stereotypical. Neither the Indian setting, the dark-skinned characters, nor the plot was demeaning. Sambo, in fact, triumphs over the tigers in a clear display of brainpower and dignity. Rather, it has been a case of title and illustrations obscuring a plot and causing the book to become one of the leading carriers of the racist image.[30]

The same cannot be said for the other works, which were unmistakably in the Sambo pattern. *Epaminondas and His Auntie,* as well as the *Nicodemus* books, stocked in school libraries and often used as standard classroom fare, were steeped in stereotypical shades. Both were vividly drawn by Inez Hogan, one of the most successful illustrators of children's books. Hogan portrayed the figures in a grabbing coal-black color, with oblong faces, thick-cherry-red lips, extended arms, and innocent-to-stupid appearance, against a background of sharp yellows and reds. *Epaminondas* was reprinted at least three times, the 1968 version being a restructuring of its basic format because of Black Power pressure at the time.

The story opens on a yellow path leading up to a black sharecroppers' shack. Epaminondas, a dull-witted boy, is given a series of errands by his Auntie. On the first day she hands him a big piece of rich yellow cake. Epaminondas takes the cake, squishes it tight, and carries it to his mother:

> "What you got there, Epaminondas?"
> "Cake, Mammy."
> "Cake! Epaminondas, you ain't the sense you was born with! That's no way to carry cake. The way to carry cake is to wrap it all up nice in some leaves and put it in your hat, and come along home. You hear me, Epaminondas?"

The following day he travels to his Auntie, who gives him a pound of sweet, fresh butter. Heeding his mother's instructions, Epaminondas wraps the butter in leaves, places it in his hat, and goes home. The hot sun melts the butter, which runs down the boy's face. Scolding him, his mother tells him to wrap the butter in leaves, take it to the brook, and cool it in the water three times. But his next item is a puppy dog, which Epaminondas proceeds to dunk in the water three times. After a series of silly episodes, Epaminondas is finally directed by his Mammy to "be careful how you step" on six cooling mince pies she has just baked—whereupon he carefully steps in the middle of each of them.[31]

Frawg, also set in the South, is not about the antics of a small amphibian. "Once, way down South, there was a little five-year-old boy named Frawg. He and his Ma and Pa and six brothers and sisters all lived in a little cabin in the middle of a cotton-field." His brothers and sisters are named John, Bush, Shine, Viney, Iwilla (shortened for I Will Arise and Go To My Father), and Evvalena. Like many five-year olds, Frawg likes to talk to bluebirds, catch fish for his mother, whose "mouf's jes' a-settin' for some good fried fish," and just kick around in the fields. He is especially fond, though, of watermelon: "Frawg liked to eat, but the thing he liked to eat most was watermelon. He could eat more watermelon than any child in the place, and more than most of the grown people. Still, he always wanted more—he just could never get enough."[33]

The most extensive series of this genre were the *Nicodemus* books written and illustrated by Inez Hogan in the 1930s. Among the many titles were *Nicodemus and His New Shoes*, *Nicodemus and His Gran'pappy*, *Nicodemus and the Gang*, *Nicodemus and the Little*

Black Pig, Nicodemus and Petunia, and *Nicodemus Laughs.* Nicodemus's features are virtually identical to those of Epaminondas, although he is not as dim-witted. Nonetheless, Nicodemus is as foolish and carefree—and, as with all the black figures in all of the children's stories, his words are in thick dialect. Nicodemus, his various friends, and his family say "er," "yo," " 'ise," "sho," "cose," "hurted," "dis," "Lawdy," "chile," "lan'sakes," "git," and "mah." All were intended to convey comedy. As a review in *Parent's Magazine* observed at the time, "The many children who have laughed over the adventures of that funny colored boy, Nicodemus, will welcome this new book. . . . This is a book to be read aloud."[33] Over the decades and throughout the country, the children's books were indeed read aloud, in classrooms, libraries, church sessions, and Scout meetings—in sum, in a full range of situations.

Not all of these books were set in the rural South. *Hezekiah Horton* by Ellen Tarry (1942) has its locale in Harlem. The illustrations by Ollie Harrington are perfectly reasonable, but the story, while not harshly stereotypical, is nevertheless negative. Hezekiah is a ten-year-old boy, well dressed and well mannered. His speech is perfectly normal for his age. Every afternoon after returning from school, he sits on the front stoop of his apartment house with his head in his hands and his elbows resting on his knees. People wonder what he is thinking about. Only his mother knows. "Automobiles!" she could tell them. "That boy is so crazy about those things I sometimes wonder if he's right bright in his head. He talks about them, he draws them, and he even dreams about them!" Hezekiah is given an opportunity to learn how to drive and to chauffeur around one of the men in the neighborhood, and the story closes with his wanting to grow up in order to drive Mister Ed's beautiful red automobile. Whereas reading materials for Caucasian children of the same period directed them toward a future profession or skilled occupation, Hezekiah is circumscribed by his obsession with a material object.[34]

From the turn of the century to the mid-1950s, virtually every popular children's series that did not turn on the antics of a white child had a black male or female jester to enliven the plot. In the *Bobbsey Twins, Honey Bunch, Tom Swift, Rover Boys, Hardy Boys,* and *Nancy Drew* series there could be found at least one entertaining black, who was always poor, conversed in dialect, feared ghosts, loved watermelon, sometimes wielded a razor, shot craps, bowed and deferred and grinned. Their names ranged from the symbolic commonplace—Henry Black in *Honey Bunch: Her First Trip in a Trailer*—to the symbolic buffoonish—Eradicate Sampson in *Tom Swift and His Airship*. When unnamed, they were referred to colloquially, as coons, niggers, pickaninnies, aunts and uncles, colored.

Although comical blacks were not the focus of the series books, they were the center of attraction in the humor books. From the minstrel years to the Cold War in the 1950s, there was an outpouring of joke books, comic pamphlets, burlesque essays, humor anthologies, newspaper and magazine tidbits, and oral jokes that traversed the country. Sambo in print appealed to all classes, but catered essentially to lower- and middle-income groups.

Printed by small houses, on poor-quality paper, these bound works were often low-cost and were widely distributed. Some, though, were marketed by powerful New York concerns such as Charles Scribner's Sons and Funk and Wagnalls. In the pre–Civil War period, the "funny nigger" took the form of minstrel compendiums and burlesque lectures. A typical collection was entitled *Black Diamonds, or, Humor, Satire, and Sentiments, Treated Scientifically: A Series of Burlesque Lectures Darkly Colored* (1855), by "Professor Julius Caesar Hannibal." The essays first made their appearance in the *New York Pickayune* and were gathered in a large volume replete with illustrations. In the form of the lectures, they centered on the explanation of scientific subjects. "Feller Sitizens," the black-complected professor begins in his first lecture, "I had come, as you all know, from 'way down in Old Warginna, what I studdied edicashium and siance all for myself, to gib a corse of lectures on siance gineraly, an events promiscuously, as dey from time to time occur."[35] It was an opening copiously repeated the century over.

The collectors of comic and humor books often stated as the

prime motivation the presentation of the "true" mirth of the Afro-American. But the contents of the works, as well as the frequent use of the name Sambo, indicated otherwise. As the national jester, the black served as the butt for a humor that was largely oppressive. Regardless of the region in which the work was published, such humor books as *Wit and Humor by Uncle Sambo*[36] (1911), *Negro Wit and Humor*[37] (1914), and *The Black Cat Club: Negro Humor and Folklore*[38] (1902) served stereotypical ends. Opening with a disclaimer, James D. Carrothers's *The Black Cat,* presumably set in Chicago, was printed to demonstrate that "the Negro is himself *everywhere,* educated or uneducated," and proceeded to emphasize the latter.[39] The most blatant statement was by Edward V. White in *Chocolate Drops from the South* (1932); he wrote that the Negro has been the "Nation's greatest source of genuine laughter and good humor." Why? "Because he looks funny, he acts funny, he is funny. Moreover, he is serious about it all. . . . It is believed that [many] will appreciate these stories about a people who are happy and hopeful, helpful and harmless. . . . "[40]

Humor books of this type were sold at bookstores and newsstands well into the 1950s. The Negro's "sense of humor," "inner peace," and "natural" inclination to please others were traits that white authors constantly extolled. "All of my life," wrote Sam Boykin Short in *'Tis So* (1952), "I have been surrounded by Negroes. They have rhythm, a keen sense of humor and a calm philosophy of life. For years I have made notes of interesting stories concerning them."[41] The main character, Ed, is an Uncle Remus type whose stock answer to any question is "Yes, suh, 'tis so"; he is the constant source of merriment down on the farm.

As in fictional literature, the self-styled authors on Afro-American humor used the books to justify the past, ensure the racial status quo, and maintain black comicality. In *Sambo's Legacy* (1870s) by the Reverend P. B. Power, the point of the sermon is humility and contriteness. Hospitalized after being struck by a cab, Sambo explains the meaning of his experience: "Ah! de legacy? All quite true, sar: Sambo try to be patient, sar, and contented, and walk berry humble, sar, and be berry thankful, and leab an example in dis yar place."[42]

This message was monotonously repeated in humor works throughout the decades. In *Adam Shuffler* (1901) by Samuel A. Beadle, the exhortation was for blacks to remain in the South and curry whites' favor. "I tells yer," says Adam in the central story, "dat de best place fer de cullud brudder am in Mississippi, 'an de best place fer fur him ter do . . . is ter git on de white side uv public opinion."[43] The antebellum period was idyllically portrayed in a quasi-biography by Orrie M. MacDonnell, *Sambo: Before and After the Civil War* (1924). "The Original Sambo," an ex-slave, peers back into his days of bondage and fondly reminisces. The author wanted his readers to view the past through Sambo's eyes: "The days of slavery beneath Southern skies as seen by Sambo, an old Slave who, though now bent with years, yet lives in the past and holds dear the days gone by with his White Folks."[44]

In one way or another, the humor books and pamphlets accentuated Afro-American ignorance, highlighted pretentiousness, and poked fun at education. Chapter headings in an anonymous book, *Senggambien Sizzles: Negro Stories* (1945), including "The Negro's Love of High Sounding Words" and "Misseducasum," focused on the inability of the black man to pronounce words correctly and use sentences properly. In jokes, blacks were boastful and uninhibited:

> Hogan: Sambo, how many chillun is yo' got?
>
> Sambo: When I count 'em las' Feb'ary, dey wuz fo'teen![45]

The popularity of certain radio programs in the 1930s and '40s inspired similar publications. W. N. Hinkle's *Funniest Darkey Stories* (1931) contained a lengthy piece, "Abie's African Rose," loosely derived from *Abie's Irish Rose*.[46] Before their show became popular fare, the blackfaced team of Charles Correll and Freeman Gosden, "Amos 'n' Andy," published a book based on their early programs. *Sam 'n' Henry* (1926) relates the story of two young black men who leave their homes in Birmingham to seek more "profitable work" in Chicago. Their eagerness for work is constantly thwarted by their innocence in a strange urban environment. They encounter a bewildering array of ethnic groups and an equally trying set of circumstances that produce the basis for humor. The program's success led to the publication of several joke book collections, such as O. M. Morris's *150 Latest Jokes* (1940s), which featured two wide-lipped black men called "Amouse and Andre" on its cover.[47]

"Black jokes" were also used as filler in many magazines. Small- as well as wide-circulation magazines—*Colliers, Hi-Jinks, Reader's Digest,* to name several—either reserved a section devoted to "Negro Humor" or printed jokes involving blacks. *Hi-Jinks,* a mid-western periodical of the 1920s devoted to wit and satire and opposed to "synthetic jin, jazz and modern artificiality," had a col-umn called "Charcoal Tablets." Several samples provide an under-standing of their character and intent:

Seven Come 'leven

Parson: "Rastus, does yo' take dis woman for bettah or wurse?"

Rastus (from habit): "Pahson, Ah shoots de works!"

A Southern restaurant serves eggs with all meat orders. A patron ordered pork chops. "Boss, how yo' want yo' eggs," inquired the waiter.

"Oh, you can eliminate the eggs."

The waiter repeated the order to the colored chef and added "liminate dem eggs."

The chef scratched his head. "Sambo, yo' tell dat customer Ah aint got no time this mawning to liminate dem eggs and that he-all will have to have dem cooked some oder way."[48]

Reader's Digest reached a much larger and diverse audience. Soon after it began publishing in the late 1920s, *Reader's Digest* filled its smaller spaces with humorous tidbits. In such well-known sections as "Life in These United States" people recounted stories from everyday experiences. Until the late 1940s, a portion of the magazine was devoted to "Negro" witticisms, sayings, jokes, and happenings. Although the magazine also reprinted serious articles about Afro-American spokesman, usually highly acceptable per-sons such as Booker T. Washington and George Washington Carver, the majority of its coverage was intended as humor. Throughout the Second World War its pages were filled with a constant patter of black comicality in familiar dialect style. Invoking the theme of superstition was this midwar declaration of "A Negro's prayer": "O Lord, help me to understand that you ain't gwine to let nothin' come my way that you and me together can't handle."[49] Buffoonish soldiers were a constant reminder of black ineptitude combined with an ability to clown their way out of difficult situations:

> Learning the phrases incidental to sentry duty proved confusing for one Negro of the 76th. An officer of the day was surprised when this gentleman challenged him with:
>   "Halt! Look who's here."[50]

As the number of joke and humor books in the late 1950s and the 1960s turned away from using blacks as America's favorite foil, a lament was heard in the South. In an effort to keep the Negro's past alive in humor's womb, a group of white writers collaborated in yet another anthology. "This book is lovingly devoted to that Happy Time," they wrote in the preface to *That Passing Laughter: Stories of the Southland* (1966), "when there was great respect and cordiality between the white and colored races in the South. . . . "[51] Although the stories were less degrading than those of the pre–World War II period, the book still reflected a reverence for the docile, optimistic, and cheerful black—and a longing for that warm time when whites viewed blacks paternalistically and could spell the word "Negro" in lowercase without criticism, which the authors did in this book.

Undergirding the image in the popular culture—validating its form and giving credence to its very being—was Sambo's active presence in nonfiction works. School texts, history books, sociological analyses, folklore collections, military reports and manuals, as well as a host of other works hidden in society's labyrinths, all characterized the black male as a variation of Sambo. "I am drawing to a close of my twenty-years' study of the Negro races," wrote sociologist Jerome Dowd in *The Negro in American Life* (1926), in which his contacts with blacks was extensively listed. "I spent my youth in North Carolina, where the Negroes constituted a very large and important factor in the life of the whites." Dowd recalled the many blacks with whom he had had contact over the years—cooks, nurses, butlers, farmhands, woodchoppers, friends, children, and an old slave who had belonged to his grandfather. His research and experience convinced Dowd that, until evolutionary change upgraded the black character, "The mind of the Negro can best be understood by likening it to that of a child." By child Dowd meant that blacks were "cheerful," "impulsive," "intolerant of discipline," had a "fondness for showing off" and "love of the spectacular," possessed a "gregarious tendency" stronger than that of any other race, and enjoyed a "lively humor."[52]

This bias was shared by a number of folklorists. Dorothy Scarborough, in her quest for southern folk songs, approached her subjects as if they were children. Scarborough was particularly interested in "darky" materials, a term she regularly employed in her work *On the Trail of Negro Folksongs* (1925). As a rule, she noted, "The Negro is an optimist and he has his own philosophy to comfort him." Ultimate happiness, however, came from his relations with animals. The Negro "has a special tact in dealing with animals, and can get more sympathetic response from them than can a white person. . . . " The implication was that "The Negro is perhaps in his happiest mood when he is making songs about animals." Scarborough concluded that, like black charity toward animals, black songs and humor were "wide and deep."[53]

At another part of the spectrum was a field report of the Army War College, *The Use of Negro Manpower in War* (1936), which described the black male in equivalent terms. The Negro was "docile, tractable, light-hearted, carefree, and good natured," the report stated. "If unjustly treated he is likely to become surly and stubborn though this is a temporary phase." Rather like a child, the Negro was "careless, shiftless, irresponsible, and secretive." To handle him, it was best to resort to "praise and ridicule," remembering that at all times "his sense of right doing is relatively inferior."[54]

Assumptions of the childlike nature and/or dependent status of blacks emanated from the writings of American historians whose early treatment of slavery—coupled with their lack of understanding of Afro-American history and culture—immeasurably fostered the Sambo stigma. Undoubtedly the most pronounced influence came from the works of Ulrich B. Phillips, *American Negro Slavery* (1918) and *Life and Labor in the Old South* (1929), the earliest scientific historical analyses of slavery. Over the decades both works were constantly reissued. Phillips's approach to slavery was known throughout the social sciences. Until 1956, when Kenneth W. Stampp[55] reversed many of Phillips's interpretations, Phillips's findings on slavery and black behavior were standard fare in hundreds of high-school and college history texts and related books.

Phillips's research was prodigious and his analyses were complicated. His insight into slave actions made him highly aware that the plantation system coerced Africans into a "self-obliterating humility" and encouraged responses "only to the teachings and preachings of their masters."[55] On the other hand, his southern background, combined with a powerful contemporary bias, forced his observations into preconceived notions. Beginning with a view of Africa as a place in which blacks had "lived naked, observed fetish, been bound by tribal law, and practiced primitive crafts," Phillips logically concluded that slavery had been a civilizing process.[56] The process of assimilation, Phillips concluded, fairly uniform and constant, succeeded not only because of coercive forces but also because the African "genius was imitative." The consequent black personality was a predominant plantation type. Its essential traits were "an eagerness for society, music and merriment, a fondness for display whether of person, dress, vocabulary or emotion, a not flagrant sensuality, a receptiveness toward any religion whose exercises were exhilarating, a proneness to superstition, a courteous acceptance of subordination, an avidity for praise, a readiness for loyalty of a feudal sort, and last but not least, a healthy human repugnance toward overwork."[57]

Taking his cue from Phillips was historian Ralph Gabriel in his work on *The Course of American Democratic Thought* (1940), a political and intellectual history that had considerable influence in the 1940s and '50s. In his analysis of slave behavior Gabriel quoted from Phillips's unpublished manuscript and argued that the children of imported slaves of the eighteenth and nineteenth centuries, and their progeny as well, "having no memory of African scenes or tribal ways or Negro languages, cheerfully made plantation life their own, for the most part accepting slavery as a matter of course and adopting their masters much as a child appropriates his parents or a pupil his teacher." Like children, moreover, the slaves had to be constantly supervised and pampered. They had to be fed, clothed, sheltered, "sanitated at all times, nursed when ill, cheered when indolent, disciplined when unruly. . . . The need of attention [was] constant."[58]

Despite his insights into the plantation tradition in American culture, Francis Pendleton Gaines was also ensnarled in the nuances of the Sambo stereotype. Aware that "categorical statements" were perilous, nevertheless, in *The Southern Plantation* (1927), a book that examined the plantation's connection to literature, theatre, and music, Gaines contended that "The negro is instinctively kind and affectionate, contented in unambitious fashion, quick to respond to the stimulus of joy, quick to forget his grief." Even though Gaines was critical of the notion that blacks were happy and contented slaves, that the average black did not fit the theatrical role of burnt-cork offering on the altar of devotion, yet "this childish race had a strong sense of dependence and returned a respectful devotion."[59]

Scholarly reassertions of the childlike black in slavery was given high credibility from the 1930s to the 1960s in the highly prestigious American history textbook by Samuel Eliot Morison and Henry Steele Commager, *The Growth of the American Republic*. Morison shared in the idea of black dependency, unequivocally declaring that although he was carried to the continent by force, "The incurably optimistic negro soon became attached to the country, and devoted to his 'white folks.'" Morison's "negro" was identified as either a "nigger," "darky," "such a one," or "Sambo."[60]

Such language and its image lost its impact in the late 1950s and early 1960s. Nevertheless, spanning at least a century and a half, the print Sambo more often than not prevailed in a national literature that only gradually came to view the black male less stereotypically. The image was severely tarnished along the way by prominent fictional works of black writers, including Richard Wright's *Native Son* (1940) and Ralph Ellison's *Invisible Man* (1949), and scholarly books such as Gunnar Myrdal's *An American Dilemma* (1944) and Herbert Aptheker's *American Negro Slave Revolts* (1943). These works, however, were obscured by Sambo's staying power in the popular culture. It is hard for society to relinquish a funny man, to view him as anything *but* a funny man, especially if that funny man is an entertainer of iconical status whose touch reaches far back into the past.

It would be wrong, however, to stress print media any more than other cultural forms. Each was in cahoots with the various dimensions of the imagic culture. Together, these diverse approaches colluded not merely in the raison d'être of Sambo's existence—but in his stretch over time.

6

Prismatic Projections

Cartoon: "It Is to Laugh"

The place is a courtroom. Present are the judge, a
policeman, and a black family. The man is looking foolish,
his wife is very heavy in her sagging clothing, and their
children are sad-appearing.

Judge—"You are charged with non-support."

Mr. Jackson—"What an idea, judge! Why, I'se kept dat
woman in jobs eber since I married her."

—*Judge* (1903)

The strange thing was that next door to Remi lived a Negro
called Mr. Snow whose laugh, I swear on the Bible, was
positively and finally the one greatest laugh in all this
world. This Mr. Snow began his laugh from the supper
table when his old wife said something casual; he got up,
apparently choking, leaned on the wall, looked up to heaven,
and started; he staggered through the door, leaning on
neighbor's walls; he was drunk with it, he reeled throughout
Mill City in the shadows, raising his whooping
triumphant call to the demon god that must have prodded him
to do it. I don't know if he ever finished supper.

—Jack Kerouac, *On the Road*

Though the print Sambo was extensive, his graphic expression was
even more pervasive, and what could have been overlooked in
print was impossible to overlook in popular culture. Reinforcing
each other, print and pictures riveted the black male's role into an
imagic straitjacket. From the early decades of the nineteenth century to the post–World War II period, the popular culture was

121

inundated with millions of Sambo representations. So overwhelming was his commercialization that it would not be an exaggeration to state that by the close of the nineteenth century Sambo had achieved iconical status. His humorous innocence, reflected in a never-failing grin, was projected everywhere, his natural buffoonery celebrated in every conceivable way.

Objects and literature interacted to present variations of a single image. Books and short stories contained illustrations by prominent artists; commercial packages displayed logos; sheet music featured cover cartoons; wooden calendars were shaped into painted figures; knickknacks showed smiling faces on dancing bodies; kitchen and barbershop walls displayed Currier and Ives prints; children's games included painted illustrations. Postal and advertising cards used both photographs and illustrations. Even dishes were adorned with happy faces, as were salt and pepper shakers, tablecloths, wooden wall reminders, and ceramic vessels.

Such fusing could be seen in the display of comic figures in bookstore window displays in the pre–Civil War years and in similar displays in department stores at the close of the century. Materially, there were jockeys on the front lawns, wooden and iron figurines in stores and homes, cardboard cutouts for commercial advertisements, and kitchen utensils next to stoves or atop eating tables. Manufacturers produced stereoscopic slides, postcards, adult and children's games. Blacks were simply illustrated everywhere: in comic strips and films, on large commercial signs and billboards. Sambo was simply as American as any pie, apple or cherry, and just as delectable.

Cartoons and lithographs dominated the scene prior to the Civil War. A particular male figure appeared on song sheet, novel, almanac, and minstrel collection covers. Portrayed as either plantation darky or urban dandy, his features were usually Africanish, and his dress was invariably shabby or foppish. Geographical location made little difference insofar as language was concerned. Dialect was typically thick and amusing. Animated faces gave the appearance of comicality. Not all political cartoons or illustrations intended foolishness; northern newspapers and magazines that supported abolitionism drew blacks more sympathetically. Yet even some of these cartoons could be interpreted humorously. And the same could be said for many of their counterparts in the South. For instance, an 1861 lithograph contrasted life for blacks in the two sections. On the left was a black man in his twenties or thirties inadequately dressed for the northern winter snows and winds, and shown leaving an inn in which a drink is being poured in the background. His features are strong and resilient; the caption reads, "A Fish Out of Water." The right segment shows the same black man down South; his dress is plantation style, but now he has a pipe in one hand and a fishing rod in the other, and he is seated next to a white man reading a newspaper while in the background happy slaves play in comfortable surroundings. Slave and master engage in an ironic conversation:

UNCLE CLEM: "Say, Massa Jim, is I wan of them onfortunate Niggers as you was readin' about?"

YOUNG GENTLEMAN: "Yes, Uncle Clem, you are one of them."

UNCLE CLEM: "Well, it's a great pity about me,—I'se berry badly off, I is."[1]

One of the most persistent graphic themes in the nineteenth century was the connection between American blacks and their African background. The measurement of intelligence, a subject of intense interest, produced a large number of lithographs and cartoons linking Sambo with the apes. This presumed relationship, given authority by many "scholarly" studies, enabled artists and illustrators to draw African-Americans in exaggerated, buffoonish strokes. Enlarged heads, extended arms, thick lips, kinky hair, and short bodies became commonplace in magazines and newspapers. Hundreds of minstrel collections and joke books featured on their covers a single figure who looked like an ape in human dress. *Brudder Bones Stump Speech and Joke Book* (1850s) was typical in showing a black figure in upper-class attire standing before a small table on which were an overturned top hat and a half-filled glass of water. He is supposedly a professional speaker, but he is rendered ridiculous by a red umbrella raised in one hand, a long yellow handkerchief hanging from his back pocket, and frazzled hair standing straight out from the intensity of his effort.[2]

Accentuating the connection was the rendering of black English in the most humorous possible style. It was a rare print, music cover, or minstrel score that showed any black using proper and acceptable grammar. Even the abolitionists, as Leon Litwack noted in *North of Slavery* (1961), were caught up in the image, and tried to coerce Frederick Douglass to speak in a thick slave accent in order to prove that he had truly been down on the plantation as one of "them."

Not surprisingly, once slavery ended, the linkage to African primitivism became more tenacious and amplified. As the institution faded in the national consciousness, the drawings of blacks became, at the very least, overstated. If whites were unable to restore their master-slave relationship, they were determined to restate that relationship by employing all of the humorous means at their disposal. In the 1880s magazines such as *Judge* and *Vanity Fair* produced several cartoons whose titles symbolized white determination: "This Way, Sambo" and "The Manifest Destiny of Sambo."

Operating within a system that clearly rewarded Jim Crow policies, cartoonists sought a form that could express black buffoonery. Various styles merged in the decades before the turn of the century. Continuing the African connection, the majority of artists extended the form: lips were widened and rendered a rosy red; teeth sparkled with glistening whiteness; hair was nappy, short and frazzled; faces were glossy, atop bodies that were either shortened and rounded, or lengthened to approximate the monkey or ape. What was understated physically was often declared explicitly. A *Harper's Magazine* cartoon of April 1903 is set in the Philadelphia zoo. Several observers are watching the antics of monkeys. One prominent white physician says to an elderly black man standing next to him, "Uncle, they seem almost human, don't they?" "Human?" replies the black man with a look of disgust. "Dey ain't no moah human dan I is." In an 1893 *Puck* lithograph entitled "Darkies' Day at the World's Fair," a group of blacks are portrayed as thick-lipped cannibals and dandies, their fairground march suddenly diverted by a tempting pile of watermelons.

Within this form all classes and groups of black society were subjected to the same type of humor. Names reflected the situation, as they had during slavery. Blacks were called, as in the "Brudder Shinbones" cartoons in *Puck* magazine, "Wakeup Misery," "Squeezeout Peabody," "G. Washington Moak," and similar appellations. Cartoon books heightened the effect by devising spurious plots. In *Coonah Town Society and Other Comic Stories in Picture and Rhyme* (1903), a black community is depicted engaging in bear hunting, dancing, midnight rides, and other activities. The story opens in revelry: "Coonah Town Sassity Makes Its Bow In a Cake Walk." Who are the people of the community? In chronological order, they are the Coonah Town Quartette; the town bully, who threatens with razor and dice; the barber who "cuts off parts of ears, eyes, noses, and a few wisps of hair"; the Dancer, described as "the best buck dancer," for when "he lights on those dainty feet/It jars the pavement in the street"; "spooks and haunts"; and the children:

> In the alley, off the street,
> Coon town pickinannies meet,
> Playing marbles, shooting craps
> Or a ten-round fight, perhaps.
>
> There are no razors in this crowd
> (To young coons they're not allowed)
> But in loafing and as liars
> They try to beat their dusky sires.[3]

Illustrations of Sambo in novels and short stories differed only in that they contained no accompanying punch line or caption. Often none was required, for the picture complemented the story and was more effective because it accompanied serious literature. The style of the image in high-culture print was more deftly drawn and powerful. Artistic techniques solidified the plausibility of the image.

Few practitioners of the genre were as effective or influential as Thomas Worth. His stylized Sambo figures achieved national prominence; he focused on the theme of black ineptness to such an extent that he set an example for other artists. Worth's drawings appeared from the 1880s to the 1920s, a period often referred to as the golden age of American illustration. Worth's name appeared throughout the culture, but he became known for his "Darktown" series in Currier and Ives prints.

Of all the popular graphics published during the past century, none reached so deeply into the culture as the prints by Currier and Ives. The earliest form of art mass production, the prints had an immense appeal to middle- and lower-middle-income groups and the institutions that served them: public schools, barbershops, churches, police stations, steamships, bars, firehouses, doctors' and dentists' offices. In 1907, when the firm was liquidated, all the stones used in the lithographic processes were discarded—except for the "Darktown Comics" of Thomas Worth.

Blacks had appeared in the firm's print catalogue long before Worth began drawing. With few exceptions, they were presented as jolly if awkward, healthy if not robust, and contented as they worked on the docks loading cotton, danced in a barn to the plucked banjo, or caught a fish. These early prints, however, had no unifying theme, no central comic force.

Worth, who had been drawing single cartoons for such magazines as *Judge*, went further to develop plots that featured a dynamic buffoon as the focal theme for an entire series. Like the many minstrel composers and performers before him, the Connecticut-born Worth presented his work as if he had been in long contact with the black community. The prints were burlesque views of the activities of blacks as they coped with the vagaries of everyday life or pretentiously aspired middle- and upper-class status. They bumbled everything in an energetic and lively comicality. The antics of "The Darktown Fire Brigade," "The Darktown Yacht Club," "The Darktown Hunt," "The Champions of the Ball Racket—On the Diamond Field," even "The Wild West in Darktown," to name but a few in the series, were simply overwhelming, because every black shared in the ineptitude. Worth also touched on various aspects of the stereotype such as crap shooting and watermelon eating, and drew his figures in the commonly acceptable way, with thick ruby lips, wide eyes, extended faces, awkward bodies, and loud clothing.[4]

Even more prolific and popular in this art form was the illustrator and story writer E. W. Kemble. When Mark Twain wanted illustrations for *The Adventures of Huckleberry Finn* (1885), he first perused several comic papers seeking an artist who could express "after his own ideas." He was particularly drawn to Kemble, whose pen-and-ink drawings appeared in *Life*. Twain declared him "a genius of an illustrator."[5] Kemble who was then twenty-three years old and had never ventured out of New York, had been drawing professionally for several years despite having virtually no formal training. His drawings for *Huck Finn*, which initially appeared in *Century Magazine* in 1884, began his reputation as an illustrator of southern themes and black life in magazines and books. His graphic work in this genre included Joel Chandler Harris's *Daddy Jake, The Runaway*, Thomas Nelson Page's *Two Little Confederates*, and Harriet Beecher Stowe's *Uncle Tom's Cabin*. In addition to his *Blackberry* and *Coontown* series, Kemble coillustrated with another well-known artist, A. B. Frost, *The Tar-Baby and Other Rhymes of Uncle Remus* (1904) and a later edition of *Uncle Remus* (1920).

Unlike Worth's accent on blacks as heavy African types, Kemble drew them "in a gently whimsical manner; his cartoons were full of wit and humor, yet drawn with simplicity."[6] Clearly, Kemble had a charming style, and his figures evoked considerable sympathy. Yet, despite his often delicate touch, his caricatures conformed to the racial stereotypes of the period. Round-faced and grinning, often in ragged clothing, beset by amusing yet troublesome situations, Kemble's blacks were as stereotypically cast as those of other artists. Indeed, his blacks were so lovingly comical that they appeared to be even more believable. Kemble's artistic as well as literary talents only added to the credibility of the Sambo configuration. As one winsome boy, in tattered clothing, shoes, and a flop hat, leaning against a barn, says in *Kemble's Coons* (1896), "I'se jes tired ob education, dat's what I is."[7] Blacks may have been tired of learning, but they were never tired of placing themselves in amusing circumstances, according to Kemble.

Kemble's drawings were among thousands—hundreds of thousands, in all probability—that appeared across the country, sketched by anonymous artists for adult and children's books, sheet music covers, posters, and short stories. These were often unrefined, frequently bordering on the grotesque, as they portrayed blacks as apes, monkeys, or cannibals in country and city dress. "A Magnificent Production of that Sterling Historical Drama, UNCLE TOM'S CABIN, Or Life Among the Lowly," began a large poster of the 1880s, followed by sketches of blacks and whites in the South. In the main, horizontal drawing were an Uncle Tom, a young dancing couple, a young man on bended knee keeping time by clapping hands, a banjo player seated on a cotton bale, a group of male and female cotton pickers watching the dance, and two prosperous whites, a master and a banker. The scene is one of merriment; all are smiling. The faces are caricatured: nappy hair, cherubic eyes and faces, upturned white or red lips, animated spirits.

Magazines attracted readers by using comical blacks on both front and back covers. Major artists such as Worth and Kemble were commissioned for their unique comical styles. The front cover of the August 1888 *Puck* featured "Brudder Shinbones and his Friends." Standing behind a small wooden fence was a mean, grizzled middle-aged black man wearing a battered top hat and lengthy tattered coat and holding an old umbrella; he is peering intently into a watermelon patch. A sign warns: "NO Trespassing in this Watermelon Patch, Beware the Dog." On the back cover of *Judge* in December 1882 was one black stealing from another: in "The Parson's Thanksgiving Turkey in Danger," a tall, dignified preacher hides behind a tree with a stolen turkey while a rifle-toting farmer in red long johns stalks him.

This practice of utilizing black figures on print covers originated in mid-century with sheet music advertisers. Because of their vaunted musical talents, which so enticed the whites, blacks were depicted frolicking in the city and the country. By the latter decades, both songs and their illustrations reflected sentimental-ized yearnings.

Blacks were shown dreaming of the wonderful plantation now destroyed by a terrible war. "Dem Good Ole Times" (1877) fea-tured a cover in which cherubic young black children romp with a dog or blow a ram's horn while Uncle Tom sits, hat in hand, mus-ing about his bygone past. The covers of "Carry Me Back to Ole Virginny" and "There's a Happy Little Home" (both 1878) show elderly men with white beards, sitting on tree stumps, dreaming of their younger plantation days, the cabins neatly pressed against the setting rays of a golden sun.

While the idyllic pre–Civil War days were presented as the high-light of their lives, songs also noted that no matter how oppressive the situation, their basic happy natures would overcome such trials. In "Sambo's Double Shuffle" (1883), a slender black man with large eyes grins as he throws a leg as high as his head and knocks his hat off in his exuberance. An entirely black community dances to "The Mississippi Barbecue" (1890s); as a banjo picker plucks out the tune to a "one step and turkey trot," a roasting animal turns slowly on the spit. A joyous scene on the cover of "Mammy Jinny's Jubilee: Shake Yo' Feet" (1880s) shows a group coming to her cabin to congratulate her; there are several dancing young children, and the minister, in his finest garb, carries a watermelon. A young man does a jig in "Pickaninny Pranks" (1900).

Urban blacks were just as happy in their environment. "Jolly Sambo" (1884), a minstrel man in top hat, cutaway tuxedo, striped trousers, with wooden knocker in hand, gaily grins as he prances to the tune. In "Nine Niggers More" (1883) there are scenes of black children at a northern seashore and in a classroom:

> You know our little nigger friends—
> You saw them once before;
> We brought them down to Rockaway
>   then,
>   and left them on the shore

But now their parents think it time they
should at school be taught,
So to instructors wondrous wise the girls
and boys are brought.[8]

In the 1890s, when the "coon song" craze was in full musical swing, sheet music covers "dealt baldly in simplistic racist emblems."[9] Even the black composer Ernest Hogan, forced to dovetail his songs to the prevailing style, had to endure seeing his songs caricatured on covers, and embellished in the most excessive ways: watermelon lips, saucer eyes, kinky hair, elongated bodies. These images could be seen in thousands of music covers. An attempt to combine them all into one song was "The Coon's Trade-Mark: A Watermelon, Razor, Chicken and a Coon" (1890s). Here the everyday stereotypes—a large watermelon, a shining razor, a succulent chicken, and a black man in bow tie with frumpled hair and a crazed expression—filled the four corners of the cover.

Yet sheet music, magazine covers, and commercial print did not even begin to approach the widespread use of other imagic forms that employed the black entertainer. Far more extensive were the penny picture postcards and the merchandise advertising cards. Combined, these two low-art forms were sold or mailed in the *billions*. During their heyday, they expressed a popularity far exceeding most commercial mass media forms even in the twentieth century.

The picture postcard had its origins in Austria and Great Britain in the 1860s and '70s. (An American had also conceived of sending a single sheet of paper through the mails just as the Civil War was getting under way, but its use was largely limited to Philadelphia.) Regardless of geography, the postcard became an instant fad. On the Continent, as in America, the announcement of their sale brought huge crowds to the post offices. In Great Britain the police were called in to control the eager public at the London General Post Office; in the United States five million cards were snapped up in several days. They were initially valued as commodity souvenirs. The earliest commercially produced postal cards in the United States began with special issues sold at the World's Columbian Exposition in Chicago in 1893.

As souvenirs and articles of correspondence, they immediately assumed a particular place in middle- and upper-income classes. Businessmen swiftly recognized the potential for sales, and advertised their products on trade cards. The public turned to them as entertainment. The postcard album assumed a special position in the parlor, alongside the Bible and the photograph album. Collections were set out for patients in waiting rooms of doctors' and dentists' offices. Hospitals requested that relatives of patients send cards, to be placed in albums for the enjoyment of others. Bridal showers often netted as many as two hundred cards. And their usage extended beyond the ordinary: in 1913 officials discovered that heavily embossed postcards were being used to smuggle morphine and cocaine into a New York state prison. At their height, in 1906, the number of cards sold exceeded 700 million.

Their fronts rendered by artists or photographed, postcards captured the massive social and technological changes occurring at the turn of the century. Further, they captured the imagination of people unable to travel to the far reaches of the globe. They recorded the styles, attitudes, even the fantasies of the populace. George Orwell regarded the picture postcard as "a worm's eye view of life," their popularity, he surmised, an acceptable outlet for feelings publicly repressed.

Orwell may have had in mind the vein of humor that coursed through the millions of cards—especially the insult variety. Wives, mothers-in-law, sons-in-law, inept housekeepers, henpecked husbands, old maids, sexually opportunistic males, suffragettes, inebriated men, foreigners, Native Americans, and ethnics were constantly lampooned. Among the various minority groups selected for their laughable traits were, of course, African-Americans: they turned out, in fact, to be the group most heavily ridiculed.

Yet, it must be noted, the cards embraced a certain realism as well. Scenes of black workers in the fields and on the docks, of uniformed black men delivering flowers, of families posing in front of shacks, of aproned black women in kitchens, of black youths and the elderly hunting for food—all these focused on aspects of black life that were easily observable throughout the South. Only a rare card recorded northern blacks.

What the cards failed to portray was the complexity of black society. The pictures were almost exclusively of southern rural workers, limited to nonskilled and menial labor, impoverished and seedy, invariably grinning, and seemingly naturally suited to their roles. Even within a framework of realism, moreover, an element of humor crept in. A 1920s card showed a young black man carrying eight animals attached to a long pole: "Nine Coons, Count 'em"; a 1940s–50s card pictured a young black male leaning against cotton bales on a wharf and smilingly plunking a guitar: "Strumming Away My Blues Down South"; two elderly black men with white whiskers and shabby suits compare "A Southern Delight, Chicken and Possum" in a 1920s–40s card.

That these items were an integral part of a dominant theme could be seen in card pictures for over three quarters of a century. Manufacturers in Brooklyn and Cambridge, Milwaukee and Chicago, Danville (Virginia) and Miami employed the humor motif in hundreds of millions of cards. In subject and style, content and color, the comedy directed toward blacks was consistent and repetitious. Within its narrow range, all groups of the community were affected.

On one level were children of both sexes. Children generally formed a substantial segment of postal cards, and black children were no differently portrayed—except that they were not only persistently funnier but their words and thoughts were always in deep southern dialect. Typical were a young boy and girl dressed in their nighties, their backsides fronting the card. They are holding hands, he with a small dog, she with a doll. In a charming pose, the way in which most children were shown in the cards, their nighties were open at the bottom, displaying their plump and rounded bottoms. A rhyming caption underneath focused on the boy's affectionate attention:

> When de golden moon comes creepin' up
> Across de fah horizon

Dah's a suttin sweet honey chile
Ah's espeshul got mah eyes on

The sender of this particular card, mailed from Omaha, Nebraska, to a hotel in Chicago on August 15, 1942, wrote underneath the girl: "Dat's you, Honey Chile."

Black babies formed a large part of the cards from the 1930s to the post–World War II period. They were usually displayed in wicker baskets containing cotton, with such titles as "Black and White Symphony," "Picking Cotton, —'Down in Sunny Dixie,'" and "Two Dixie Products—Greetings from the Sunny South." Older children were shown cavorting. Cards produced at the turn of the century had young boys "Playing Hookey" (1902), posing as "A Typical Coon" (1905), or fishing as a "Sportsman in Dixieland" (1910s). Occasionally there was a northern scene. A brightly colored New Year's greeting card showed a young black boy, his head encircled by a red scarf, pulling a female on a sled who sported a pink hat and muffler, and bore the message "I'se mighty glad dat I can wish yu all de good fings dis season."

Most cards, however, were set in the South and extolled the region's virtues. Postcards, after all, were printed for the vacationer's trade, and whites rarely went to Harlem for their vacations. Thus, there were many shots such as the one of a young girl in a wide blue farm hat, her ragged dress down on one shoulder, who smilingly assuages the consciences of anyone concerned with racist practices: "Yas Suh, Of Course I'se Happy Down South" (1930s–50s). It was a message repeated over decades.

Teenage antics was a highly popular theme. Groups ranging from several to eleven youths, in rural dress, often barefoot and sporting different types of hats, were shown carousing in clubhouses, cruising in homemade autos, shooting craps, sharing molasses, and devouring watermelons. Especially did they feast on watermelons. Artists and photographs rendered luscious green watermelons and bright red watermelon slices about to be consumed by eager grinning faces. It was always, it appeared, as one card said about a group about to gorge on watermelon, "Dinnertime." Watermelons were fondled in "Anticipation"; fought over in "Give Us De Rine?—Ain't Goin' Be No Rine"; extolled in "We's in Heben." One card showed a man with a melon under each arm, eyeing a loose chicken: "Dis am de wurst perdickermunt ob mah life!" On another:

> I'm an American, same as you
> And my favorite flag is red, white and blue
> But when I'm hungry 'tis plain to be seen
> My favorite is red, white and green.

One postcard simply showed three round circles that read from left to right, "Watermelon Into Coon." Straight lines within the first two circles gradually descended into a grinning type of pumpkin face. It was entitled "Evolution."

Nor were youths the only class of blacks addicted to the melon. Thousands of Uncle Tom cards pictured elderly men seated in the fields, on farm equipment, at the side of barns, munching away, their faces wreathed in contentment. It was, as the captions simply stated, "Melon Time."

The region's peculiar topography produced unique settings in which black antics could be further accentuated. An intriguing subject for northerners was black men and youths riding the backs of alligators in Florida. Like cowboys astride their horses, the blacks dangerously rode the gators with a simple rope affixed to the animal's mouth. A small boy in a dark red riding outfit rode an alligator in an early 1900s card, "The Home Stretch in Florida." A group watched a young man ride an alligator out of a river in "The Spring Run." Many, though, were not so lucky. In a curious reversal, a large number of cards portrayed blacks in the grip of a gator's jaw, usually by the seat of the pants; well-dressed young boys and men were about to be punished for unspecified sins. In a swamp, a gator held fast a man in white shirt and tie, who, on his knees, hands and eyes turned upward, asked for deliverance in his "Darky's Prayer, Florida" (1930s–40s):

> Deah Lawdy, please bless dis po' nigger.
> He won't be had no mo',
> His sins was accidental like
> What he done sinned befo'.

Oh, Lawdy! Swing wide de pearly gate
'Cause dere ain't much mo' time to wait.

Cartoon cards supplemented artistic portraits and photographs. Beginning in the 1920s and extending through the 1970s were a series in which the figures were a continuation of the worst of the Jim Crow period. Overly plump bodies and faces, half-moon smiles, extended ruby-red lips, rotund eyes—even cats looking like minstrel singers—caricatured every level of black society. A portly woman hangs her wash: "That Reminds Me—I'm Just A Little *Behind* in My Writing." Another woman, well dressed, with her three children looking identical despite their ages, inquires about white gloves to a white female clerk and receives an answer: "Madam, Could I Interest You In A Pair of White Kids?" A young man in a loincloth held together by a large safety pin plaintively asks, "I'se *Pinnin'* A Lot of Hopes On Gittin' A Lettah From Yo' All . . . Why Don't Yo' Write?" These cartoon cards were done in brilliant color and sharpness.

Postcards for all occasions—Valentine's Day, Christmas, Mother's and Father's Days, birthdays, births, patriotic events, anniversaries—and for no particular occasion all supplied mirth for over three quarters of a century. Although the East and Midwest were the suppliers of these cards, they were sold in stores across the country, and every year hundreds of thousands passed through post offices on the way to a public that clearly responded to their contents.[10]

During its first years of use, the postcard also served the function of advertising products. A picture of the product underscored by details of its significance adorned one side, leaving the reverse side for an address. Eventually, however, the two formats were separated out and the advertising card, in size and character almost identical to its relative, assumed its own place in the commercial world. Older businesses and new products announced themselves to millions of potential customers, and also reminded the faithful to reorder. Despite its mailing cost, virtually every consumer industry used the card in the decades before and after the turn of the twentieth century.

Various purposes were fulfilled by the advertising card. It announced the coming visit of a "drummer," a sales representative; it served as an order form; it was used as a receipt of an order; and it pictorially extolled the product. As a device it became the ancestor of the newspaper and magazine advertisement. One of its prime techniques was humor as a visual grabber.

Sambo sold many products via the advertising card. His face beckoned benignly on different types of goods, but especially household items: soaps, polishes, gas ranges; a variety of foods: coffee, cereal, ginger, shrimps, soda pop, jellies and marmalades; and home medicines: cough syrups, kidney plasters, liniments. Before the coming of the twentieth-century female who combined sexual allure with motherly innocence, there was the black male with his enticing smile and good-naturedness as the consumer come-on. It is easy to discern why blacks of both sexes were employed to sell household products: it was assumed that, as servants, they knew which products were among the best. In fact, as *natural* servants, their folk wisdom directed them toward the superior good. "My missus says dars no good coffee in these yer parts," intoned a pearly-toothed elderly man in an 1888 ad for Chase and Sanborn coffee. "Specs she'll change 'er mine when she drinks SEAL BRAND."

But blacks were used to extol goods unrelated to their servile positions. On this level, it was their comicality that supplied the incentive. Manufacturers and businessmen felt that humor was an essential pathway to the consumer heart.

> Clark's O.N.T./Spool Cotton/
> George A. Clark/Sole Agent/
> In WHITE, FAST BLACK and BRIGHT Colors/
> SOLD EVERYWHERE

read an 1890s card. On the flip side was a smiling young black male in patched overalls, red shirt, and hat, seated astride a large cotton spool with the agent's name, testing his fishing rod thread. "I reckon Dis Yere's Strong 'Nuff Suah." A cigar company entitled its 1890s card "Little African" at the top and "A Dainty Morsel" at the bottom. In between were a snapping alligator coming ashore and a small naked black baby crawling away. Occasionally a gallows "joke" was employed. The Elgin, Illinois, company, supplier of horse and buggy springs, reins, and whips, mailed out a card in which the whip was prominently highlighted. It certified its power in the card's title, "HANG 'EM!", by showing a lynched black hanging from a tree along with the message "And Keep 'Em Straight."

Advertising cards possed certain advantages. They were a low-cost, highly personalized form of communication. More, they crammed a wordy message with image into a limited space. The success of the card led advertisers to other techniques. An ingenious offshoot was the postal stamp, a noncommercial, decorative stamp that was usually stuck to the rear of the envelope. The advertising stamp, like its predecessor, became a technique of personal persuasion and was later used by nonprofit organizations to solicit funds.

Sambo became a commemorative stamp. An 1½ × 2½-inch stamp was not uncommon, done in bright colors, drawn by artists, and containing all of the imagery and messages found in the cards. Food companies used them extensively. Some were highly detailed affairs. Such a stamp was dispersed by the Armour meat company in 1915–16. Against a brilliant green background with the Armour "Star" Ham emblazoned on top was a black chef in a white hat and coat, holding a large ham in one hand and pointing to it with the other. It was, he announced, in a slogan that became the company's trademark, "The Ham What *Am*." Another stamp showed the back of a black maid in a red bandanna, against a yellow background, holding a tray of biscuits and announcing, "I'se Comin'!" It was the ad of the Atlanta Milling Company of Georgia: "Miss Dixie Self-Rising Flour Makes Better Biscuits."

Advertising, however, was moving away from restricted space and limited audiences in order to capture a larger segment of the public. The new immigration and urban migration were ensuring a huge market, and manufacturers sought other ways of reaching the consumer. Techniques developed in the decades before the turn of the century were applied to other media forms in the twentieth century. As advertising tapped into newspapers, billboard signs, magazines, and product packages, there was the ubiquitous Sambo.

As in previous years, the smiling black hawked various goods, but especially those associated with pleasure: foods, toys, household items, clothing, and tobacco. Tobacco actually led the way. Ads for cigars appeared as early as the 1850s. Engravings of various black couples walking down country roads, a plantation house and field hands in the background, worked in both the dandy and darky for Southern Rights Segars in 1859. Later in the century blacks chased away giant wasps, sat smoking on porches, traipsed down rural roads, and got married in the ads. Mirth was supplied by blacks of all classes and types. At times merely the stereotypical label was given, as in Old Coon Cigars and Nigger Head Tobacco. Usually, though, ads lampooned specific groups. An 1890s lithograph ridiculed the most prestigious class, the black preacher. Standard Durham Smoking Tobacco of Durham, North Carolina, displayed a color ad in which the humor revolved around the wedding of two sets of identical twins. The participants were dressed in tuxedos and long evening gowns. Seated before a white-haired preacher were the wedded twins at the dinner celebration. Read the rhymed caption:

> O Joy! O Rapture! Happy Mokes!
>   The Pious Parson Came
> And Joined The Twins in Hyman's Bands,
>   So That the Four Were Twain.
> The Wedding Feast The Guests Declared
>   Had Never Yet Been Beat
> And When They'd Drank All They Could Drink
>   And Eat All They Could Eat—
> "Dis Am De Triumph Ob De Feast,"
>   The Pious Parson Spoke.
> And Of The *Standard Of The World*
>   Each Darkey Had A Smoke.

In the decades following the First World War the tobacco ads, like many others, eliminated distended physical faces and bodies. Dialogue was softened. The connection to African primitiveness was rarely seen. But the black male as entertainer remained fast.

In *The New Yorker* of September 27, 1930, for instance, a cigarette ad for Old Gold brought together Marilyn Miller, a star dancer in the *Ziegfeld Follies,* and the furnaceman of an apartment house. "That's Why They Got There . . . So Quickly" was the theme. She dances before him as he encourages her: "Mar'lyn chile, shake yo' feet." The ad credits the "kinky-haired old furnaceman" for being the "first to educate Marilyn Miller's feet. At those same feet a few years later, Old New York laid its heart."

It was the food industry that made the most extensive use of Sambo in its promotions. At one time or another, hundreds of products were displayed with blacks. Although most were ephemeral—newspaper advertisements and billboards regularly changed their pictures—others remained in play for years. In 1922 Hendler's Ice Cream, "The Velvet Kind," hoisted a billboard showing a bare-bottomed, moon-faced black boy holding a red-and-green watermelon on his lap. "Eat Seeds 'n All!" he smilingly boasted. Labeled "Pickinanny Freeze," the product sold for five cents, and was heralded as "A Pal For Your Palate." It was but one of many, many such signs that remained in one place for a considerable length of time.

Eventually, three human figure trademarks attained national recognition and appeared in cards, on signs, and particularly in newspapers and magazines: Uncle Ben (rice), Aunt Jemima (pancake mix and syrup), and the Cream of Wheat chef. Originating at the turn of the century, two of the food figures became classical representatives of the house servant. Always clean, ready to serve with a crisp smile, intuitively knowledgeable, and distinctively southern in their spoken words, they epitomized servility with exceptionally natural cheerfulness. Their faces conveyed an innocence, their ages cut across the scope of a lifetime—one young, one middle-aged, and one elderly—but all were primed to offer health through food and cheeriness. Dressed in a high white chef's hat, bow tie, and white jacket, the Cream of Wheat man strums on a banjo: "A Merry Heart Goes All The Way." A youngish Aunt Jemima, her head wrapped in a red polka-dot bandanna matched by an identical shirt, draped in a red shawl, grinningly beckons: "I'se In Town Honey." The Uncle Tom-ish Ben, partly bald, partly white-haired, joyfully proclaiming his rice with twinkling eyes, joined the pair in the 1930s.

Few food trademarks rivaled them. Their familiarity was often extolled by the company who presented them. An old white-bearded black man in a battered top hat and patched pants, leaning on a cane, peers directly into a large Cream of Wheat sign. "Ah Reckon As How," he joyfully proclaims, "He's De Bes' Known Nigger in De Worl'." ("Nigger" was changed to "Man" in the early decades of the twentieth century.) Aunt Jemima's reputation was enhanced by her rag-doll family—a husband, "Uncle Mose," and several children, "Dawn" and "Wade." Aunt Jemima and Uncle Mose also became handy utensils, salt and pepper shakers, and a syrup pitcher.

Certain products associated with the home were closely linked to Sambo. Stove and gas companies used blacks because, as the Lorain Oven Heat Company declared in its 1922 ad, " 'Mammy' would have told you that her chief trouble was in getting the *right heat.*" Soap ads cleaned bodies and the family wash, sometimes with magical consequences. In a Pears Soap ad in 1888, two young boys, a black and white, bathe in metal tubs, their heads and upper bodies showing. The white emerges clean; the black emerges with his body cleaned white. Joining the popular trademarks in the soap area was Fairbank's "Gold Dust Twins." The pair was the conception of E. W. Kemble, who as a staff artist drew them for the *Daily Graphic.* The N. K. Fairbank Company of Chicago compiled a number of Kemble's drawings and published them in a booklet, *Fairbank's Drawing and Painting Book Showing the Gold Dust Twins at Work and Play as Sketched by the Famous E. W. Kemble* (1904). Consisting of seven color and black-and-white sketches, it was intended as a coloring book for children, offered with the purchase of the soap and also sold separately.[11] Imprinted on all sides of the washing powder package for nearly seventy-five years were two small boys, twinish, naked except for a small skirt. Arms wrapped around each other, they were intensely black against a yellowish-orange background. Eventually their skin was lightened and the Africanness diluted, but their mirth remained intact. The logo and particularly the name seeped into the stock of American colloquialisms. "We looked like the Gold Dust Twins," wrote a woman, "Boiling in Tulsa," to Ann Landers in the 1980s, complaining about a sister-in-law who wore the same dress to a charity ball.[12]

The advertising prism included many goods totally unrelated to black status. Here the enticement was also strictly a humorous one. The Fisk Tire Company in the 1920s and '30s used as its logo a small, yawning, cherubic white boy in woolen pajamas, holding a small lantern in one hand and a tire in the other. It was, the color ad reminded car owners, "Time to Re-tire, Get a Fisk." The picture was actually an ad within an ad, and invariably there was a funny black figure in the foreground. At times it was a bandannaed black maid holding the wash and fending off a goat with her umbrella. Or it could be a barefoot youth, his tattered pants held up by suspenders, looking disappointedly at the broken watermelon at his feet.[13]

Package images, then, often fused with print advertising, and both frequently merged in the material culture. Sambo fixtures filled kitchens and other rooms. In addition to the Aunt Jemima and Uncle Mose salt and pepper shakers and syrup pourers, there were Sambo plates, cookie jars, potholders, tobacco humidors, pincushions, bottle openers, clocks, cigarette holders, and toys. Toys for adults and children were sold in department stores and through mail-order companies such as Montgomery Ward and Sears, Roebuck. The 1927 edition of the Sears catalogue offered for forty-five cents a "Chicken Snatcher": "One of our most novel toys. When the strong spring motor is wound up the scared-looking negro shuffles along with a chicken dangling in his hand and a dog hanging on the seat of his pants. Very funny action which will delight the kiddies. Nicely lithographed metal. Height, 8½ in." In the 1920s–30s, large department stores offered a target set entitled "Sambo," a donkey shooting game. Surrounded by concentric circles for different points was a large picture of a widely grinning black youth with a tooth missing. The game was done in bright brick colors, the boy appearing silly in his outfit. A similar game was marketed by the Milton Bradley Company, "The Darky's Coon Game," in which the contestants had to lob a little wooden ball into Sambo's mouth. For adults as well as children, there were elaborately detailed playing cards. Crown Cards distributed "The Fireside Game" in the 1890s, a deck of cards with photos of blacks eating watermelons, shoe-shining, conversing in dialect, lounging in different poses. In the same decade the L. D. Baldwin company sold cards that depicted a different aspect of "pickaninny life" with such captions as "The Crossing Sweeper," "The Virginia Pine Chopper," "An Alabama Coon," "Little Wharf Rat." Playful gift items were the magnetic dancing team "Tip 'n Tap," music boxes, and earrings. Symbolically conveying this array of household material objects was the iron jockey on thousands of lawns.[14]

Thus, the imagery was essentially an extended cartoon. The obvious power of a cartoon lies in its ability to focus on a person or object and convey an unequivocally sharp message. Repetition of the basic idea ensures its impact. The traditional cartoon appearing in newspapers and magazines from the latter decades of the nineteenth century into the early part of the twentieth century, in which blacks were the objects of humor, was but a further indication that Sambo was America's earliest laugh-in.

In *Puck*, December 2, 1894, an elderly black gentleman in a top hat and long coat, hands tied together behind his back, peers at a rooster in a cage. His wife, "Uncle Rastus's Better Half," explains to a guard about her husband's hands: "He wuz boun' to see de poultry show, sah, an' he had me do it foh fear he might get absent-minded, sah!"

In *Life*, November 20, 1890, a tall African, in a top hat and loincloth, pokes a stick into the stomach of a fat white man hanging upside down; there are other whites hanging alongside. The sign in the marketplace reads: "Fresh Lot of Missionaries for Thanksgiving Day."

In *Judge*, May 12, 1904: "A Little Rough." A bulbous man is seated at a table devouring a meal of fowl. The waiter—black, short-headed, long-legged, with small rounded eyes—is on his way back to the table carrying half a watermelon and muttering to himself: "Ah wondah ef dat southern gent ordered watahmilyun br'iled chicken jes' ter tantalize dis poor cullud waitah?"

In *Life*, December 22, 1904, shortly after President Theodore Roosevelt invited Booker T. Washington to dine with him at the White House, for which he was severely castigated: "Harvard's Football Eleven of 1909, Under President Roosevelt, of Harvard." Underneath the heading was a picture of eleven black men, differing only in size but not in ferociousness. All sported the athletic letter "H" on their jerseys. In place of a football was a large watermelon.

It was natural that Sambo would also make his appearance in the first generation of comic strips. The earliest strip, "The Yellow Kid" by R. F. Outcault, was printed in the last decade of the century and tended to be simple and crude. Comics mirrored the vast demographic changes occurring throughout the eastern and midwestern sections of the country. A vast outpouring of immigrants from Eastern Europe and a smaller but nevertheless substantial number of people migrating into the cities forced a different perspective on the character of American society. Everywhere was seeming massiveness. Sprawling factories, burgeoning cities, huge machines matched by millions of newly arrived ethnics forced a redefinition of space. As Arthur Asa Berger aptly observed in *The Comic-Stripped American,* the comics portrayed an ambience of chaos, "with bodies everywhere and crowding the space of the cartoon, just as it was felt that we were beginning to get crowded in America."[15]

The early strips encompassed them all. Caricatures of Germans and Jews, Irish and blacks, even mangy dogs, were commonplace in the comics. Afro-Americans were among the many groups stereotyped. The comic that first initiated sequential action, Rudolph Dirks's "The Katzenjammer Kids," which came into being at the turn of the century, revolved around the antics of a German couple and their extremely winsome but equally mischievous boys. Located in a typical setting, the action brought together the natives—Africans—with the Germans. With few exceptions over its fifty-year existence, the natives were dressed in skimpy loincloths, with bones through noses and as necklaces, top hats, and crowns for royalty; they conversed in southern dialect. Among their various names were "Captain Oozy-Woopis," "King Doo-Dab," and "Skinny Snowball." To a certain extent, however, the blacks in the strip, while conforming to the Sambo image, nevertheless possessed visual dignity and authority.[16]

At the same time, the theme of African cannibalism played on all levels of the media. The funnies often used it over the next seventy-five years. African tailors constantly measured whites, and the stewpot-over-roaring-flames was a familiar sight. This African connection was a not-so-veiled threat to whites, a connection that stirred up subconscious anxieties of black retaliation. From Frederick B. Opper's "Happy Hooligan," syndicated in the 1910s and '20s, to the revamped "Mutt and Jeff" in the 1970s, the king always wanted to know "what size platters to put you on."

When not preparing tasty whites for their next meal, African-Americans were ridiculed for other habits, the most threatening being their assimilative urges. In one episode of "Welcome the King of Dahomey" (1911) by Kemble, a group of upper-class black women in gowns greet the Duke of Dahomey at a special reception. He is appropriately attired in a long-tailed tuxedo. However, the Duke is rather short and the tails are rather long. He is hardly attractive in his buffoonish dress. Informed by a fawning woman that "De men is all in de smokin room," he graciously replies, "De gemmen kin wait. I gotter pay ma respects to de ladies." The women immediately size him up as a prospective husband for their unmarried daughters. One hopeful mother turns to her daughter: "Mabel, ah wants you to sing one ob you tender lub songs fo de Dook." "Pray do," affirms the Duke. "It will calm my fevered brow." He is leaning with one elbow on the piano, his face in a contented smile, eyes closed, when the open piano top suddenly crashes on his head. Mother and daughter beat a hasty retreat from the room. "You suttnly did make a mash on de Dook," sarcastically exclaims one of the remaining debutantes.[17]

Buffoonery was standard fare in many of the earlier comic strips—but blacks more than most seemed to excel at this type of behavior. Especially did "Sam" epitomize this brand of humor.

Sam was a cartoon character of the 1900s whose egg-shaped body supported a pool-ball head and moved on tree-rooted legs. Sam's smile truly extended from ear to ear, his thick red lips were equally wide, and he was always convulsed in laughter. Often Sam was the protagonist, and his aggressive laugh induced retaliation—which caused Sam to laugh even harder and louder. He frequently shared the action with other ethnics, on one occasion with a German whose corpulent body was clothed in striped green pants, a red vest, and a Tyrolean hat. Sam has failed to stop a thief who has just stolen some goods from the German. When asked why, Sam merely guffaws and declares, "Ho! Ho! Ho! He looked like a comic Valentine." Another situation involved Sam's family—their physical features were even more exaggerated—who howl with laughter when a very heavy-set, well-dressed white man crushes a small stool. The man proceeds to hit Sam on the head with the stool after several "Ho! Ho!"'s. Sam laughs on and finally shouts, "Sakes alive, wuzn't that fat? Wow."[18]

Many of the funnies in the early years sported at least one black character for additional comic effect. Their physical appearance varied considerably, some drawn in heavy colors and lines, others with lighter skins and with normal dimensions. In a substantial number of strips—"Kitty Higgins," "Gasoline Alley," "Toots and Casper," "The Katzenjammer Kids"—it was an Aunt Jemima maid, whose wide mouth was matched by her rotund torso and who always addressed the white folks in plantation English. A simple designation rounded out their identities: "Dinah," "Mammy," "Mirandy." Not all secondary figures were female. In the strip "Moon Mullins," it was "Mushmouth," whose clownish face was not unlike that of his "Boss," and who was just as good-natured. The difference between the two lay in "Mushmouth"'s mushy language. And there was "Asbestos" in the strip "Joe and Asbestos." He sported a black bowler hat, holes in his shoes, and a checkered suit, and possessed the ability to communicate with horses—a skill amply projected in movies in the 1930s and '40s.

From its earliest beginnings, photography used blacks in identical fashion. Always the accent was on a humorous aspect of black life. As in the rest of the popular culture, photography made little distinction between ages and classes. Turn-of-the-century group pictures of black children invariably displayed kinky-haired, moon-shaped children, sometimes well dressed, other times in tattered clothing, but always in some comical circumstance. An exception-ally large 1897 group portrait of young boys in fourteen different poses was captioned "All Coons look a-like to me"; another showed both sexes in nine different naked poses with the heading "ALLIGATOR BAIT."[19] Even the most serious situation was bent in a humorous way. In Mark Sullivan's popular history of the late nine-teenth and early twentieth century, *Our Times,* there was a picture of a black soldier holding a gas mask in his hands—and laughing. His wide-open mouth, prominent white teeth, and half-closed eyes made superfluous the caption, "A War-time Smile."[20] Many blacks in white high-school, college, and university yearbooks, those perennial publications devoted to encapsulating the personalities of graduating students, suffered similar fates. In 1924 three Afri-can-American males received degrees in dentistry from Tufts Den-tal School, one of the most prestigious in the country. They all possessed identical traits in the yearbook, *The Explorer:* one was listed as being "one of our merry-makers, and has brightened the path leading us through many weary days. He has a rare sense of humor, for never has been known to admit a sorrowful moment . . . "; another was popular "due to his radiant personality, and pleasing disposition . . . a smiling 'Chip off the block'"; and the third was even more cheerful than the others: "The sun smiled kindly when it first smiled on 'Bob White' and in so smiling some of the sunshine stuck to him, for he has spread happiness wher-ever he has gone."[21]

Moving photographs, the precursors of the motion picture, which developed in the latter decades of the nineteenth century, projected the same Jim Crow images. Lantern slides were popular in business establishments and middle-class homes. These oper-ated on a roller arrangement, giving the appearance of movement. Like the stereoscope, which conveyed a three-dimensional picture, lantern slides were easily operated by hand and were intended for all ages. Blacks ate watermelons, picked cotton, hunted coons, merrily pranked, and inadvertently fell prey to some accident in different types of slides.

The comic strips, cartoons, knickknacks, advertising and postal cards, food packages, newspaper and magazine covers, prints and lithographs, posters and signs, lantern and stereoscopic slides—all these and more bounced the black image around the different and complementary levels of the popular culture. If history is a consequence of the meshing of tiny as well as sizable images, it can be said that whatever which way the prism was turned, Sambo was always there, always grinning, always comical, always entertaining.

It has been argued that in the period prior to the turn of the century "the coarseness and grossness [of depictions of blacks] typical of the 1880s and 1890s began to yield to more attractive and pleasant characterizations between 1900 and 1920," that "the ugly image did not disappear, but it did have new and vigorous competition." That competition, it was suggested, came from German and Jewish characters. Moreover, blacks no longer were forced to don blackface makeup, and black spirituals and jazz came to be appreciated as serious music.[22]

While these changes were notable, while the caricature of blacks became more refined and whites became more attuned to the nuances and depth of black culture, the essential core of the stereotype remained fast. Long after the ethnic comic stereotyping was gone, the black comic image was still present, intact and operative. Only its outer edges changed during this period, not its intrinsic format, the black male as sublime comic, as natural entertainer.

When the prism of Sambo is turned to reflect the popular culture in the first quarter of the twentieth century, yet another visual angle is revealed. Now it was another moving picture, the film, a cultural form capable of creating and manipulating a national consciousness, that seized upon the image. Not surprisingly, Sambo became a movie star.

7

The Camera Eye

Roll on, reels of Celluloid, as the great Earth rolls on!
—Frank O'Hara, "To the Film Industry in Crisis"

"I ain't askin' you, is you ain't . . .
I is a askin' you, is you is?"
—*Hearts in Dixie* (1929)

Never in history has so great an industry as the movies
been so nakedly and directly built out of the dreams
of a people.

—Max Lerner, *America as a Civilization*

How to convey a moving image?
How to connect a moving image to a larger schema?

John Dos Passos wrestled with these questions as he worked into his trilogy of American society in the 1920s. His mission in *U.S.A.* was to depict the powerful economic forces reshaping the country and redefining private lives with their presentation in the mass media. Photographs and films were becoming the prime shapers in the perception of events—as well as with the sense of history. They were public eyes presenting the complex changes into private brains.

Quickly, Dos Passos had come to understand that the twentieth century had created new forms of seeing. New eyes that were attached to technological apparatus: *The Camera Eye:* clicking, flickering, flowing, zooming, sweeps. It was a new order of coding the past, recording the present, and scouting for the future. Consequently, multiple eyes, human and technical, interact and interpret.

The Camera Eye searches out the moving images of Sambo on film . . .

The Silent Camera Eye: 1890s–1910s

Eyes peer into the darkness, ears attend to the piano music. "Young Darkey, Slave Scenes, Southern Characters or Scenes." The images on the screen, some black, some blackface, are mirrored in the titles:

- *The Wooing and Wedding of a Coon* (1904),
- *The Slave* (1905), *The Rastus Series* (1910s),
- *The Sambo Series* (1909–11), *For Massa's Sake* (1911),
- *In Slavey Days* (1913), *Coon Town Suffragettes* (1914),
- *The Nigger* (1915), *Our Gang Series* (1910s–1930s),
- *Birth of a Nation* (1915)

The number of reels are many, the number of images but two: blacks are comical, blacks are scary; blacks are buffoonish, blacks are frightening. Pathé Film announces a one-reeler, the opening film in a series that presages the future:

RASTUS' RIOTOUS RIDE
A One Reel American Comedy

Rastus is a Comical Darky With a Faculty for Getting into Scrapes. His Ride is Really Riotously Risible![1]

The images are of the minstrel character, Jim Crow, still connected to the previous decades, not a fully developed screen character. The industry has yet to present the flip side of the image. D. W. Griffith—southern, conscious of history, attuned to cinematic innovations—freezes a decade of American time. It is the Reconstruction period, when deeply submerged fears of black legislators, black voters, black educators, black skilled workers, black landowners disturb white cherished ways. His remarkable film

Birth of a Nation (1915), called by the progressive president of the United States "living history," gives a gripping gift to Anglo-Saxon civilization: to the rescue ride hundreds of Ku Klux Klanners, determined to put blacks in their place. Protests of the film by racially sensitive whites and outraged blacks fuel nationwide controversy; crowds at the theatres bring attention to racial themes. *Birth of a Nation* changes moviemaking, becomes a classic, becomes a training film for the KKK, becomes one of the most-watched films of the century, becomes too divisive, becomes a liability to film makers and producers.

The Silent Camera Eye: 1910s–1920s

The darkness is now highly familiar, the music more refined, the images are tightly fashioned. The protests over the racist film subside, leaving movie moguls with an unspoken, unwritten, unannounced decision: no more the explicit savage black, no more the status-seeking black, no more the politicized black, no more the respectable black—no more upsetting whites. Rather, the black in his natural overseas setting, a reminder of his origins, his evolutionary status: Africa in *The Drums of Fate* (1923). Instead, the fieldworker in his sentimental American home: the plantation in *Uncle Tom's Cabin* (1904, 1914, 1918, 1927). Instead, the comical plantation in Mack Sennetts's *Uncle Tom Without the Cabin* (1919). On to the jolly, jazzy, dancing black in *One Exciting Night* (1922). Applause for the blackface popular stage singer transforming the silent film into a talking vehicle, the minstrel man Al Jolson warbling and caressing the plantation mother in *The Jazz Singer* (1927):

> Mammy, Mammy,
> I'd walk a million miles for one of your smiles,
> My Ma-aa-mmy.

Laughter for the pickaninnies—Farina, Sunshine Sammy, Pineapple—in the *Our Gang* series. Yuk-yuks at the scenes of adult black men shivering and yammering at ghosts and spooks and ha'nts and thunderstorms, solemnly swearing tribute to superstitions: the rabbit's foot, the voodoo doll. Addicted to gambling, shooting craps, playing cards secreted in shoes and socks in a World War I comedy, partly with blackface actors, called *Ham and Eggs at the Front* (1927). And always cheerfully serving whites as chauffeurs, porters, valets, doormen, janitors, maids, cooks, stableboys. What's in a silent-film name? "Smoke," "Molasses," "Buckwheat." Addicted to laziness, drowsiness, shuffling.

Title: *In Old Kentucky* (1927). Sheet music opens to "My Old Kentucky Home." Script: "An old colored man. He is listening to the music with a smile on his lips, but a tear in his eye." A plantation boy, young and slack-jawed, named Stepin Fetchit. Film ends to the tune "Dixie."[2]

The Camera Eye & Ear: 1930s–1940s

The Nation's House: small/cavernous: garish, colorful, carpeted: small town/metropolis/hamlet: Saturday-afternoon baby-sitter, Saturday-night date, weekday-night contest: popcorn/jujubes/Milky Ways: feet moving, eyes straining, hands reaching: an interior universe/an external image: cartoon, serial, newsreel, short subject, two features: the nation's immersion, the nation's escape, the nation's fantasy, the nation's laugh

The black image cast in the silent period expands in the new technology of the next decades. The emergence of the screen Sambo feature: malapropisms, superstitious gyrations, rhythmical patter, buffoonish repartee, childish actions. A range of comical scenes, a mélange of humorous moves, a panoply of entertaining enticements. The screen Sambo becomes an art form, a particular typed character whose centuries-old tradition is adopted, extended to countless millions who have never known a black person—to those millions born in the 1910s and '20s whose first contact with a black person is on the screen in the Nation's House.

Whose only contact is image and name. What's in a talking-movie name:

> Sambo, Algernon, Caesar, Streamline, Napoleon, Speed, Willie, Lamar, Birmingham, Eight Ball, Rome, Lucius, Sylvester, Gummie, Uncle Billie, Jupiter, Jonah, Mose, Acorn

Different ages, different sizes, different looks, different dress, yet all the same, all one.

Old forms in a new medium. Minstrelsy is rejuvenated. White performers don blackface, yah-yah to minstrel songs. Little kids in *Our Gang* put on a minstrel show; Mickey Rooney and Judy Garland in *Babes in Arms* (1939) stage a minstrel show; minstrel scenes appear in countless films, including a Marx Brothers movie. Two exemplars of the burnt-cork tradition stage their acts before the camera. Al Jolson and Eddie Cantor—scions of Jewish immigration—don blackface, rounded white eyes, rounded white lips. Of Jolson, like dozens of nineteenth-century practitioners, it is guiltily written: "Jolson acquired his Southern accent more honestly than most professionals who yearn for the Swanee River: he learned it from the Negro playmates of his boyhood."[3] Jolson carries his style to such films as *Hi Lo Broadway* (1933) and *Wonder Bar* (1934), musicals in which the images are crass. In his declining years, films of his career again bring attention to minstrelry and the whites' affection for it: *The Jolson Story* (1947) and *Jolson Sings Again* (1949) star Larry Parks, who applies blackface and syncs his words to Jolson's off-camera voice. The films are box office hits, as they say in the "biz."

Cantor, called "Banjo Eyes," a star in the *Ziegfeld Follies,* sells Liberty Bonds during World War I in blackface and minstrel costume. His rendition of "If You Knew Susie" makes him sole proprietor of the song. Becomes a favorite with the public, with his energetic boyish body and his saucer eyes, which roll around in circles. Combines burlesque comedy with traditional blackface and performs as bootblack, butler, tramp, waiter, song-and-dance man, sometimes in different dialects. Makes many movies, with numerous minstrel-type scenes, the most incongruous being *Roman Scandals* (1933), a sort of blackface in toga.

Minstrelsy plays but a small role in the larger entertainment. The screen Sambo is the big hit, the performer, the star. No name, of course, ever appears in lights, on the marquees, in the opening credits. But every moviegoer knows, if not by name, that Sambo is ever present, a black face with comedic intent in his or her soul.

Script descriptions reflect the silver-screen images. In a highly popular movie, *The Littlest Rebel* (1935), set in the South during the Civil War, starring Shirley Temple, Bill "Bojangles" Robinson, and Stepin Fetchit, the black figures are "negroes," "colored," "pickaninnies." In other films, they are "Darkies," "Mammy," "Sambo." Directions are strikingly clear about their actions:

> The skinny colored boy is playing up to his audience, working for laughs.[4]

> Mumbling to himself, he carries dish out of scene.
> . . . keeping up an incoherent chatter.
> He laughs good-naturedly.
> He looks around cautiously—evidently not quite sure of himself.[5]

Southern scenes in the antebellum period sentimentalize the plantation, the lost cause, the slave's natural place. To the tune of "Roll, Mississippi," the opening shot in the film *Mississippi* (1935)—starting Bing Crosby, Joan Bennett, W. C. Fields, and the Cabin Kids—focuses on a riverboat. The *River Queen* is heading upstream. Suddenly, the camera flashes to "a couple of negro boys dancing." It's the "Cabin Kids slapping hands in time and harmonizing on four bars of the number. . . . " One of the "small colored kids" walks behind the Commodore and yanks the whistle cord, blowing his nose with a loud snort timed to the pulling of the cord. They are introduced by the Commodore as "a group of sun burnt youngsters." Later, in their "Swanee River" number, they are joined by a group of delighted slaves who add their voices to the song. It's a typical movie scene of happy and contented slaves.[6]

There was one focus, but always variations within it. The camera eye and ear pick up black workers at jobs menial and subservient. Never at jobs of power or authority. Always,

- they sing: cotton workers hauling bales on the gangplanks sing "Ah hate to see the evenin' sun go down" and "Ah got troubles" in *Banjo On My Knee* (1936).
- they aim to please: a black baker aboard a submarine in *Gung Ho!* (1943), the story of a special group of Marines known as Carlson's Raiders during World War II, proudly exclaims, "Dat's de best cake ah evah baked."
- they just ain't very smart: a black doorman in a New York hotel replies to the question "Where's Borneo?" from a young white girl in *Just Around The Corner* (1938).

  > "Borneo? He done moved up to Harlem."
  > "It isn't a man, it's a place."
  > "It is? Well, . . . it's way up in the sky."
  > "Way up in the sky?"
  > "Yeah, it's part of that Aura Borneo."

- when they don't sing: a black servant in *Unconquered* (1941), a movie about the French and Indian War, is unusually quiet. "What's wrong, Jason? How come you're not singing?"
- they connect to the Deity: a black sailor shipwrecked with whites in *Lifeboat* (1944) plays the flute, pickpockets a hidden compass from the secret German agent, and does not participate in killing him. "When we killed the German, we killed our motor," says one of the white survivors. "No sir, we still got our motor," answers Joe quietly, and peers upward.
- they connect to African origins: a black janitor in a New York clinic in *I Take This Woman* (1940), wearing a funny ski hat and carrying a mop and pail, says, "Well, bust me for an ape's uncle."
- they are superstitious: a "colored caretaker" in *High Sierra* (1941) gives advice to two white fishermen:

ALGERNON: Yessuh, that fellow better fish the banks and watch his step. He better never go out in no boat because that little dog has put the hex on him for sure.

The men laugh.

FISHERMAN: Put the evil eye on him, huh?

ALGERNON: Yessuh . . . the evil eye! That lil' ole dog got the evil eye! His left eye . . . kinda shines in the dark like a cat's eye.

SHAW: If it's in the dark, how do you know which eye it is?

Algernon scratches his head. The men laugh.[7]

- they gamble and drink: three black chauffeurs and a doorman are needled in *Louisiana Purchase* (1941): "OK, boys, here's a deck of cards to play gin rummy—only cut out the gin this time."
- they really are dumb: a black caretaker in a hotel picks up the telephone which has been accidentally dialed by "Cheetah," Tarzan's chimp companion in *Tarzan's New York Adventures* (1942). He carries on a long conversation and, after many confusing moments, exclaims, "Don't you fool with me, colored boy."
- they are funny even without trying: a black waiter in a comedy-mystery, *Florida Special* (1936), addressed by a patron with a Hungarian accent:

    "Hey, waiter, do you have spinach? Do you like spinach?"
    "Yessah, we have spinach, but ah don't like it."
    "Ha, ha, vot an accent."

- they aren't responsible: a black stableboy in *Breezing Home* (1937), one of countless flicks in which the stable hand grooms and talks to the horse, on women and marriage: "Ah don't know—too much trouble in women folks . . . ah got married once so to have some button on mah shirt—then I didn't have no shirt a-tall!"

How can one trust workers such as these? How can one hire these people for anything other than menial tasks? But are they funny!

A particular comedic form is finely honed in this period. It is a type of action that goes to the core of gullibility, goes to the heart of innocence, goes to the soul of a child. It is the comedy that warps/wraps itself around the primitive. It is comedy that centers on the mysteries of the supernatural, the workings of another dimension no longer accepted in an industrial society, which prizes the scientific method.

What could be funnier than the anxieties that arise from superstitions? The anxieties of grown men who, learning of the presence of ghosts, haunts, spooks, and devils, do anything they possibly can to avoid such spirits. First they chatter and shake, then lips quiver and mouths stammer, then eyes bulge, then nappy hair stands on end, then they sometimes turn albino, then they take off as swiftly as they can, passing locomotives in their haste to get away, saying, as they move into flight, "Feets, do your thing," "Feets, don't fail me now," "Feets, don't desert me now."

Not only grown men. There had always been, after all, a female counterpart. Not quite as prominent, not quite as extensive, not quite as comical, but always present nevertheless to reassure whites that biology was a rigid enforcer.

What's in a female movie name?

Lollypop, Gossip, Aida, Stella, Daisey, Aunt Dilsey, Aunt Petunia, Hester

What's a female movie Sambo like?

good-natured, light-headed, motherly, yet sassy, direct, surly

What's in a female part?

maid, cook, maid, seamstress, maid, baby-sitter

Men had no monopoly on Sambo traits. Gambling?

"My sister's baby was born on 4:03 and I bet two dollars on 4:03 right on the nose . . . but I didn't win."[8]

Ignorance?

WHITE MISTRESS: I don't know why he gave me all those presents. I know him as well as I know Shakespeare.

BLACK MAID: Who is Mr. Shakespeare? I don't recall any Mr. Shakespeare ever called on you.

WHITE MISTRESS: That was before your time.[9]

Gossipy?

COOK: You didn't tell me you wuz gonna hire a man for your paper.

EMPLOYER: It just happened.

MAID: Well, you didn't tell me.

EMPLOYER: She has to know everything. If I don't tell her, she has a misery of the spirit.[10]

Befuddled?

MAID: [Reading a newspaper story to her mistress] An' after Lieutenant Abrams' discovery of the we—wee—weepone—

MISTRESS: Weapon, Stella.

MAID: Yes, ma'am . . . mm—de weepons wit' which de jockey was murdered, de famuous slee-uth—

MISTRESS: Sleuth . . .

MAID: Yas'm . . . Nick Charles, who is collo—bore—atin' . . .

MISTRESS: Collaborating . . .

MAID: Dat's it—announced dat . . . a single criminal . . . per—perpat—per-per—pat—

MISTRESS: Perpetrated . . .

MAID: Per . . .

[she gives up][11]

As the custodians of whites, as the providers of goodness, black women gruffly give advice, openly empathize with troubles, cite from "De Good Book," oversee the antics of little children, maintain order and discipline, and stand fiercely as protectors of their masters-employers. They pose little threat, sexual or otherwise. In these films they are simply loyal and lovable.

But the female of the Sambo species takes second place because she is not *the* entertainer. To entertain! That's what it is all about! Not only did black men entertain in whatever line of work they perform, they also entertained *as performers*—in the same way that whites desired them in the big house on the plantation and in the streets, circuses, and theatres in the northern cities. Films permit a wide range of movement, and movement enables black talent to expand and soar. In musicals, comedies, dramas, short subjects, cartoons, documentaries—yes, regardless of plot or subject or event—the camera watches, the boom records the black entertainer:

> tap-tap dancing, jitter-bug gyrating, plantation wheeling . . .
> piano-playing, harmonica-humming, big-band soaring . . .
> choral-singing, blues-winging, spiritual-evoking . . .

What did it matter that Rick never actually said "Play it again, Sam" in *Casablanca* (1943)? The line has stuck. The symbolic act of Sam playing for his white master is overlooked; sunk below consciousness.

The Camera Eye & Ear: The Black Star

> Name: Lincoln Theodore Monroe Andrew Perry
> Origins: So named after four American presidents in Key
>   West, Florida
> Performing Name: Stepin Fetchit
> Motto: "Take your time—time ain't gonna take you"[12]

Small roles in several films, but a standout. Then flashing recognition. *Hearts in Dixie* (1929), a movie exclusively about black life on the plantation, a first. *Hearts in Dixie* has serious intent: are blacks to remain in the past or move into the present? The plot revolved around ignorance and enlightenment. Which way will they go? Answer: superstitions—a voodoo ceremony. Answer: a happy place—blacks singing "Ring, Ring de Banjo," "Peter, Go Ring Dem Bells," "Oh, Dem Golden Slippers," "Deep River," "Swing Low, Sweet Chariot." Answer: the past triumphant. Reviews of *Hearts in Dixie*:

Louella O. Parsons, a white columnist, in the *Los Angeles Examiner,* March 8, 1929:

> There is nothing in *Hearts in Dixie,* however, at which either race can take offense. It is such a true and sympathetic picture of the

colored folk. The pitiful superstitions of some of the uneducated Negroes, their simplicity, their love of a good time, and their psychology are all graphically presented. . . . The real Southern plantation melodies are so sincerely sung that one glimpses the real soul of the Negro.

Unnamed columnist in a black newspaper:

This would have been a great picture if it had been allowed to stay on the screen just fifteen minutes . . . the producer preferred to adhere to the old tradition that the American public loves to see our people singing in the cotton fields and dancing in the sand, barefooted.[13]

Stepin Fetchit becomes the most prominent practitioner of the black fool in films. It is more than an act: it becomes an art form.

Stepin Fetchit—from the movement of Step and Fetch It—is catapulted to stardom. Not quite equal to comparable white performers, but one of the most recognizable, most bankable, most comic blacks in Hollywood. Begins his career on minstrel shows as "Rastus, the Buck Dancer." Doesn't like that name, changes it to the "Jolly Pard," then to "Skeeter Perry," then to "Step 'n' Fetchit." Goes over to M-G-M to audition for *In Old Kentucky* (1927). Asked at the screen test if his name is really "Stepin Fetchit," he replies, "Sure." Told to see the director, he slouches into the office and flops into the chair nearest the door.[14]

Starts at seventy-five dollars per day, collects over a million in his short movie career, possesses six houses, employs a host of Oriental servants, drives around in a fleet of limousines, one of which is pink with his name in neon lights on the side. His formula:

s-l-o-w-s-h-u-f-f-l-i-n-g-a-l-o-n-g-f-r-o-m-p-l-a-c-e-t-o-
p-l-a-c-e-s-l-a-c-k-j-a-w-e-d-d-r-o-o-l-i-n-g-w-o-r-d-s-
i-n-c-o-h-e-r-e-n-t-c-h-a-t-t-e-r-l-a-z-i-l-y-l-o-u-n-g-i-n-g-

An act? A black reporter interviews him:

I was surprised. I had expected to see a mild "Gummy," not quite so lazy as the original in *Hearts in Dixie*, but enough to be known and recognized. That is why I had to adjust myself to this energetic man with a collegiate look and a nervous vitality that showed itself in his gesticulating and restless movements.[15]

Many movies, many buffoonish scenes, many laughs. Criticism from black quarters. Hardly anyone notices. Whites don't read black newspapers or journals and don't listen to or even hear black speeches or protests. They are laughing too hard. Whites do read trade papers, warm to the comforting words in an advertisement:

> Calafurnia here I'se am/Right from sunny Alabam,
> De lan' ob cotton, corn, un moonshine/Dat taste jus' lak dis
>   moobin pitcher gib ob dine.
>
> I'se lak Dixie, deed I do/But you'se raise watter mullons, too,
> An' your chicken jus' as grand—/Calafurnia, here I'se am!
>
>   Yours fo'de
>   axin'
>
>   Stepin
>   Fetchit[16]

Stepin Fetchit, like Epaminondas in the children's storybook before him plays the fool. But does it really matter? Does it really matter that Bill "Bojangles" Robinson possesses dignity and charm when he dances with Shirley Temple, that Canada Lee, the dramatic actor, does not drawl as "Joe" in Alfred Hitchcock's *Lifeboat*, that Louis Armstrong and Count Basie in countless musical numbers demonstrate extraordinary talent, that Mantan Moreland and Willie Best finesse the comic role as chauffeurs and valets in the *Charlie Chan* series and dozens of other films? What *do* whites see? Are they aware it is all act, all put on, all comic survival within imagery long established?

Stepin Fetchit outshines them all. In *Stand Up and Cheer* (1934) he is exceptionally bright. *Scene:* he is interviewed and asked if he's ever been employed. "Yassah—I'se been workin' in the Army of Refrustration." "Refrustration, eh? What kind of trees did you plant?" "Er—wooden ones." *Scene:* a hillbilly named Dinwiddie looks him over and nastily exclaims, "Ignoble Hottentot!" An undaunted Fetchit exclaims, "You can't fool me, boss—that's pig latin!" Other scenes show him confusing a "talking" penguin with the comedian Jimmy Durante and claiming to be the English writer George Bernard Shaw.[17] He is always the hapless, lovable victim. In *David Harum* (1933), one of the many horse-racing pictures of the period, he is of course inseparable from the horse, even being sold with him on the auction block. *The World Moves On* (1934) has him as a recruit in the French Foreign Legion: how could he ever have been mistaken for a Frenchman? he wonders. In *Steamboat 'Round the Bend* (1935), one of several pictures with Will Rogers, he is inside a moth-eaten, discolored whale. He emerges from the whale's distended mouth, "a shiny black knob-like head and two staring white eyes," to a viewer's declaration, "it's Jonah hisself." Not so, says Fetchit, "I'se hidin' from dub jail-man." Baptized "David Begat Solomon," he actually is "Jonah." Aboard the showboat he plays "duh banjo—and duh harp—and duh drum—and duh tringle—and duh—" to the delight of passengers.[18]

He embodies a range of stereotypes. In another comedy with Will Rogers and Hattie McDaniel, *Judge Priest* (1935), set in a small Kentucky town on the Mississippi River, Fetchit plays a prisoner, "a gangling lazy mumbling negro boy" named Jeff Poindexter. He is accused of chicken stealing and appears before the judge, played by Will Rogers:

SCENE 9:

CLOSE SHOT—JUDGE PRIEST as he leans back in his chair and we see his face clearly for the first time. He pulls out a bandanna handkerchief from his breast pocket and a corncob pipe tumbles on the desk accidentally. He disregards that and wipes his forehead with the bandanna, then drawls quizzically at the prisoner.

JUDGE PRIEST: Where you come from, Jeff?

JEFF [Pointing with his thumb over his shoulder]: Aa-a-a-a-ah m-m-m-m-m-m-m-m- yassah, y'onor.

JUDGE PRIEST: Who give you the name Poindexter?

JEFF: [stammering naturally]: M-m-m-m-m-m Mistah Ranny.

JUDGE PRIEST [Interested for the first time]: You don't mean Major Randolph Poindexter—down yonder at Pine Bluff?

JEFF: Yassuh. Thas' him.

JUDGE PRIEST [His eyes twinkling reminiscently]: Well, salt me down!—Major Ranny! 'Pears like you Poindexters always gettin' mixed up with chickens. . . . You, Jeff. What you got to say for yourself?

JEFF [Stammering]: No, suh, y'onor. Ah-ah-ah I wan't near them chickens dat night. Ah was fishin'.

JUDGE PRIEST [Leaning forward]: How's that? Fishin' where?

JEFF [Pointing his thumb off vaguely over his shoulder]: A-a-a-a-a-aah mmm-m-m-m-mmm Sleepy River.

CUT TO:

SCENE 14

CLOSE SHOT—JIMMY BAGBY as he shakes his head positively.

SARGEANT JIMMY: Ain't no fish in that river.

CUT TO:

SCENE 15

CLOSE SHOT—DOC LAKE and HERMAN FELSBURG, profoundly interested as DOC dissents with conviction.

DOC LAKE: 'Tis too.

HERMAN FELSBURG: Doc's right, Jimmy—[Slyly] if you know how to ketch 'em.

CUT TO:

SCENE 16:

CLOSE SHOT—JEFF as he nods and stammers.

JEFF: Yassuh, white folks. Ah-ah-ah ketched me a bull-head cat-fish a-a-a-a-aaah [Stretching his hands away out] dat long.

CUT TO:

SCENE 17

CLOSE SHOT—HORACE MAYDEW, looking very annoyed and indignant, as he cries out oratorically.

SCENE 17

MAYDEW [angrily]: There's your proof he's lying.

CUT TO:

SCENE 18

CLOSE SHOT—JUDGE PRIEST as he leans forward, deeply interested, but unhurried.

JUDGE PRIEST: Hold on there, Boy. What'd you use for bait?

CUT TO:

SCENE 19

FULL SHOT—GROUP AND FRONT OF COURTROOM as JEFF begins to stammer and pantomime in explanation as if baiting a hook and

all lean forward with intense interest except MAYDEW who is close
to the bursting point.

JEFF: A-a-a-a-aaaah Ah gets me a hunk of beef liver—and ah puts
it on duh hook . . .
[He is baiting an imaginary hook as he talks and as he comes to
the word]

DISSOLVES TO:

SCENE 20
MEDIUM SHOT of JUDGE PRIEST and JEFF POINDEXTER walking away
from CAMERA down a path that leads to Sleepy River and beyond
on the river we see an old paddle wheeler chunking up the river,
seen through a break in the trees, and JEFF is carrying several
cane fish poles and a demijohn in the other hand, while the JUDGE
is carrying his own prize fishpole.[19]

Later, in the sixties, when the career had faded and the criticisms were pointed, Lincoln Theodore Monroe Andrew Perry
would counter, would bring suit, would argue that he was after all
only playing a role, the *only* part he could have gotten at that time
in Hollywood, no different from any one of a dozen black actors
at that time, only people don't remember or recall what it was like,
how rigid the system was, how locked in they were, prisoners to an
image. "I was only playing a character, and that character did a
lot of good," he exclaimed in an interview. Then, as a counter to
the image: "Just because Charlie Chaplin played a tramp doesn't
make tramps out of all Englishmen, and because Dean Martin
drinks, that doesn't make drunks out of all Italians."[20]

8

The Radio Ear:
The Odd-Couples Connection

A friend of mine tells me his father would turn on the
hulking Crosly console on Sunday evenings and say, with a
beaming smile: "There's good listening tonight!"
                    —Jim Harmon, *The Great Radio Comedians*

For an amazing phenomenon [*Amos 'n' Andy*] which stands on its
own merits and needs neither explanation nor analysis. I'd
like to offer my own modest theory even though it happens
to be the theory which many others before me have offered.
I claim these two stout fellows have won a place in the
popular taste and have held it against all comers because
they are so natural, so simple, so full of an unforced
joyousness, so dogged human.
                    —Irwin S. Cobb, in *Here They Are—Amos 'n' Andy*

It is difficult to fathom, even sixty-odd years later, precisely why
the change occurred. Did it have anything to do with the difference between seeing and hearing, between the visual and the oral?
Did it relate to the institutional demands of the two media forms,
films and radio, themselves? Was it connected to the liberal atmosphere of the New Deal and the publicized sensitive activities of
Eleanor Roosevelt? Or did it arise from some inchoate, emerging
sense within the Caucasian community that the black image was
archaic, that, while blacks might well be, undoubtedly were, intel-
lectually limited, they were not exactly buffoons either? Comical,
yes, yet not fools.

What does seem certain is that in the 1930s radio presented the black image markedly differently from films and advertising. Not that the radio industry was free from racist perceptions or practices. Quite the contrary. But it was able to alter the image as the newest large-scale medium, decades removed from the Jim Crow formulas that had ensnarled American culture so thoroughly at the turn of the century.

In the early years, to be sure, it did not appear that radio programming would express itself any differently from the other forms of popular culture. The African-American presence was restricted largely to musical formats, to bands and singing groups. And when dramas replaced musicals as the main thrust of radio programming in the 1930s, only the spiritual chorales remained. Occasionally in this vast wired empire there would be performances by Marion Anderson and Paul Robeson, for they were so gifted that they could not easily be denied. These, however, were the exceptions in a system that was open only to those willing to perform as servants, and then only if, like Bert Williams before them, they could project themselves as "black black." More than one actor was rejected on the grounds of not sounding "like a Negro." At the same time, the black community was also rejected as a "topic" for analysis on public affairs programming's highly popular format throughout the period. Overall, then, the radio studios and their structure were lily-white.[1]

Yet blackness of a sort existed on radio, a blackness wrapped within white images, which took an odd form, the "odd-couples" shows. Three syndicated programs offered the only sizable black "presence" from the 1920s to the mid-1940s, and it was the comical black who was given prominence in every one. Ironically, this presence involved actually only a single black man, for the others, four in all, were whites in blackface.

Moreover, in only one of these three shows could be heard the buffoonish sounds emanating from the screen. *Pick 'n' Pat* which became *Pick 'n' Pat Time* during the 1940s, began its prime-time programming as *Molasses 'n' January* on the CBS network at the beginning of the New Deal and continued through World War II. In terms of performers, content, and style, *Pick 'n' Pat* was a throwback to nineteenth-century blackface comedy. Extolled by

the announcer as "America's foremost exponent of blackface buffoonery"—"two dusky delineators of devastating dumbfoolery,"
"two dusky dynamos of comedy," "two dark clouds of joy," "two
storm clouds of joy, who shower you with laughs"—the program
was hardcore stereotyping. Support characters, dialogue, and sit-
uational humor reflected its crass qualities. Pat's girlfriend was
"Ducky Pew," who hailed from "Chitling Switch," and her sister
was "Juicy Goosey Pew." His close relatives were "Uncle Anthra-
cite" and "Aunt Carbona"; his cow was named "Beulah."

In all probability, the show was initiated as a competitor to the
extraordinarily popular *Amos 'n' Andy* program. To detract from
the performers' origins, there were references to their blackness:

PICK: Well, Pat, I want you to meet my gal friend, here, sweet
smellin' Bethesda.

BETHESDA: Hello, short, dark and repulsive.[2]

DUCKY: We better start dancing, Pat, 'cause I can't stay very late.
My kitchen sink is full of dishes.

PAT: Suppose your kitchen *is* full of dishes. You don't have to
get home for that.

DUCKY: Yes I do. My brother wants to take a bath.

PAT: You mean to say your brother bathes?

DUCKY: Yes, on alternate July's [After Laugh]. But this time he's
doing it in May for a change.

PAT: What's the idea of your brother bathin' in the sink?

DUCKY: Well he'd done it ever since I took the landlord in the
bathroom to show him where we needed some repairs. The landlord looked around and said, "Miss Ducky, what do you mean by
keeping coal in the bathtub?" My brother said, "That ain't no
coal. That's me."[3]

PICK: The more war bonds you buys the sooner the war will be
over, and the sooner we'll have no more things like black-outs.

PAT: You know, that reminds me of the last time I was in a black-
out, with my fat juicy sweetheart, Ducky Pew.[4]

The range of buffoonery was bolstered by distorted words and
phrases. "Graduated" became "granulated"; "catastrophe" was
misunderstood and phonetically pronounced as "a cats who's-is-

free"; calcium was for shooting craps with "pet calciums." Jokes connected to contemporary affairs but always had a twist and a touch of ignorance and stupidity. *Pick 'n' Pat* simply pandered to the Jim Crow tradition with its accent on mindless joking and crass dialect.

Yet the show was an anachronism. Compared to rival comics, Amos 'n' Andy and Rochester, it appeared out of place, out of touch with the war effort against the antidemocratic tenets of Nazi Germany. It went off the air when the war ended.*

On the air before *Pick 'n' Pat* was the series it attempted to emulate. It was bound to fail; it simply could not compete with the daily fifteen minutes of *Amos 'n' Andy,* a series continuously broadcast from 1928 to 1943, which reflected its extraordinary popularity. During World War II the show expanded another fifteen minutes, and it was adopted by television in the early 1950s. A decade later, with pressure brought by the NAACP and other groups, it was terminated. Begun in 1926 on a local Chicago station, under a different name, *Amos 'n' Andy* had been on the airwaves for almost four decades in all, for over ten thousand programs.

Amos 'n' Andy was not simply the first nationally syndicated radio show; its longevity suggests a national psychic connection based on humor. Its time slot, from 7:00 to 7:15 P.M. brought family activities to a virtual halt. Throughout the country during the Depression, people rushed to get home in time for the opening number, "A Perfect Song." Dining-room service in hotels across the country was held up until the show ended; movie theatres began their programs after the closing musical number. George Bernard Shaw declared after touring the country, "There are three things that I shall never forget about my visit to the United States—the Grand Canyon, Niagara Falls, and *Amos 'n' Andy.*"[5]

Decades after its cancellation, the Hallmark Company issued a birthday card with the heading " . . . Do You Remember?" It showed a middle-aged person sitting in a chair listening to a

---

*I am extremely grateful to Mort Lewis, the principal writer of the show, who made available the scripts of the show and answered all questions openly and with enthusiasm.

chapel-shaped radio, and the inquiry, "When nobody had a TV and we'd sit around the radio and listen to Fibber McGee and Molly, Amos and Andy and Fred Allen?"[6]

It was in 1928 when the manager of a local station asked two white troupers working in Chicago to do a program after the highly popular comic strip "The Gumps." Charles J. Correll and Freeman J. Gosden had been involved in amateur theatricals and had also promoted and produced minstrel shows and musical comedies. Applying a blackface model, Correll and Gosden created *Sam 'n' Henry,* a narrative of two Negroes who had migrated from Birmingham to Chicago in search of work. Within a year after they began broadcasting—when approximately twelve million families owned a radio set—the show became the first serial program to be nationally aired. Its move to a wider audience also led to a change in locale. On the rationale that taxicabs were more in demand in New York—the format flowed around the actions of the "Fresh Air Taxicab Company of America, Incorporated"— the show's setting was shifted to Harlem.

In many ways it was a complicated, brilliant show, an intricate meshing of characters, dialogue, antics, and situations, all contrived and acted by Correll and Gosden. They described their conception in *All About Amos 'n' Andy,* in which they immediately dispelled questions about identity.

> Question: Who are Amos 'n' Andy?
> Answer: Freeman F. Gosden and Charles J. Correll.
> Question: Are they white or colored?
> Answer: White.

The show's focus was to revolve around the eccentricities of two men:

> *Amos:* Trusting, simple, unsophisticated. High and hesitating in voice. It's "Aint't dat sumpin'?" when he's happy or surprised, and "Awa, awa, awa," in the frequent moments when he's frightened or embarrassed. . . . Andy gives him no brains but he's a hard earnest worker and has a way of coming across with a real idea when ideas are most needed. He looks up to and depends on

Andy: Domineering, a bit lazy, inclined to take credit for all of Amos's ideas and efforts. He's always "workin' on the books" or "restin' his brain," upon which (according to Andy) depends the success or failure of all the boys' joint enterprises. He'll browbeat Amos, belittle him, order him around, but let anyone else pick on the little one—then look out![7]

Like an old-fashioned minstrel show, it had characters with farcical names—the Kingfish, Madam Sapphire, Brother Crawford, Lightnin'—who spouted jokes and malapropisms, foolishness and patter, rejoinders and quips in a rhythmical repartee. It was all in the Sambo vein. Never were there family or full names; rather, it was "Amos" and "Andy." Always there were atrocious dialect and mispronounced words and phrases. Frequently there was ignorance and presumptuousness and simplemindedness. The dialogue was heavily larded with colloquial expressions, stock phrases, trite words, and familiar quotations. Often the malapropisms were used as a comic device to keep the conversation flowing or to overcome a lull in the action. The political description "socialist" became "social-risk," its definition being "Dat puts ev'vybody on de same basis." "Syrology" was the word for "psychology," which Andy defined as "eatin' on a man's brain." Correct language was obviously not one of their strong points. An "inferiority complex" was twisted to "infy-oratory reflex," and its definition was "Dat's when you think dat you aint nuthin—even if you AINT, don't nevah think dat." Mutilated phrases became their trademark: a business proposition was "Here's de propolition"; an adverse reaction, "I'se regusted"; a cry of dismay, "Holy mack'el." The men displayed large areas of ignorance. On language:

ANDY: You aint re-gressive.

AMOS: Whut do re-gressive mean?

ANDY: You know whut re means, don't yo'—R-E?

AMOS: R-e—re I know whut dat mean alright.

ANDY: Well, gress like you gress sumpin—den sive like a sieve. Dere you is.

AMOS: Oh yeh—dat's RE-gressive.[8]

On politics:

LIGHTNIN': Whut do it mean when I hear 'em say "de senator at large"?

ANDY: Dat's a fat senator—a large fat senator.

LIGHTNIN': Nosuh, dat aint what I talkin' 'bout—"At Large"— he's "at large."

ANDY: Oh well—dat's a senator dat done run out o' stuff down at Washington—he's like a bear in de woods dat's lost—he's at large.[9]

On historical events and the origins of July Fourth:

ANDY: Well, Sittin' Bull was sittin' 'round—Columbus came oveh an' made him mad—den dat fellow Paul—a—dat man dat rode dat hoss—whut was his name?

AMOS: Paul? Jus' call him Paul—dat's alright.

ANDY: He was ridin' round carryin' on—it was hot dat summeh—de war was goin' on—Columbus, he was discoverin' America—George Wash tryin' to git across the riveh—Liberty Bell had a crack in it—things was in a mess.

AMOS: Well, whut did dey do about it?

ANDY: Well, all of 'em got togetheh an' had a meetin'—it was so hot dey jus stopped ev'thing—it happened to be de Fourth o' July—it was so hot dat ev'body said dey would take a day off.

AMOS: Ev'body said dey'd take a day off huh?

ANDY: So dey took off de Fourth o' July—en' ever since den peoples is been doin' de same thing jus' layin' 'round—tired an' hot.[10]

The full range of stereotypical dispositions was exploited. Good-natured stealing and a happy-go-lucky work style were prominently featured. Their representative was the "Kingfish," introduced as the joyous and clever thief. The Kingfish makes his appearance when Andy is jostled by a man and discovers that his watch chain is suddenly gone: "Say," Andy exclaims, "'scuse me for protrudin', stranger, but aint you got ahold of my watch chain?" "Your watch chain?" Kingfish ingenuously answers. "Well, so I does. How you like dat! One of dese solid gold cuff links o' mine musta hooked on your watch chain dere."[11]

Kingfish was a confidence man in the tradition of Mark Twain's "Duke" and "King" in *Huckleberry Finn*, those who make their living by posing as actors, preachers, phrenologists, and quack doctors. The Kingfish's frenetic energies were directed toward avoiding work through dubious schemes or by conning Amos and Andy into underwriting questionable enterprises. But he was not the only one actively pursuing laziness. Andy, who frequently fretted about unemployment, once exclaimed to Lightnin': "I got a feelin' dat I wanna go to work." Lightnin' quickly shot back, "I had dat feelin' once, but I snapped out of it."

There was a pretentiousness about Amos and Andy that was evident not only in their quest for sophisticated language, for success in the business world, but in their imitation of Caucasian social life. The show introduced the radio audience to the world of the black fraternal lodge. Though a spoof of the fraternal activities of small-town life of the twenties in general, the machinations of the pair and their friends in the lodge propelled them into clownish proportions. The lodge was called "The Mystic Knights of the Sea," and its members were named after fish. Lower-order members "Sardines"; officers were titled after a specific variety of fish, such as "Shadfish" for the secretary of the order, "Swordfish" for the Guard of the Door, and "Kingfish" for the head of the lodge. The benefits of the brotherhood were explained by the Kingfish in his sales pitch to Amos and Andy: "Oh brothers—we has great meetin's. Whenever a sardine gits sick, de jellyfish sees dat he gets plenny to eat an' in case any of de sardines die dey is buried wid fishly honors."[12]

Not surprisingly, the show was based on whites' black dialect. Like Joel Chandler Harris before him, Freeman Gosden, who played Amos, was viewed as "a virtuoso in Negro dialect" and on the banjo. He had been reared in a Virginia household, where he was attended by a black maid and befriended by a black playmate, "Snowball." By contrast, Correll was a northerner, yet much of his musical education either bordered on or was directly tied to the black idiom, such as soft-shoe dancing. Soon after the two met, they developed a blackface act. To deflect criticism of their work, the pair wrote that they had frequent associations with "colored folk" in order to ensure that their black creations were "true to life." As seeing is a form of believing, they also posed with blacks in selected publicity sessions over the years.[13]

Amos 'n' Andy was an amalgam, a blending of stage minstrelsy with radio imagery, adapted for a mass audience. In its minstrel format, the announcer (interlocutor) opened the show by introducing the entertainers (end men), asking straight questions at the proper time, laughing when necessary, and responding to their rejoinders. Like the minstrel, the end men outwit the announcer, who manages dignity in the face of insult and foolishness. Since Correll and Gosden could not employ burnt cork in the traditional minstrel manner, they had to stress certain features of black life. Consequently, both dialect and situations were graphically hyped. Sociologist Arnold Rose acutely assessed the relationship between dialect and image: "To the Northern white man, although seldom to the Southern white man, the speech of the Negro seems unusual. In fact, the Negro dialect is an important cause of the Northern whites' unconscious assumption that Negroes are of a different biological type from them."[14]

As the show's hold over white imagination increased, Correll and Gosden seized upon advertising and other means to offer themselves as white black men. In these pictures Amos and Andy often appeared as mulattoes. In one ad, Amos wore a loud plaid shirt with sleeves rolled up to expose long underwear, dirty dungaree trousers, and a porter's cap. His partner wore a cocked derby hat, dented, with one hole in it, and smoked a cigar in a presumptuous manner.

Yet, while the show sustained the derogatory historical image, it also transformed it by carrying it to another dimension. From the very beginning, *Amos 'n' Andy* was a complex show with nuances of plot and character. It operated on many levels and at times contradicted itself in ways that reflected white confusion about the black world. This was partly the consequence of its locale and connection to events. *Amos 'n' Andy* was essentially an urban show, it connected to the problems and confusions of metropolitan life; and it further related to dominant social values of the twenties and thirties, for black humor, or, rather, the humor of "white blacks," worked within black language and rhythm, made the contradictions of the decades—the twenties with its accent on exalted material expectations and the thirties with its constricted economic realities—far more palatable than they actually were.

The dominant themes of the series were completely consistent with white bourgeois aspirations. The search for work and the dreams of success dominated *Amos 'n' Andy* for over thirty years. The various schemes pursued by the pair and their friends to achieve status and prestige, to enter the stolid middle classes, was totally attuned to the Dream. When they spoke of going beyond the middle class, of actually becoming rich—"Dere you go—wimmen on de brain," exclaimed Henry to Sam in their very first broadcast in 1926, "how we gonna ever be millionaires in Chicago when you always talkin' 'bout wimmen?"—they were connecting to a larger fantasy.[15] The critic for the *Literary Digest* was quick to note the relationship between the program's success and the American religion: "A & A is built around the theme of money. . . . This is the drama in which we are all engaged. In this universal plot there are no villains, in the ordinary sense, nor heroes, nor heroines, either."[16]

In important ways the motivations of the blackface pair undercut the traditional stereotype. In their quest for status they rejected the "worker" label, refused work relief, and avoided government projects. Their aim was to become entrepreneurs. One of their more "successful" ventures was their joint partnership in their first and really only company, the Fresh Air Taxicab Company. It was begun with a twenty-five-dollar investment in a convertible car. Andy immediately appointed himself president and made Amos "de chief mechanic's mate, fixer of de automobile, head driver of the company an' chief bizness gitter." Two divergent sides of black life emerged as Amos performed all of the work, while Andy, when not asleep with feet propped on a desk, was busy talking to one of his girlfriends.

Ownership of a business accorded the entrepreneurs high status in Harlem. Friends visited the company ostensibly for social reasons but in reality to ask for a loan, sell a policy, solicit for a fund, or seek membership in the fraternity.

The Fresh Air Taxicab Company was just one of many business ventures. At various times Amos 'n' Andy owned and operated "The Reducingest Reducing Company," "Okeh Hotel," "The Fresh Air Garage," a grocery store, a filling station, a lunchroom, and a furniture store. But these businesses failed, as did many during the Depression; Andy was forced to sell greeting cards, or work as a hotel doorman, or a process server.

Despite the poor management decisions, labor problems, or shortage of capital, despite the adversities and false starts, the pair maintained a cheerful disposition and rarely complained about their predicament. On the contrary, they appeared endowed with endless grit and optimism:

ANDY: Yo' know Amos, times like dese is bad.

AMOS: Yet, but on de other hand, times like dese does a lot o' good 'cause when dis is over, which is bound to be, an' good times come back again, people like us dat is living today is goin' know what a rainy day means. People is done used de respression, "I is savin' up fo' a rainy day," but dey didn't even know what dey was talkin' 'bout. Now, when good times come back again people is gonna remember all dis an' what a rainy day is— so maybe after all, dis was a good thing to bring people back to dey're sense an' sorta remind ev'ybody dat de sky AINT de limit.

ANDY: Yeh, yo' git some good out o' ev'thing, don't yo'?[17]

Although such enterprises as the Fresh Air Taxi Company were never a financial success, the program exposed white listeners to the ingenuity of fictitious Harlemites attempting to cope with the harshness of the Depression, earn a living with scheming decency, and never lose hope. Amos and Andy were stereotypically cast within a historical mold, but they possessed enough positive characteristics to offset, if not contradict, the worst features of Sambo. Laziness was offset by work preference, stupidity by connivance, buffoonishness by clever repartee, and language atrocities by smart thinking. With their perseverance and doggedness, they exuded an inner resourcefulness that gave them dignity. At a time when the visual media generally were still mired in Jim Crow imagery—Madison Avenue ran ads showing benign Uncle Toms teaching whites how to dance and perform, uniformed porters smilingly transporting beers and luggage for whites, cherubic faces beckoning hungry Americans to devour Uncle Ben's rice and Aunt Jemima's syrup; postcards displayed black groups eating watermelons and hunting possums; and cartoons and comic strips featuring blacks talking to horses—the *Amos 'n' Andy Show* was a step closer to reality, a step away from the rigidity of the stereotype.

Still, the program gave a stilted version of African-American life. How could it have been otherwise? Gosden and Correll were white men, after all, who were isolated and remote from the world they were portraying. Even more peculiar, whites themselves were largely absent from all the activities in *Amos 'n' Andy,* an absence that probably comforted white listeners who preferred keeping blacks at a safe distance. It recalls de Tocqueville's perceptive remark a century earlier regarding the termination of slavery in the north. The legal barrier down, whites "shun the Negro with the more pertinacity since he fears lest they should someday be confounded together."

The *Amos 'n' Andy Show* had been on the air for almost a decade when that isolation came to an end. In 1937, Eddie Anderson, a bona fide black actor, had a bit role as a Pullman porter on another popular radio comedy, *The Jack Benny Show*. The scene involved was part of a train sequence. Because the program was being shifted from its broadcasting locale in New York to Hollywood at the end of the season, the script simulated the changeover. There were three separate but connected sequences in a stock Sambo routine between the star, Jack Benny, and the train porter:

JACK: Hey, Porter, Porter!

EDDIE: Yas Suh.

JACK: What time do we get to Albuquerque?

EDDIE: Who?

JACK: Albuquerque.

EDDIE: I dunno, do we stop there?

JACK: Certainly, we stop there.

EDDIE: My, my.

JACK: Hm!

EDDIE: I better go up and tell the engineer about that.

JACK: Yeah, do that.

EDDIE: What's the name of that town again?

JACK: Albuquerque.

EDDIE: [Laughs] Albuquerque, what they gonna think up next.

JACK: Hm, fine porter we got.

JACK: Hey, Porter!

EDDIE: Yas suh?

JACK: When I got on the train yesterday, I gave you a suit to press, where is it?

EDDIE: Gee I'm lazy, don't I remind you of Stepin' Fetchit?

JACK: Yeah. And did you find out about Albuquerque?

EDDIE: He can't press it any better than I can.

JACK: ALBUQUERQUE is a town.

EDDIE: You better check on that.

JACK: I better get off this train, too. . . .

EDDIE: Say, boss, did we just pass through a town?

JACK: No.

EDDIE: Then what did I throw all that baggage off for?

JACK: I don't know and I wish I was baggage.

[The train stops at Albuquerque]

JACK: Hey, Porter!

EDDIE: Yas-suh?

JACK: How long do we stop here?

EDDIE: Where?

JACK: In Albuquerque.

EDDIE: [Laughs] There you go again.

JACK: Hm, no use talking to you.[18]

This exchange had not been the first on the program. In a 1932 show, Benny beckons "a Colored Porter"—listed in the script—as he alights from a train en route from Chicago. "Right this way, Boss, I'll get you a cab." "All right, Porter. Leave my grip here." "Yas, suh." Suddenly, sounds are heard of a loud crash. "Hey! I told you to be careful with that grip." "Sorry, Boss . . . Say, ain't you Jack Benny?" Benny puffs up: "So, you know me, eh . . . Well, here you are, Porter." "Thank you, Boss . . . wait a minute. This is a nickel you gave me." A pause. "Well?"[19]

The porter in this particular scene was played by Hotcha Gardiner, a white member of the staff whose specialty was dialect roles. There was no black member of the Benny program, although there were occasional scenes involving different minority persons over the years. Eddie Anderson's voice, however, lyrically raspy and infectiously comical, brought an instant response from the staff and public. A little more than a month later, they wrote him into another show. This time he was a waiter named "Pierre." In a saloon with other cast members, Benny calls for a waiter. "Yas-suh, boss, did you call me?" "What have you got that's good to eat?" Benny asks. Pierre informs him that he's in the wrong place for good eating. "Say, waiter," Benny suddenly inquires, "didn't you used to be a Pullman porter?" "Yas-suh, will you ever forget Albuquerque?" The connection made, the waiter joins in a skit involving the commercial, a singing homage to Jell-O. Declares Pierre the waiter: "Make mine watermelon."[20]

Accepting Anderson's growing popularity, the writers expanded his role. In a show several weeks later he was cast as "a Colored Fellow." Again, the main interchange was between him and Benny. On this occasion the issue was a found watch, and it led to a favorite topic of the show, a "financial skirmish" between the two principals. Remarkably, it was the "Colored Fellow" who came out ahead in the bartering. Like others before him, all of whom had been white, Anderson was permitted to better Benny.

On the very next show, Anderson was a fully integrated performer in the proceedings. He had become Benny's butler, eventually his chauffeur as well, and he had been given an identifiable name. Eddie Anderson had become "Rochester." Years later, when queried about its origins, both Benny and Anderson agreed that it had been Benny's idea. "When I'd get mad and shout 'Rochester!' it had a really good ring to it."[21]

In contrast to other members of the show, who were regularly announced by their full names, Anderson was known simply as "Rochester," and by members of the show simply as "Roch." A year after he joined the staff, in fact, the name replaced "Eddie" in the scripts. It became one of the most widely recognized names in the popular culture. Eventually he received a family name in an off-hand manner several years later when Benny, in a pique, shouted "Rochester Van Jones!" Every now and then Benny would refer to him this way. But this was not meant to expand his identity or dignify him.

Regardless, Anderson's place as a regular member of the Benny family was unique for a black performer. For Anderson, his popularity propelled him into limited parts in films, though mainly allblack, and in television, again as Benny's manservant. He had entered show business at the age of fourteen in an all-black revue and later went on the vaudeville circuit with his brother. In 1925, he moved up in billing when he appeared as a song-and-dance man at the World Theater in Omaha and followed the vaudeville troupe to Los Angeles, where he worked in local clubs.

By the time Anderson had become a full member of the show— his gradually expanding role eventually led to star billing in the early 1940s—the program had become a national habit. Its prime attraction was Jack Benny, who, like many radio comedians, had developed his talents in vaudeville. Benny had entered radio in its formative years, billed as "The Canada Dry Humorist." The accent on "dry," though attached to soda pop, was insightful, for his humor was indeed very droll. At the same time, it was a contradiction, because neither Benny nor his humor was very bubbly. Not a comical person, he possessed rather a fine sense of comic timing, an inert body, and a slow voice that could freeze a funny moment and capture a whimsical theme over time. His persona was plugged into certain compelling American values, at once endearing and repelling. He was, to put it succinctly, Everybody's Miser: a family relation, a close friend or neighbor, a distant businessman or banker. Unlike Dickens's Scrooge, however, Benny was neither bitter nor recriminating. He could be petty, cowardly, scheming—even egotistical and mildly tyrannical—but never was he overwhelmingly disdainful. He would attempt to be many things—a virtuoso violin player, a leading film star, a graceful athlete—but more often than not he wound up being ineffectual. He appeared aloof, but the gentleness and warmth would eventually prevail. He could posture and puff up, yet his self-deprecating side would win out. Benny sensed these various contradictions and communicated them to the audience.

His approach to comedy altered the course of radio shows. Benny's programming "de-emphasized timeworn vaudeville routines by reducing the number of puns, he-she jokes and 'feed lines' by the stooge." The humor emanated from contrived situations rather than haphazard wildness and involved an extended family, called the "gang," rather than a single person.[22]

But the core of the show, the *idea* around which the action flowed, was Benny himself. Anyone could best him, and did, including Eddie "Rochester" Anderson. Over time, it was Rochester who got the better of him in *personal* situations more than anyone else. This relationship with Rochester became extraordinary in its depth and sensitivity. The pair became, in fact, the oddest racial couple in American culture. They shared intimacies and domestic arrangements on radio and television that went far beyond the typical employer-employee association. In developing a symbiotic relationship, they reflected subtle changes occurring in American society that would ultimately alter the stereotype of the black male.

All this, of course was not evident at the beginning of their relationship. In the initial stage, Rochester's place in the program's comic structure was largely tied to the essentials of the stereotype. Not unexpectedly, Benny had engaged in such humor in previous shows. A take off on *Uncle Tom's Cabin* was the main theme of a 1932 "New Orleans" show, done in dialect; there were the usual egregious grammatical errors, circumstantial foolishness, and an occasional play on the black penchant for "cutting." Exclaims a janitor after being asked who will assist him in removing Benny from the scene: "Me and dis razor . . . Ah've been totin' dis *razor* fo' five years . . . an' everybody knows I ain't no barber."[23]

Ten years later, during Rochester's reign, the half hour was devoted to an orchestrated minstrel show. The entire cast performed in dialect, with Benny serving as the interlocutor, and Rochester sang "Somebody Else—Not Me," which contained the lines "two iv'ry bones with eb'ny dots: which 'oft leads to cemetry lots." In an aside during the performance, Benny quizzically points to an item on Rochester's expense account. It was for burnt cork. Rochester explains that, although he didn't need it, he spent the money anyway—for a "cork with a bottle of gin round it."[24]

There were many such asides about Rochester's habitual imbibing. "Did you ever use any of the Sympletely Soothing Syryp," Benny asks him in a spoof on commercials. "Boss," offers Rochester, "if it's in a bottle, I've tried it!!" Don Wilson, the show's announcer, gives him a Christmas gift. "M-mm," says Rochester, "it looks like a bottle." "Yes, Rochester, it's hair tonic." "Oh," exclaims a disappointed Rochester, " . . . *Well,* a little White Rock will fix that!" An avidity for gin, though, is his drinking weakness. Giving instructions over the phone for a party for the gang, Benny tells him to prepare a nice bowl of punch. Rochester informs him that there "ain't nothin' to put in."

> JACK: Wait a minute. What became of that quart of gin I bought last week?
>
> ROCHESTER: What's that?
>
> JACK: That quart of gin, where is it?
>
> ROCHESTER: What? . . . I think we got a bad connection.
>
> JACK: Rochester, what became of that quart of gin I bought last week?

ROCHESTER: Now you're talkin' too loud.

JACK: Rochester, for the last time . . . what became of that bottle of gin?

ROCHESTER: I had a headache.[25]

Another of Rochester's frailties was gambling, which consumed much of his leisure time. He was often engaged in shooting dice, which he artfully described as "African Badminton," "Ebony Roulette," "Ivory Gin Rummy," and "African Handball." On one occasion he succinctly declares: "The only game I play only involves three moves . . . get down on your knees, shake gently, and wish 'em a Happy Landing." Ordinary or unusual questions frequently elicited a drinking or gambling retort. "Do you know any famous sayings?" Benny asked him one night. "I know one," Rochester answered affirmatively. "What is it?" "Don't shoot till you're faded!" Even in his sleep Rochester would dream of the game. "Let me see them dice!" he shouted in a sequence overheard by Benny. Often, "up in Harlem" or "on Central Avenue" (the main street in the black section of Los Angeles) Rochester would phone Benny. "Up here at Lenox Avenue" in Harlem one day, he told Benny he was a member of the "If at first you don't succeed, roll again" club.[26]

These vices naturally dovetailed with another shortcoming: Rochester had a shady side. He stole, fabricated tales, and regularly cheated. Not big things, to be sure, but a constant reinforcing of the notion that he cut corners, that he was a trifle amoral. The items purloined were, for instance, chicken wings from a Benny dinner or a watch or suit of Benny's to be used for gambling. Presumably married, he nevertheless had a bevy of girlfriends. "Did you ever hear of Fidelity," Benny says in one scene, explaining, "I mean you should be true to one girl." Rochester is astounded by Benny's innocence: "Oh, Boss . . . Re-consider!" He tried to sneak his woman, sometimes called Josephine, in or out of the house, or to a location as close as possible. On the phone one day with Benny, he disarmingly inquires as to whether Miss Livingston— Benny's girlfriend, played by his actual wife—needs a new maid, or something. "A new maid? . . . No, not that I know of," replies Benny. "Okay, so long," says Rochester, thinking he has hung up the receiver, "I'll think of something, Honey." In a parallel reference to the "Big Three" leaders of World War II meeting to discuss postwar issues, Rochester had his own Big Three: "She, me, and her husband!"[27]

Reflecting the scope of Sambo, Rochester's shortcomings were reflective of its basic elements. As clever as he might be, Rochester operated within intellectual restrictions. There were constant references, at times outright declarations, of his inability to read. His inital role as a porter who could not read or understand the word "Albuquerque" had established this fact. It was reinforced throughout the radio years. "Say, Boss," he asks as he chauffeurs Benny on a trip to Yosemite, "are you sure this is the right road to the hotel?" "I think so, Rochester . . . We just passed a sign back there, what did it say?" Attempting to squirm out of an answer, Rochester replies, "It was printed, Boss, I'm a *longhand* man." More direct was the answer he gave Benny in an exchange over Benny's illness. Despite receiving medication all week, Benny still feels sick. Rochester suggests that it might be the medication itself and offers that Benny "ain't never gonna have any dandruff in your stomach." Benny feigns upset. "Good heavens, Rochester, did you give me that hair tonic? . . . I told you a thousand times to read the labels." As adamantly as possible, Rochester explains, "I told you a thousand times I can't read." Benny relates that he should get glasses. "That ain't gonna help any" is Rochester's final statement.[28]

Superstition was the flip side of ignorance. Rochester had an abiding fear of danger and ghosts—even electricity. Many skits followed the format devised in films presenting blacks as cowards. A two-part 1938 series revolved around the formation of a submarine crew. "There might be a lot of danger ahead," declares the undaunted commander, Benny, "so keep on your toes. One little slip on the part of anyone of you, might mean death to all of us." Immediately Rochester responds, "Hey, Chief . . . Make way for a deserter!" Later, as the imaginary destroyer attacks the submarine, Rochester conjures up safety through his rabbit's foot. Unseen dangers also plagued him. Decorating the Christmas tree, an annual rite, Benny asks him to fix the tree lights. "Fix 'em?" says the concerned Rochester. "I ain't foolin' around with electricity." Benny wants to know what he's afraid of. "I don't wanna get hit by nuthin' I can't hit back!" Similarly, ghost scenes incite panic. In one typical farce, the gang is spooked by a phantom voice in a scary situation. Even Jack declares that he doesn't "feel so good either." But Rochester is more out of whack than any of the others. "Well, guess I'll be runnin' along now." Jack tells him to stay put. So does the Ghost: "Yeah, stick around." "Don't count on it," retorts Rochester. "What are you scared of, White Boy?" askes the Ghost. Just as anxious as ever, Rochester corrects him: "I ain't no white boy." "Wait until you look in the mirror," exults the Ghost.[29]

Rochester's eating habits were not less stereotypical. The symbolic garden served as his showplace. When a group of chickens attack Benny's backyard, Rochester is called to chase them away. "Shoo! Shoo!" he admonishes the chickens, and then exclaims to himself, "Dawgonne, how I can have so much willpower when I'm droolin'." And there was always the watermelon. In the garden assisting Benny, he plaintively asks him to plant "these seeds instead" of the string beans and tomatoes. Benny demurs because he wants tomatoes. Rochester is insistent. "But these are mighty appetizin' when they reach maturity." Says a rather exasperated Benny, "We've planted enough watermelons . . . That's all you think of . . . watermelons. We've planted more *now* than we can eat." "Than *who* can eat," rebuts Rochester.[30]

At the core of these characteristics was Rochester's blackness. If there were any doubts in the radio audience regarding Rochester's identity, the various pointed and comic references to his features and hangouts dispelled them. In a two-program sequence involving a trip by Benny, Mary, and Rochester to Yosemite, for instance, Benny refers to his skin color on several occasions. Arriving at night, Benny inquires about his whereabouts. "Right beside you, Boss, it's dark," Rochester informs him. "Well," Benny suggests, "either open up your eyes or smile. . . ." Along the way they stop; Benny gets out of the car and instructs Rochester to remain there. Rochester, however, wants to walk around. "All right," says Benny, "but don't get lost in the snow." "Who, me?" replies Rochester. "Oh," Benny agrees, "that's right. . . ."[31]

Rochester's ancestry enabled him to spot an impostor in Indian dress on another of their trips. He knew that the man selling merchandise was not a Native American, he noted, because he was eating a pork chop sandwiched between two watermelon slices.[32] And he knew his way around those black hot spots, Harlem and Central Avenue, where he spent much of his leisure time. So much so that, early in his employ, Rochester suggested to Benny that he be appointed "Ambassador to Harlem," a symbolic title he held over the radio years. Raucous and swinging, guzzling and cutting, by and large sum up the ways in which Harlem and Central Avenue was portrayed. "I've been weekending up in Harlem," Rochester joyously informed Benny, "we had a Gin Barbecue. . . ." The Central Avenue drink was "Vita-Min" or just plain "Oomph." The sense of time, Benny and the audience further learned, was quite different in the black community. "Rochester," Benny inquired in the 1939 New Year's Eve broadcast, "I thought you were going out and celebrate." "No hurry, Boss . . . on Central Avenue, Father Time lingers till we get rollin'." Celebrating, however, was not limited to the last night of the year. Black joints *moved* all the time. "I suppose you know all the Hot Spots," Benny once said of the Harlem clubs. "There ain't no cool ones there" was the terse answer.[33]

Overall, then, Eddie Anderson's role appeared as merely another version in the long line of Sambos. Yet there were discernible differences between Rochester and previous figures. In a subtle, structured way, the stereotype was constantly being undermined through a form of inner spoofing. Even the most hardcore stereotyping was defused, rendered unbelievable, by some phrase of byplay that occurred in the middle or at the end of a skit. This defusing process was begun soon after Anderson became Benny's full-time butler and valet. And it became more sharply defined as the character's show time increased and his role expanded. While paying obeisance to the fashionable image, the Rochester figure never fully conformed to it and actually mocked it at the same time.

How was this verbal-imagic trick accomplished? Often, some derogatory trait would be offset by Rochester's playful and down-right ridiculing phrase "Oh, come now, Boss." At other times, an assumed feature was punctured by acknowledging its presence and again ridiculing it. For instance, when they are at home waiting for guests, the doorbell rings, and Benny calls out, "Hey, Rochester, see who's at the door." The request is simply stated. Rochester, however, responds sarcastically, "Yes suh, I'll shuffle right over." Shortly, the telephone rings, and Benny asks him to answer it. This time a different response: "That ain't in my contract." But Benny is, after all, the employer who cannot let his servant overstep his bounds. "Answer that phone!" he exclaims with some force. "YES, SUH," Rochester shoutingly complies. It is a picture of a servant who is not exactly very servile or dimwitted. As the action further unfolds, Benny enumerates the persons coming to the dinner table; there will be seven, including himself. Quickly Rochester asserts himself: "That's eight including me."[34]

From his early introduction, Rochester's character is infused with this mocking quality. In one of their many disputes over contractual arrangements—this episode occurring three years into their relationship—Rochester demands a written document. Benny explains in his skinflint manner that they have a verbal agreement. "A-huh," says Rochester. "That means," continues Benny, "we have a mutual understanding . . . Why put it on paper? The amount of money involved is too small." Rochester persists, telling Benny to "get it up" and informing him that his attorneys advise "where-as and to-wit." Benny is surprised that Rochester has an attorney. The implication revolves around the strangeness of black men hiring lawyers. Benny inquires as to their names. They are, Rochester sarcastically informs him, "Sambo, Tambo, Sugarfoot and Smythe." In this sequence, another aspect of the stereotype was undercut. In a reassuring tone, Benny relates that Rochester need not have financial worries. "I'm going to give you a substantial raise next year." "Substantial?" asks a curious Rochester. "Yes . . . ," answers Benny in a condescending way, "you know what that word means don't you?" Rochester is up to the challenge. "I ain't illiterate," he declares, "I'm skeptical."[35]

So, too, with the notion of black superstitious tendencies. In the previously stated episode involving Rochester's fear of electricity, for instance, the remainder of the dialogue actually restores his dignity while undermining Benny's. To the previous query as to his fear of electricity, Rochester asserts: "I don't wanna get hit by nuthin' I can't hit back." In his rejoinder Benny treats him like a child but then makes his own error. "Oh, Rochester, imagine being afraid of electricity . . . Suppose Robert Fulton was afraid . . . He never would have invented the electric light . . . would he?" Mary corrects Benny, who feigns ignorance of Edison and asks what Fulton accomplished. Rochester answers with the patriotic phrase "Don't give up the ship." He is informed by Benny that John Paul Jones made that statement. It was, then, a zany scene in which both white man and black man played at the game of ignorance. Yet it was not over. Fixing the lights, which Benny had initially ordered, Rochester mumbles to himself the scientific underpinning of the electricity in a version of a Groucho Marx routine: "Let me see now . . . There's the electrons and the electrodes . . . then there's the *positive* and the *negative* . . . but I ain't *positive* which one is *negative*." "Hmm," responds Benny in his characteristic manner. "Then there's the atoms . . . Now the atoms are supposed to go from the positive to the negative . . . or . . . maybe they go from the electrons to the electrodes . . . Then again, maybe they go from *Natchez* to *Mobile!*" "Rochester!" "Now as long as these atoms keep passin' each other everything is all right . . . but when they meet halfway and start fightin' . . . they're gonna turn on anybody who tries to butt in!" On and on goes the byplay between the pair in a seemingly endless routine of joint fears and foolishness.[36]

Even more significantly, many of the Samboisms associated with Rochester's character were gradually downplayed, and some were entirely eliminated. Gradually, yet inexorably, Rochester's identity was heightened, steered toward a more affirmative stance. Several years into the role, the show's writers took a swipe at blackface practices. Chauffeuring the famous Maxwell car—a wheezing automobile that had seen much better days and lacked a radio— Rochester sings a love song for his boss and Mary: "Careless. Now that you've got me loving you careless, careless in everything you do, are you just careless, as you seem to be, or do you just care less for me . . . I said for *ME!*" Benny compliments him and requests yet another song, a number entitled "Scatterbrain." "Now wait a minute, Boss—" Rochester protests. "Rochester, I said sing 'Scatterbrain.'" At this point Mary joins in, saying that Rochester should be permitted to rest after an hour of singing and relaying his complaint that "at eight o'clock he wants me to imitate Amos and Andy." "Well—," says Benny. "*I* can't do that blackface stuff," declares Rochester. "You can try, that's all I ask . . . You don't hafta be perfect," tried Benny in a halfhearted attempt. And that's where the scene comes to abrupt halt.[37]

This was not the first swipe at blackfacing, either. Intriguingly, it was Benny who took a shot at the practice in a short exchange with Rochester. Explaining over the phone that Benny's manager has called for his presence at an opening of a "Drive-In Stand" and requested that he be there in full dress, Rochester adds that Benny should also "put on some *cork*" since he is "workin' *with* him." "*Oh no you're not and goodbye!*" says Benny abruptly. To himself after the call ends, Benny declares, "Hmm, none of that Sambo-and-Tambo stuff for me. . . . "[38]

Moreover, the ignorant servant eventually was replaced by the informative and therefore helpful assistant. A decade after his introduction as the Pullman porter who couldn't comprehend the name Albuquerque, fathom directions on medical bottles, and read street signs, Rochester displays a command of the language. When asked by Benny to spell the words "superfluous" and "discrepancies," he does so with ease. Largely gone, also, were ghosts and spooks and the urgent need to remove himself from seen and hidden dangers.

Yet it was not only the mocking aspect of the character that signaled the change in the image. Much more expressive was Rochester's aggressive behavior, his willingness to confront Benny, to criticize and even, under certain circumstances, ridicule him. The term "sassy" has been used to describe this behavior, and in some respects it has validity. Anderson's servant jived Benny and took liberties not previously accorded a black man in public. At the same time, the response went beyond sassiness. There were certain boundaries beyond which things could not be said or implied. But Anderson possessed a latitude within which he could express his own desires and dislikes. Moreover, since humor is one of the prime tools in human weaponry, it was remarkable that a black man—even more remarkable in this case, in that the black man was also a servant—could openly taunt and satirize a white man. It was the first such media encounter, and it paved the way for the comedic confrontations of Dick Gregory and Godfrey Cambridge in the early 1960s.

At its most acceptable level, Rochester joined with the other members of the gang in twitting Benny's miserly habits. There were numerous scenes involving Rochester's supposedly meager pay—Rochester's low salary produced many protest letters from listeners—and his unsuccessful attempts to secure a written contract. Rochester also took many swipes at Benny's lifestyle. Told to wear a chauffeur's uniform, Rochester countered, "You mean these gloves?" On another occasion, singing a blues song while driving Benny around, he is ordered to cease his warbling. "I'll [have] to put a radio in this car," Benny exclaimed. "A radio in this car," Rochester retorted, "would stand out like a bathroom in a log cabin."[34] Benny's attitude toward money, however, was on-limits to everyone, including the gang and guests. Rochester's comic license extended to all mundane matters, and to intimate ones as well. For one thing, Rochester could countermand almost any order. On many occasions, for example, when told to be ready for a trip to go hunting or to visit another city at 4:00 or 5:00 A.M. he would blithely state: "If you want me to go, you better make that *seven.*" In a scene with Benny atop a ladder trimming the

Christmas tree, the doorbell rings. "There's the door, Mister Benny, you want me to answer it?" asks Rochester rather innocently. "Look, Rochester," replies Benny sarcastically, "I'm up here on the ladder, my arms are full of ornaments, so what do you think?" Undaunted, Rochester suggests another possibility: "Well, how long before you'll be down?"[40]

More to the point, Rochester was able to needle Benny personally, to zap into the inner workings of his employer. Trying to spruce him up for a special occasion, Rochester trots out his sport shoes to go with a full-dress suit. "Where did you ever see sport shoes with a full dress suit?" Benny inquires. "In the Harlem Esquire." "Well, run over to my dressing room and get my plain *black* ones, and hurry." "Black coat, black shoes, black pants . . . ," assesses Rochester, "you is the most *monotonous* man I ever worked for." Accused of having pawned Benny's wristwatch—which in fact he has—Rochester declares: "You're the third-degreeinest man I ever worked for." He deflated Benny's ego. Doing a scene based on the movie *Golden Boy*, with Barbara Stanwyck, Benny is chided for his performance. "Now wait a minute, Barbara . . . I put a lot into that speech. I felt the part and was very emotional," protests Benny. Chimes in Rochester, "I wasn't carried away."[41]

It should be immediately noted that this bantering was kept within recognizable class boundaries. Few of these jibes went unanswered. After most such episodes, Rochester was made to know his place. In the *Golden Boy* skit, as in many other situations, Rochester is subsequently told to "keep out of this. And get the tea."

Still, that a black man could razz a white man, subject him to barbs, and counter his orders in a public display of aggression was extraordinary. It offered a picture of a black man who hustled but with dignity, was indolent but with resourcefulness, was imbued with shiftiness but with openness, and, over time, was servile but with growing stature. He was still the entertainer, yet there was none of the buffoonery and ineptness. And there was a humor filled with retaliatory wit.

Had the character remained at this level of development, it would have constituted exactly what it represented, a marked change and the beginning of a new type of black entertainer on the white circuit. Something more fundamental occurred, however, a unique interaction for which there was some literary precedent, yet which also represented a metaphorical expression of centuries of racial wrenching. It was the fusing of Benny and Anderson as the oddest couple in the popular culture. In every generation, as Leslie Fiedler wrote intriguingly on the complex relationship between Huck Finn and Nigger Jim, Americans *"play out"* the impossible mythos:

> and we live to see our children play it: the white boy and the black we can discover wrestling affectionately on any American sidewalk, along which they will walk in adulthood, eyes averted from each other, unwilling to touch even by accident. The dream recedes; the immaculate passion and the astonishing reconciliation become a memory, and less, a regret, at last the unrecognized motifs of a child's book. "It's too good to be true, Honey," Jim says to Huck. "It's too good to be true."[42]

The Benny-Rochester motif played out this "impossible mythos" for over two decades in the national media. And in the dream, they touch.

This process of coupling began shortly after Rochester was integrated into the show as Benny's valet-chauffeur. And it opened in a symbolic manner: a new house in Beverly Hills into which the pair move together. Entering the house on the first day, Benny is startled to find his servant sleeping in *his* bed, and he informs his servant to move into his own quarters, over the garage. Rochester counters with a territorial presence statement, but he is emphatically ordered to "Get to your own quarters!" At first, there is an awkwardness in working together, a temporary shyness that is reflected in a special type of comic episode. About to appear in a new film with Joan Bennett, a particularly attractive woman, Benny feels the need to rehearse the romantic scenes. In this setting, as in the others that would follow over the years, Rochester takes the female role. The difficulty is reflected in the interplay between them:

JACK: . . . I can't be romantic working opposite Rochester.

EDDIE: You cramp my style, too.

JACK: All right, let's call it a draw.[43]

Gradually, as their strangeness gave way to an ease of familiarity, they shattered the "impossible mythos." As their relationship deepened, so did their physical interaction. In a similar scene three years later, the pair rehearse for another movie, in which Benny has to propose to his leading lady. The action unfolds in the studio dressing room. The words and interchange are affectionate and playful. "Oh, Connie," says Benny to Rochester, who has taken the part of Ann Sheridan, "you've made the happiest . . . " Suddenly the door opens and in walks Mary. "Hello, Jack, what's Rochester doing on your lap?" "Huh?" Benny answers, as if unaware of the situation. "It's quite all right, Miss Livingston," Rochester assures her, "he just asked me to marry him." The action doesn't end there, of course, for that would be too confusing, a bit too close to the cutting edge. "All right, Rochester," says Benny as the roles are clarified again, "I think I know the scene . . . You can start getting my clothes ready." Rochester, though, remains playful: [Sweetly] "Yes, Bill." "I'm *Boss* now . . . ," Benny reminds him.[44]

Between those scenes, a pattern emerged that typified the employer-servant relationship. As a servant, Rochester performs the usual chores: he prepares dinner, shops for groceries, does the chauffeuring, keeps to-be-done lists, inventories household requirements, borrows supplies from next-door neighbor Ronald Colman, cleans and sweeps and dusts and polishes and generally maintains the house. As the employer, Benny usually directs and orders the situation and always has the final word. But their relationship went beyond those class bounds and strayed into another dimension. They became entwined, as odd male couples do, as surrogate spouses.

Underneath the bantering—in fact, the bantering crucially reflected the actual relationship—were white and black men symbolically acting out the marriage in which the races had been inextricably connected for centuries. That marriage had gone sour for whites after slavery was abolished. In coming together now, after a century of segregation, the odd couple represented a reunion, a reconciliation based on powerful differences that could be partially surmounted.

This could have been accomplished only with a comic structure, because whites continually refused to recognize—indeed, fled from—the notion of black aggression. Yet once in a while the Benny program did permit physical interaction. Benny and Rochester sparred with boxing gloves on several occasions, with Rochester fooling Benny with the shoelace gambit and knocking him along with his bridgework to the floor.[45]

In this surrogate arrangement with Rochester as the dutiful spouse, his domestic activities expanded. He brought Benny breakfast in bed, read to him at bedtime, bathed him, secretly perused his attic-stored love letters, gently watched him snore at night, tricked him into taking his medicine, nursed him over the trauma of being robbed, carried him over the threshold upon his return from a London trip, and overall expressed sensitivity to his whims and idiosyncrasies.

It was not only these actions that reflected Rochester's "other half" status, it was his disposition—the tone of his approach to Benny. Sassiness remained throughout the years:

> ROCHESTER: I'd never leave you, Boss . . . I'd work for you for *nuthin'*.
> JACK: That's mighty sweet of you, Rochester.
> ROCHESTER: I'm working for *next* to nuthin' now.

but now there was an overriding tenderheartedness:

> ROCH: Oh, Mr. Benny . . . Mr. Be—[*Softly*] Look at him curled up in the chair fast asleep . . . I won't wake him . . . I'll just pick him up, carry him upstairs and put him to bed . . . [*Grunts*] . . .
> JACK: [*Snores*]

[*Sound: Slow footsteps . . . then up stairs*]

ROCH: [*Softly*] Just look at him . . . not a care in the world . . .

JACK: [*Snores*]

ROCH: Look at the way he snuggles in my arms like a little child . . .

> [*Sings softly*]
> He must've been a beautiful baby . . .
> He must've been a beautiful child . . .
> When he was only startin'
> To go to kindergarten
> I'll bet he drive those Indians wild . . .
> And when it came to winning blue ribbons
> He must've shown the other kids how
> [*Music sneaks in*]
> I can see his big blue eyes
> When they handed him the prize
> I'll bet he made the cutest bow.[46]
> [*Applause*]

He coos to his mate: My, my . . . Mr. Benny is still asleep . . . I better wake him up easy . . . I'll tickle his feet . . . hitchy kitchy kitchy koo!

[*Snores*]

Hmm . . . He doesn't feel it at all. Maybe I oughta take off his sox . . . Hee hee hee . . . The minute the nights get chilly, he doesn't take any chances . . . sox, corduroy pajamas, ear muffs, and a derby . . . [47]

and exudes affection: "Hee hee hee . . . *Love* that man!"[48]—but always teases, as when he washes Benny's back:

> "You and me, we Sweat and Strain,
> Working all day and rocked with pain
> Tote that Brush, Lift that Soap
> Sometimes I wish I was *with* Bob Hope."[49]

As in most relationships, a process of role reversal is built in, in which power is momentarily shifted, giving the semblance of sharing and goodheartedness by the partner holding the superior position. At various times over the years, Benny would relinquish his status and supplant Rochester as the servant. These usually occurred on special occasions, as, for example, on Rochester's birthday or after Benny had lost to Rochester in a card game. "And now let's go out to Jack Benny's house in Beverly Hills," announcer Don Wilson intones at the beginning of a program, as he has for the years. Suddenly he expresses surprise: "Where we find (Hm, there must be something wrong here . . . No, that's what it says) . . . Where we find Jack down on his knees scrubbing the kitchen floor."

[*Sound: Scrubbing with brush . . . brush in water . . . more scrubbing*]

JACK: [*Grunts*] Hm . . . I didn't know a floor could get this dirty . . .

[*Sound: Scrubbing*]

JACK: [*Sighs*] Well, anyway, the floor's scrubbed . . . What a job . . . Now let's see . . . what else is on that list of things I have to do.

[*Sound: Paper rattling*]

JACK: Oh, yes . . . I've already dusted the bedrooms, turned the mattresses, changed the linen on the beds, did the dishes, washed the—

[*Sound: Phone rings . . . receiver up*]

JACK: Hello.

ROCH: Hello, Mr. Benny, this is Rochester. I just finished eighteen holes of golf.

JACK: Oh, you did, eh?

ROCH: Yeah . . . Did you wash the living room windows?

JACK: Yes, yes.

ROCH: Did you put out the garbage?

JACK: It's out, it's out.

ROCH: Did you scrub the kitchen floor?

JACK: I just did that.

ROCH: Good . . . When will dinner be ready?

JACK: SEVEN O'CLOCK AND IT'S THE LAST TIME I'LL PLAY GIN RUMMY WITH YOU . . . [50]

Reversals were not always connected to unusual circumstances; those that occurred in more mundane situations are perhaps even more revealing. On a train trip, the two men race to the sleeping quarters. Rochester manages to beat Benny to the lower berth, forcing Benny to call a porter for a ladder.

This occasional rearrangement of positions, while offering the appearance of equality, never strayed far from accepted status roles. Note that they happened infrequently, and, as in the instance of the gin rummy bit, Rochester addressed his live-in mate as "Mr. Benny." Nevertheless, after a decade of being together, the pair had achieved a remarkable media breakthrough. They had become a racially liberated, aging male couple who also managed to avoid the stigma of gayness.

That it worked within an environment of odd-couple purity could be seen from yet another kind of reversal. This centered on Benny's borderline jealousy of Rochester's activities. Paralleling his servant's actions of reading his love letters, Benny surreptitiously peeks into Rochester's diary. Rummaging through his library in search of something to read, Benny comes across *My Diary* by Rochester Van Jones. For a split second, Benny debates opening the book, but he gives in, of course. "I think I'll take a look and see if . . . No, I better not . . . Oh, I'll just read it a little bit . . . it can't hurt."

Rochester's diary opens with "the little secrets that dwell in my heart," which Benny thinks "cute." To the sounds of rustling pages, Benny reads of a meeting of "the Central Avenue 'Roll out the Barrel and Dice Club,'" a dream of a woman who caresses and kisses him, and about Benny himself. It's in the form of a tender insult: "Mr. Benny is one of the kindest, most considerate, most generous bosses I ever had . . . and he never gets mad when I ask him for a raise . . . I know this because I've asked him *thousands* of times. . . ."[51]

The play on Benny's miserliness was typical fare; audiences expected it. As the audience anticipates, Benny is caught in the act and tries to hide his indiscretion. Rochester refuses to let him off the hook, and the scene concludes with the pair bantering tenderly. In a mock argument, they accentuate each other's foibles and sore spots. All indiscretions, all insults are thereby forgiven.

In humor, they had forged an intimate coupling. By the time

they had reached into television in the 1950s, Benny and Anderson had become a media fixture. Their relationship had encompassed several generations of listeners and viewers who had experienced an extraordinary situation: a black man and a white man who shopped, played cards, partied, sang, and played, cavorted, and wrangled without rancor or subversive intent. Perhaps the ultimate compliment to their togetherness was the New Year's Eve they spent together. It is 1950. The scene opens with Rochester intending to spend the evening on Central Avenue (a continuing play to black rowdiness), but quickly turns on Benny's remaining home. Faithful, to be sure, Rochester insists on staying with his boss. "Say, we might have fun at that," Benny says, " . . . if you're willing to stay home with me on New Year's Eve, we're gonna do this thing right . . . We're gonna open a bottle of Champagne." It is Rochester who hastens to get the bottle, opens it, and fills the glasses, his servant role demanding it, and it is Rochester who offers the toast, "Happy New Year, Boss . . . and I hope we'll be together for many more." Benny affirms, "I hope so," and the two join in singing "Auld Lang Syne."[52]

Throughout, although both men remained fixed within prescribed social bounds, significant changes had occurred. The Benny-Anderson relationship played against the prevailing stereotypes of black and *also* white men. By the late 1930s and into the next decades, Anderson was not a Stepin Fetchit comedian but one with considerable dignity, perseverance, intelligence, and talent. Gone was the buffoon who displayed ineptness and dim-wittedness, whose humor derived from a natural childishness. He one-upped his white boss both psychically and physically.

It could be argued that all this was relatively easy for a Rochester to accomplish. Benny, after all, presented himself as the antithesis of the American male: totally unthreatening, undemanding, and practically everyone's foil. Both his radio and television personality actually possessed female qualities, apparently a reflection of the inner person. His friends, in fact, often teased him about some of these traits. Phil Harris, the wisecracking bandleader of the show, once asked everyone to watch Benny walk.

"You know," Harris declared, "you could put a dress on Jack and take him anywhere."[53] Benny presented himself as limited in virtually every aspect of life but two: he was a dogged miser and he could elicit a laugh.

To dismiss the changes because of Benny's characteristics, however, is to overlook the odd-couple relationship. By integrating themselves in the confines of a house, by locking themselves into permanent bachelorhood, and by forcing themselves to deal with each other's imagic shortcomings, they presented the most optimistic racial portrait possible in that time.

To a considerable extent, the pair's entwining was symbolic of the changes that were occurring on various cultural levels, shifts in attitudes and politics that would be mirrored in the civil rights movement of the 1950s and early '60s. It cannot be finally demonstrated that this media relationship actually eased the way for the changes that were to come. Nor can it be fully shown that the Jack Benny program influenced the coming of a later show, the *I Spy* series of the 1960s, in which Robert Culp and Bill Cosby played detectives who were an interracial odd couple.

Even without these various direct connections, however, the program set the stage for envisioning the black male in a different light. For Anderson as Rochester had loosened the grip of a hardcore Sambo in the media and gone far to pave the way for the figure's demise in the popular culture.

9

The Fool as an Emancipator

Don't ask f'r rights. Take thim. An' don't let anny won
give them to ye. A right that is handed to ye fer nawthin'
has sometin the mather with it. It's more thin likely
it's ony a wrong turned inside out.
> —Finley Peter Dunne's Mr. Dooley

This race has the greatest of the gifts of God: laughter.
It dances and sings; it is humble; it longs to learn;
it loves men; it loves women. It is frankly, baldly,
deliciously human in an artificial and hypocritical land. . . .
If you want to feel humor too exquisite and subtle for
translation, sit invisibly among a gang of Negro workers.
The white world has its gibes and cruel caricatures; it has
its loud guffaws; but to the black world alone belongs
the delicious chuckle.
> —W. E. B. Du Bois, *Dusk of Dawn*

When Godfrey Cambridge, his heavyset body topped by a big grin,
came onstage in the early 1960s, he frequently trotted up to the
microphone and, panting, told his audience: "I hope you noticed
how I rushed up here. No more shuffle after the Revolution. We
got to be agile."[1] Contained in that comic instant was the symbolic
act of Sambo's fall.

An interval of several decades had transpired between Rochester's raspy voice jiving and caressing his sidekick-employer
Benny and the emergence of nationally recognized black comics
like Godfrey Cambridge. A World War and a civil rights movement
had immeasureably altered the image of the black male in the mass

media. Barely five years before Cambridge's assault on nightclub stages, in fact, James Baldwin had already declared the death of Sambo. "Aunt Jemima and Uncle Tom are dead," he wrote in his prophetically acerbic *Notes of a Native Son* (1955), "their places taken by a group of amazingly well-adjusted young men and women, almost as dark, but ferociously literate . . . who are never laughed at. . . . "[2]

The change in the image had crept in slowly in the labyrinths of the culture. In all probability, as Richard Dalfiume has perceptively argued in his study of the impact of the Second World War on racial affairs, it was the hypocrisy and paradox contained in the war's meaning that forced serious alterations of attitudes. For Afro-Americans, the crisis of the 1940s highlighted the gap between the American creed and its practices. "The democratic ideology and rhetoric with which the war was fought stimulated a sense of hope and certainty in black Americans that the old race structure was destroyed forever." When that hope failed to materialize, "the ground was prepared for the civil rights revolution of the 1950's and 1960's; the seeds were indeed sown in the World War II years."[3]

Within the white world, certain changes had simultaneously occurred. Gripped by the most popular war in American history, whites were pushed to confront, if not all of their personal racist notions, at least the presentation of their racist images. Democratic ideals clashed with the racism of fascism and made whites squirm with embarrassment. Consequently, the nature of the global struggle forced the media to loosen their stereotypical grip on all minorities, and women, too. Ironically, the war against another racial minority didn't hurt either. To an extent, anxieties over the Asian enemy deflected racist ideas against blacks.

Concern about America's image during the war had a curious unsettling effect on the news and entertainment media. Uncertain about the type of black male to present, media managers often refused to show any blacks whatsoever, including those participating in the armed forces. Early in the war, the NAACP received reports from local branches indicating that black soldiers had been totally deleted from the newsreels. "Inevitably white people get the impression Negroes are doing little if anything to win the victory," protested an editorial in *The Crisis*.[4] Eventually these complaints would take effect on media policies, but they also produced a Catch-22 backlash as criticisms often reinforced the policy of invisibility.

Even startling changes remained hidden from public view. When two black actors, one portraying a soldier and the other a young doctor, appeared on the highly popular radio soaps *Our Gal Sunday* and *The Romance of Helen Trent*, the event was not even mentioned in the trade papers.[5]

Still highly visible, though, still prancing around the layers of the media and popular culture, were clips of Sambo. There were the usual blackface minstrels onstage and in films; the scared antics of Mantan Moreland as Charlie Chan's valet in films; the mumbling shuffles of Stepin Fetchit; the ungrammatical dialect routines of *Pick 'n' Pat;* the sale of knickknacks; and the mailing of thousands of postcards displaying comical Sambo scenes. Buffoonery could be found virtually everywhere: in a newsreel showing a frightened black soldier, an anecdote in a newspaper, or a children's storybook. Comedy abounded in the humor sections in the *Reader's Digest*, which consistently printed jokes about funny Negroes, in and out of uniform.

As the war progressed, though, protests against the stereotype from black organizations and civic groups grew sharper. Gradually, inexorably, Sambo began to recede. This was, after all, a *democratic* struggle, involving all minority groups in the country. Buffoonery was crossing over the line, at odds with the momentous character of the struggle itself. Consequently, the war undermined the jester's place; the coexistence of the seriousness of global struggle with the comic antics of black men was just too unbalanced, too anachronistic. Without much fanfare and with little awareness, Sambo was actually playing to his final audiences.

The immediate postwar years provided the first clues, the sense that the stereotype was on his way to the cultural dustbin. But unlike Humpty-Dumpty, who had a great fall, Sambo's descent was gradual and at times barely perceptible. As in the nursery rhyme, though, once the fall had begun and the cracks appeared in the shell, there could be no restoring the form.

What obscured the change was the appearance of additional Sambo figures on the popular-culture scene, such as in the name and logo of the Sambo restaurants. Begun in southern California in the postwar years, the pancake houses quickly expanded their franchises in the next decades. Standing atop the entrances of the family restaurants was a figure wrenched from the nineteenth century: a young boy, unmistakably black, with rounded white eyes, thick red lips, vaguely Indian garb, a comical statue who could hardly best anyone, let alone a bunch of tigers.

Appearing at the same time was *Song of the South* (1946), a Disney film based on the Uncle Remus stories. In flashing colors and charming cartoon figures, a storytelling old black man in white whiskers related the trials and escapes of Br'er Rabbit to a small white boy against the backdrop of an idyllic plantation system. *Parents Magazine* presented the picture with an award, as as did the Motion Picture Academy to the actor who was the voice of Uncle Remus.

The stereotype was challenged, however, by changes occurring within the entertainment industry. The film factories pared down the number of pictures showing black chauffeurs and servants running from spooks, moved away from the Stepin Fetchit productions, and issued a spate of racially and ethnically conscious stories. *Lost Boundaries, Pinky, Home of the Brave,* all produced in 1949, reached into the lives of blacks caught up in a racist society and dealt with the issues in a sensitive manner. The radio industry canceled the heavy-handed *Pick 'n' Pat* show and introduced *Beulah,* the female counterpart to Rochester, starring the powerful actresses Ethel Waters and Hattie McDaniel. Comic strips withdrew such figures as Asbestos and portly maids. Sambo was being toned down.

That the racial environment had become highly charged, that protests from the NAACP and other organizations were reaching into media culture, was evident from the response to a Jack Benny program one Sunday evening in February 1950. Unable to come up with a new script because of the illness of several of the show's writers, the producers substituted a broadcast from ten years earlier. Rochester's behavior on that occasion was typical fare for the time: he brazenly chased women and shot craps. Now, at mid-century, there was an immediate protest to the studio. Telephone calls lit up the switchboard, followed by letters urged on by the NAACP. "Jack Benny certainly laid an egg," the *Los Angeles Sentinel*, a black newspaper, sharply wrote in an editorial. Benny publicly apologized for the program.[6]

Sambo's growing unpopularity was further hastened by the emergence of an electronic medium that almost totally rearranged the entertainment industry. Like radio before it, television reflected the racial sensitivities of the period. Although the *Amos 'n' Andy* and *Jack Benny* shows were adjusted to a visual form—the former replaced Gosden and Correll with an all-black cast but maintained the same format, to the consternation of many blacks—there was a noticeable absence of Sambo figures or programs. In its early stages, television stayed with traditional programming, such as vaudeville-type and variety shows, but also experimented with newer forms. Interestingly, in its quest for audiences, it sought out not the comic black but rather the entertainer black. Well-known singers and groups, Nat King Cole and the Ink Spots among them, made regular appearances on such prime-time shows as Ed Sullivan's *Toast of the Town,* Sid Caesar's *Your Show of Shows,* and Fred Waring's musical General Electric program.

Even this change was not without its obstacles. Producers and network executives were highly skittish about allowing black men to perform in roles other than as singers or dancers. Deviation from this policy of compartmentalization brought protests from community vigilante groups, largely based in the South. In 1955 the Philco Playhouse offered *A Man Ten Feet Tall,* starring Sidney Poitier, a rising black dramatic actor who had been acclaimed for his role in the film *Blackboard Jungle* that year. It was the first starring role for a black actor in the new medium. Threats against the company and network for this perfidious act were extensive.

Newspaper editorials, petitions to the network, and declarations never to purchase the company's products kept blacks confined to limited appearances and roles.[7]

From the other side came protest and exasperation as well. For decades, the NAACP and other organizations had decried stereotyping throughout the media. In the 1950s they stepped up their campaign to bring changes in films and television programming. As evidenced by the films prior to the fifties, the movie industry had proved difficult to change. Television, on the other hand, was still in its formative development. Blacks petitioned the industry to include more black actors in dramatic roles, to produce programs about blacks, indeed, to have a black star host his own network show.

The results were dismal. When CBS responded to pressure in 1960 by issuing an edict that black actors be sought for roles in dramatic series, the response by producers and others often bordered on subterfuge. "How to handle the situation honestly without acceding to social pressure?" asked the executive producer of *Gunsmoke*. The program was among the most popular on prime-time television, and blacks had had an occasional part in the series. However, the producer argued that to include more blacks in order to satisfy contemporary social sensitivities would interfere with the program's historical authenticity. His own extensive research showed, he erroneously argued, that "the Negro was treated despicably during a time in history when the country was terribly bigoted. He was used mainly to sweep out saloons or clean latrines."[8]

Several networks met the black offer to produce a program with a name performer. ABC made a pilot called *Three's Company,* featuring Sammy Davis, Jr., and the Will Maston Trio. After eight months of rehearsals and an introductory showing, the project was canceled for lack of a sponsor. A second pilot starring another highly popular singer did make it onto the airways, but it was short-lived. NBC produced *The King Cole Show* for thirteen months in mid-decade before it was discontinued for lack of advertising underwriting.[9]

While the networks avoided using blacks in dramas and shied

away from starring the black entertainer, at the same time they also killed the black jester. In the mid-1950s the *Amos 'n' Andy Show,* still highly popular, was canceled in response to a chorus of protest from black organizations. Apart from reruns of older films, Sambo was nowhere to be found within the electronic media.

The forces that undermined and doomed the jester were faith and laughter. For to undermine a jester, it is first necessary to render him irrelevant, unseemly, and, even more important, blasphemous to the time in which he exists. Then, to destroy him, it is essential to replace him with a different persona, a character capable of deflecting and overturning the oppressive laughter by forcing it in the opposite direction.

The initial event was the electrifying emergence of the civil rights movement. "From the moment that Mrs. Rosa Parks, in that bus in Montgomery, Alabama, resisted the Omnipotent Administrator," wrote Eldridge Cleaver in *Soul on Ice,* "contact, however fleeting, had been made with the lost sovereignty—the Body had made contact with its Mind—and the shock of that contact sent an electric current throughout this nation, traversing the racial Maginot Line and striking fire in the hearts of whites."[10]

Throughout the 1950s and into the mid-1960s, the movement affected the media in ways that no direct attack on its policies could have. The thrust of the movement, the nonviolence from which it derived its tactics and its moral conviction, had more of an impact upon the idea of the jester than all of the black protest could have achieved. For the movement was bound up not only in faith but in humor as well.

"Humor," wrote Reinhold Niebuhr, "is, in fact, a prelude to faith; and laughter is the beginning of prayer. Laughter must be heard in the outer courts of religion; and the echoes of it should resound in the sanctuary; but there is no laughter in the holy of holies. There laughter is swallowed up in prayer and humor is fulfilled by faith." The juxtaposition between faith and humor, Niebuhr continued, emanates from the fact that both involve the

incongruities of existence. "Humor is concerned with the immediate incongruities of life and faith the ultimate ones."[11]

To an extent, the movement contradicted Niebuhr's observation of the connection between faith and humor. At its basic level,
the tone of the movement was essentially one of deep moral intensity and religious zeal. In the sermons from the pulpits, in the
exhortations made by civil rights leaders and workers, in the songs
and chants of the marchers, in the entreaties to the older generations, inner sustenance was derived from the justice of the cause.
The language of the movement was often couched in religious
terms and expressions. There was a joy of spirit, a oneness with
history, coupled with a sense of inner conviction. Exclaimed
Hosea Williams, an aide to Dr. Martin Luther King, Jr., "Negroes
in Alabama are redirecting the history of mankind. You can't
understand it—it's too magnificent—any more than the children
of Israel understood what was happening when they walked
through the Red Sea."[12]

In the inner courts of the movement were constantly heard the
resonant sounds of the faithful. Conceiving of themselves in accordance with the principles of the Judeo-Christian code of ethics,
leaders and followers, black and white, were often motivated by an
acute sense of Biblical mission. The rightness of the cause was per-
force the consequence of the gaping disparity between the ideal
of brother-sisterhood of God's people, the American creed of
egalitarianism, and the denial of Afro-Americans as beings of
social worth. The letter Dr. King wrote to white clergymen from a
Birmingham jail in 1963 sharply focused on the dichotomy
between historical rejection and existential affirmation: "If the
inexpressible cruelties of slavery could not stop us, the opposition
we now face will surely fail. We will win our freedom because the
sacred heritage of our nation and the eternal will of God are
embodied in our echoing demands."

With faith in the rightness of their actions, activists unhesitat-
ingly placed themselves in dangerous situations. Being jailed for
the cause was a mark of the calling. Wrote one black student to his
parents from jail, "Try to understand that what I am doing is right.

It isn't like going to jail for stealing or killing, but we are going to jail for the betterment of all Negroes."[13] Civil rights workers who had served time in jail received special distinction in the "jailbird hour." The Reverend Fred Shuttlesworth, of the Southern Christian Leadership Conference, called for two-minute expressions from those who had been incarcerated. "No one speaks but those who have been to jail, making it at once a privilege and an honor. The youth who takes to the floor makes no effort to conceal his pride and joy in the fight." Those who had not served time were put down with the retort "Don't bug me, man. You haven't served your time yet."[14]

The jailings were also intended to symbolize the contradictions between religious values and the political system. While those who demanded their constitutional and moral rights were beaten and jailed, their antagonists were legally untouchable. Soon after the sit-ins began in the early 1960s, King traveled to Durham, North Carolina, and addressed a group of students at a church. "Let us not fear going to jail," he counseled, "if the officials threaten us for standing up for our rights." The objective was national arousal. "Maybe it will take this willingness to stay in jail to arouse the dozing conscience of our nation."

At the preliminary meetings that led to the formation of the Student Nonviolent Coordinating Committee, the idea of jailings as a gesture of faith was particularly affirmed. One established committee was called "Jail vs. Bail." Its chairperson suggested that all students arrested remain in jail rather than be released on bail or pay fines. "This will show that arrest will not deter us."[15] In the summer of 1960, more than four thousand people were arrested for participating in sit-ins at restaurants, kneel-ins at white churches, wade-ins at beaches, stand-ins at movie theatres, and swim-ins at pools. Aaron Henry, president of the NAACP in Mississippi, expressed its Biblical connection: "We'll make these jails temples of freedom."[16]

The driving sense of mission was infused with sense of urgency. "The Negro knows he has a God to serve, a soul to save and a society to elevate," declared Shuttlesworth at a civil rights rally in Pasadena, California.[17] Symbolic of the accent on immediacy was a sign at SNCC headquarters that displayed outreaching arms with a single word, "NOW." It was an expression that presaged and laid the foundation for the thrust of political activists of the 1960s. "They are not thinking about pie in the sky, in the bye and bye, but a piece of that pie, now."[18] Civil rights demonstrators wore lapel buttons bearing the inscription "It's NOW Baby." At marches and the "ins" actions, there was often a rallying interplay between leaders and workers:

> What do you want:
> Freedom?
> When do you want it?
> NOW!
> How much of it do you want?
> All of it!

Before hundreds of thousands of marchers at the Washington Memorial in 1963, King spoke of "the fierce urgency of *now*." When he launched into his "I have a dream" sequence, blacks responded by exhorting, "Tell 'em, tell 'em." But as he moved on in his vision of a future America where the humanity of colors would finally prevail, there were those who could not bear the thought of some distant time. "Fuck that dream, Martin!" a man screamed. "Now, now, goddamit, NOW!"[19]

As the movement asserted itself, impatience became both an organizational force and a personal goal. *"Impatience,"* wrote Howard Zinn, "was the mood of the young sit-in demonstrators: impatience with the courts, with national and local governments, with negotiation and conciliation, with the traditional Negro organizations and the old Negro leadership, with the unbearably slow pace of desegregation in a century of accelerated change."[20]

Nowhere was this impatience more clearly demonstrated than in the spontaneous expressions that sprang from adversity. White reporters were noticeably moved by the participants' inner conviction. A *Time* writer was struck by a small black girl who walked out of a church after a community rally and marched straight toward a solid, menacing phalanx of southern police. Suddenly, she stopped, turned, and called to a slower friend, "Hurry up,

Lucile. If you stay behind, you won't get arrested with our group."[21] A younger generation of blacks, knowledgeable about past behavior but antagonistic to it, had decided to confront it and change it.

In the inner sanctuaries, then, were heard the sounds of the faithful secure in the belief that their time had come—for overturning not only racist laws and practices but the ideology upon which the system rested. The objective of the movement, not always understood by whites, was not merely the obliteration of Jim Crow practices but the overthrow of Sambo himself. The use of nonviolent tactics, the placing of bodies on the line, the acceptance of jailing, all were consciously conceived to demonstrate that blacks would no longer accept white definitions of black culture, black personality, black history; no longer would they permit the existence of the natural jester in the mass media. Fully aware of media concentration on the movement since its inception, blacks were sending a message, in fact, a very charged message that the life of the jester was simply and irrevocably over. A minister at the height of the movement wryly informed his congregation that they should finally and openly tell the white folks the truth. It was well known, he stated to parishioners' nods, that whites would prefer to have lies about the Negro perpetuated. "So," he playfully admonished them, "stop fooling white folks. When they ask you if you're participating in the movement, don't scratch your head, just tell them YES. Ye shall know the truth and the truth shall make you free."[22]

Truth was to be found in the laughter coming from within the holy of holies. Different types of laughter, from mocking to gallows entwined with prayer. In the struggle against a powerful majority in the South, humor was used as an antidote to the omnipresent tension that accompanied nonviolent demonstrations and to tweak and undermine whites and their racist institutions. Humor often made possible the unthinkable in situations for which few were prepared. Mary Hamilton, a freedom rider jailed in Jackson, Mississippi, in May 1961, was suddenly confronted with a vaginal examination by a person who was clearly not a doctor. "When I went in, and saw what was happening, I practically went out of my mind with anger; but rather than say anything I just made a joke of it. That was the only way I could handle the situation without blowing my top."[23]

Jiving humor was frequently an integral part in churches, at rallies, and at the "ins" activities. Vocal inflections and physical gestures—difficult to convey in print—buoyed workers, demeaned the opposition, and offered release from the unrelenting anxiety. Typical was an extemporaneous talk by James Forman, executive secretary of SNCC, at a charged meeting after a major confrontation in Selma, Alabama. The aim, to increase voter registration, was bitterly opposed by many southerners. The meeting was held in a church, and the day's emotions still churned in Forman. "We ought to be happy today," he told his clapping workers. "Jim Clark [sheriff] never saw that many niggers down there!" Snickers began to build in the audience. "Yeah, there was Jim Clark, rubbin' his head and his big fat belly; he was shuffling today like *we* used to!" The crowd roared with laughter.[24]

At times, laughter would suddenly erupt during confrontations—and with harsh consequences. "What y'all niggers marching for anyway," asked a cop of a group of teenagers on a church lawn during a meeting break. "Niggers? Niggers? Niggers? You don't see no niggers out here," one of the teenagers said. "If you mean us *Negroes,* then we are marching because we are aiming to taste a bit of that freedom you white people are enjoying."

> "'Freedom'?" one of the cops asked.
> "Y'all wouldn't know what to do with it," the other cop said.
> "Well, we are on the road to getting it. When we do, we'll show you all what we'll do with it," another teenager said.
> "That's telling him, man," someone shouted as others pitched in.
> "Yes, we gonna eat in your restaurant, drive your police cars, vote and everything else," they were saying.

Suddenly, "the air was filled with laughter from the teenagers on the church lawn. At that moment, the two cops jumped the little ditch between the street and the church lawn and began pulling a young man . . . toward the street by both arms. . . . They thought he was resisting them. One of the cops cracked him across the head with his billy stick, and the other one joined in."[25]

Expectedly, the focal point of the humor centered on the absurdity of racism. "I say we can protest an unjust situation on an intellectual level," wrote actor and playwright Ossie Davis. "We can show it is ridiculous and therefore laughable. . . . Now I can imagine no other institution more ridiculous on the face of the earth than the institution of segregation."[26]

Jim Crow practices were constantly subject to ridicule. Fifty Fisk University students, jailed for participating in the Nashville sit-ins in 1961, made their situation more bearable and the cause of their predicament more absurd by telling stories related to segregation at eating establishments. "Dig this," said one student. "There is this cartoon of a Negro student sitting alone at a lunch counter. The caption reads: 'The Customer is always white.'" Said another, "Hey man. I sat down in Kress and the white waitress told me, 'We don't serve Negroes here.' I told her that was good because I don't eat them." The story was identical to an exchange between a CORE official and a bartender in a confrontation in central Baltimore in the mid-1960s. A dozen CORE members attempted to integrate a street known as "The Block," an area of liquor and burlesque entertainment establishments. "May I have a beer, please?" one of the demonstrators requested. "We don't serve colored in here," rasped the bartender. "I didn't ask for a colored," replied the worker, "I just want a beer."[27]

A combination of biting satire and good-natured triumph was directed against the ideology of segregation. To the contentions made by antagonistic whites that man is unable to withstand sudden social stress, that civil rights could disrupt traditional racial patterns and social institutions were being desegregated too rapidly, blacks would reply, "How fast is slow, baby?" To the argument that gradualism would produce the desired results, King responded by sarcastically saying that segregation is "the adultery of an illicit intercourse between justice and immorality and it cannot be cured by the vaseline of gradualism."[28] To the statement that integration would undermine the purity of the white race, Jennifer Dawson, a SNCC worker in Alabama, commented,

"There has been integration for years. Half the children in my community are half white." James Baldwin sardonically quipped that "At the rate things are going here, all of Africa will be free before we can get a lousy cup of coffee."

Much of the humor originated within the currents of the movement. Situations were lampooned; authority figures were belittled. The ironic twisting of names as a means of retaliation could be traced back to slavery. Ralph Ellison wrote that the black community "is deadly in its ability to create nicknames and to spot all that is ludicrous in an unlikely name or that which is incongruous."[29] In Selma, where demonstrators were doused by heavy jets of water and attacked by police dogs directed by sheriff Jim Clark, he and law officials were styled "Jim and the Clark Boys." The Alabama Safety Director, Al Lingo, and his aides were dubbed "the Lingo Kid and His Deputies." Acts of barbarism were sarcastically excoriated. The city of Birmingham, scene of at least eighteen bombings in the late 1950s and early '60s, was renamed "Bombingham." CORE freedom riders who traveled throughout the deep South and were subjected to intimidation, beating, and jailing regarded the Greyhound Bus advertisement "Travel is *safer* by Greyhound" as a side joke.

Gallows humor filled the air during the planned marches. Poet Robert Penn Warren, curious about the uniform of the workers, which consisted of overalls or Levi's, was told that it made it "easier for them to drag you when dragging-time comes. You want to make it nice and easy for them."[30] Mississippi's reputation as one of the most dangerous places for civil rights activists prompted this story by James Farmer. Farmer, head of CORE, had led the freedom bus rides into the Deep South; the riders had been severely beaten and their buses set on fire in Montgomery. "Don't go into Mississippi," Farmer said many had warned him. "Go anyplace you like, go to the Union of South Africa, but stay out of Miss." Farmer recounted a tale by one minister who argued against the trip:

Once upon a time there was a Negro who had lived in Miss, lived for a long time running from county to county. Finally, he left

the state, and left it pretty fast, as Dick Gregory would put it, not
by Greyhound, but by bloodhound, and he went to Illinois to
live, in Chicago. And unable to find work there after several
weeks of walking the street unemployed, he sat down and asked
God what he should do. God said, "Go back to Mississippi." He
said, "Lord, you surely don't mean for me to go back to Mississippi. There is segregation there!" The Lord said, "Go back to
Mississippi." The man looked up and said, "Very well, Lord, if
you insist, I will go. But will you go with me?" The Lord said,
"As far as Cincinnati."[31]

Gallows humor often turned on Mississippi as the symbol of
black repression. Even during the liberating march on Washington
in 1963 it was the focus of a spontaneous remark by Dick Gregory.
Sitting on the steps of the Lincoln Memorial with writer John A.
Williams and publisher Bob Johnson, Gregory looked up at the
airplanes that were continuously circling overhead and exclaimed,
"How do I know that isn't the Mississippi Air National Guard up
there?"[32]

Laughter reverberated throughout the meetings and marches,
taking the edge off the anxieties by belittling and demeaning the
opposition. Irony often combined with ridicule. The Reverend
Ralph Abernathy, in introducing King before an extremely large
audience on a drizzly day in March 1965, when the movement was
winding down, exclaimed with a broad smile: "We come to Montgomery not with sticks, stones, or guns. We come to love the hell
out of Alabama." Anxiety was lessened and authority figures were
taunted by chants during the many demonstrations. One target
was George A. Wallace, then the Governor of Alabama, whose
opposition to black enrollment at the university brought in federal
marshals. To the first part of a chant, "Give me," the crowd
responded with a specific reference:

> Give me a   W
> Give me an   A
> Give me an   L
> And another   L

Give me an A
Give me a C
Give me an E
And what've we got?
NOTHING

The chanters then reversed the words:

Give me an N
Give me an O
Give me a T
And an H
Give me an I
Give me an N
Give me a G
And what do they spell?
WALLACE

The sit-in demonstrators in Knoxville, Tennessee, who succeeded in desegregating the restaurants in that city after a protracted struggle, used a nursery rhyme to register their facetious protest. At the sign-carrying stage of the action, a white picketer carried a placard that read: "This Little Pig Had Roast Beef." Directly behind him was a black demonstrator whose sign completed the rhyme: "This Little Pig Had None."[33]

As the movement's momentum built during the early 1960s, taunts directed at the police became more direct, more defiant. In the clash between law officers and demonstrators, young blacks assumed a mocking stance. "One way to conquer fear," wrote a reporter of the Mississippi situation in 1964, "seems to be an over-compensating, taunting, plucky bravado." As an example, the reporter described a scene involving a teenager who was about to join a picket line in Greenwood in which he was sure to be arrested. Approaching, he suddenly "clapped his hands and did a mocking bent-knee dance close to a policeman." Another policeman within viewing range bristled with anger: "That's one nigger boy I want to get in the jail house." Undaunted, the teenager turned his attention to the man and began teasing him with a song. A few minutes later, he was on the picket line and immediately arrested.[34]

The Reverend Wyatt Tee Walker, executive director of the Southern Christian Leadership Conference, observed the identical behavior in young blacks in Birmingham as they confronted firemen dosing them with heavy streams of water. Rather than run from the hoses, the demonstrators played with the water, sliding along the pavement, getting up and getting knocked down again. "This went on for a couple of hours. All in good humor. Not any vitriolic response. Which to me," concluded Walker, "was an example of changing spirit. Where Negroes once had been cowed in the presence of policemen—here they had complete disdain."[35]

Discomfiting whites produced an elated sense of triumph and a number of humorous stories to be used to boost morale. Civil rights workers recounted tales of whites who reacted to their tactics and presence with jitteriness and buffoonery: of waitresses who dropped plates and cups; of store managers who fidgeted nervously or sweated profusely, staining their shirts; of cashiers who were led off in tears. An oft-repeated incident occurred during the sit-ins led by Fisk University students in 1962. Two female students, who had led the action at a lunch counter, were in the ladies' room at the very moment when an older, white patron sought refuge from the scene in front of the store. Upon entering the door and encountering black women inside, the woman threw up her hands and tearfully burst out, "Oh, Nigras everywhere."[36]

The ultimate satire is that which reverses the roles of antagonist and perpetrator. Reduction to absurdity means not only the demolition of an opponent's arguments but also the placement of the opponent in the position of the victim. An example of this situation was a tale told at the height of the movement:

> A Negro woman entered a southern restaurant soon after it was desegregated and asked the white waitress, "Y'all got some fried chicken?" The waitress said that they were all out of fried chicken. The woman inquired, "Y'all got some black-eyed peas?" The waitress replied that they were all out of black-eyed peas.

Exasperated, the woman asked if she could have some chitlins.
Again the answer was negative. "My, my," the woman countered,
"y'all ain't ready for integration yet."[37]

A number of the tales were told in a tone of admonishment. To
the accusation that integration would lead to mongrelizing the
races:

> In the late 1950s, in the corridors of the U.S. Senate, a northern
> senator chanced to bump into a Dixiecrat senator and saw him
> wink at a colored girl. "Why," said the northerner, "I thought
> you didn't believe in integration."
>
> "I don't," replied the southerner. "You northerners never
> understand anything. I don't want to go to school with that
> girl—just to bed with her."
>
> Two Negroes in Charleston were walking along with nothing
> to do. One finally turned to the other and suggested that they
> visit a brothel in the white district. The other protested. "Let's
> not. They'll lynch us for sure." The friend calmed him down and
> persuaded him to go to the house.
>
> But he refused to enter and stayed outside. He waited and
> waited. Finally, unable to contain himself, he yelled up at the
> window, "Moe, Moe, are you all right?" Out of the window
> popped the head of his friend, who replied, "Of course I'm all
> right. They just don't want us to go to school with 'em, that's
> all."[38]

With blacks so vulnerable to white retaliation—many who
openly supported the movements either lost their jobs or were visited by terrorist groups late at night—some of the humor
employed contained a double-entendre. "Fooling whitey" was an
old technique that had been highly refined during and after slavery. Consider the subtle story that circulated during the Montgomery bus boycott, when whites wreaked their vengeance on
those who backed the action:

> A white family called in their colored maid and asked her if she
> supported the strike. "Oh, no, ma'am," said the maid. "I won't
> have anything to do with that affair. I plan to stay away from the
> buses as long as there's trouble."

In a similar way, a young black boy who walked before a Birmingham police station wearing a T-shirt with the initials SOB was suddenly confronted by a group of white policemen. The boy quickly explained that the letters actually stood for "Southerners of Birmingham." At times, though, the tales revealed a humor that deflected retaliation. Shortly after the Watts riot in 1965, a teenager walked into a cafeteria and requested a cup of coffee. When the white counterman asked for ten cents, the teenager replied, "Sorry, don't you know we're not paying for anything this week!"[39]

Quips similar in tone circulated during the drive for voting rights. Prior to the Voting Rights Act of 1965, humor reflected a certain cautious optimism about the possibility of change. "When the Negro gets the vote," went a catchphrase, "it's no longer going to be Miss Anne, it's going to be Hey Baby!" Another tale, however, suggested not optimism but frustration, a tale of the status quo:

> A Negro who went to register in his town was given an application form and the standard literacy test.
>
> "What is the first line of the thirty-second paragraph of the United States Constitution?" the registrar inquired. The applicant answered perfectly.
>
> "Name the eleventh President of the U.S. and his cabinet." The applicant again answered correctly.
>
> Unable to trip him up, the registrar asked, "Can you read and write?" The applicant nodded and was handed a Chinese newspaper. He wrote his name and then studied the paper.
>
> "Well, can you read it?" asked the registrar.
>
> "I can read the headline, but I can't make out the body of the text," replied the applicant.
>
> Incredulous, the registrar asked, "You can read that headline?"
>
> "Oh, yes," said the Negro, "I've got the meaning all right."
>
> "Well, what does it say?"
>
> "It says," concluded the applicant, "that this is one Negro in Mississippi who's not going to get to vote this year."[40]

Understandably, the laughter was tinged with bitter irony. Southern justice, southern patterns were assailed for their respective ways and legitimized violence. An acidic joke made the rounds at the height of the movement:

> A Negro civil rights worker active in a Southern town suddenly disappeared from the scene. When he failed to show up after a week, it was decided that he had been killed and a search was begun. Some days later they located his body at the bottom of a nearby river. They pulled him up and observed that he was tied and bound with chains and locks. "Look at that damned nigger," exclaimed the sheriff of the town. "He tried to swim across the river with all them chains he stole from the store."[41]

A tale that appeared in the waning days of the movement used specific political figures but was similarly harsh:

> President Lyndon Johnson was flying back to Washington when he looked and noticed a man water-skiing. He directed the pilot to descend and observed that the skier was black and was being pulled by several whites. Heartened that his efforts in the area of race relations were finally being realized, he ordered the plane to land in order to congratulate the men.
>
> As he beckoned to the sportsmen, he noted with astonishment that the skier was Dr. Martin Luther King, Jr., and the Caucasians were Governor Wallace of Alabama and sheriff "Bull" Connor. Shaking the hands of Wallace and Connor, Johnson declared, "Ah want y'all at the White House for a Texas cookout. You men are a shining example of brotherhood." He boarded his plane and returned to Washington.
>
> As soon as the plane took off, Wallace turned to the sheriff and said, "That stupid Johnson. He still don't know how we troll for alligators down here."[42]

Caustic and contemptuous, these were the angry feelings upon which the humor fed. Still, a note of triumph came to coexist with it and eventually would assume priority. From all areas, the air was filled with quips and barbs openly directed against whites, giving expression to Robert Frost's description of humor as "good-natured triumph." The asides encompassed the range of prejudice; some were apocryphal, while others were heard at conferences and meetings:

> A Negro to a friend: "I'm not prejudiced. I have a lot of white friends. When I see them I treat them just like people."

On amalgamating the races, the Reverend Ralph Abernathy in a speech in Washington: "We do not want to be the white man's brother-in-law. We want to be his brother."

On the economic boycott as a weapon, the Reverend James Cameron of Hattiesburg, Mississippi: "It's amazing how a man who hates you the night before will throw his arms around you the next morning if you withold the dollar from him. All dollars are integrated."

President Lyndon Johnson on the telephone with Dr. King: "But look here, Reverend King. It's been called the 'White' House for over a hundred years."

On the KKK practice of burning crosses on the front lawns of Negro homes: "A white couple moved into a Negro neighborhood. That night a watermelon was burned on their front lawn."

Question: "What happens to civil rights workers after they die?" Answer: "They disintegrate."[43]

Faith and humor entwined, then, to produce a decade of awareness of black resiliency in facing up to violence and black dignity in confronting legalized injustice. The black jester who had for so long played center stage was suddenly a bit player in the media. The antics of a buffoon, of comedic foolishness, were just too incongruent with the objectives and actions of the civil rights movement. That the day of Sambo's demise had finally come was signaled by King in a civil rights speech in Los Angeles in the summer of 1964: "I say goodnight to you by quoting the words of an old slave preacher who said: 'We ain't what we ought to be and we ain't what we want to be and we ain't what we're going to be. But thank God we ain't what we was.'"[44]

While the movement was the catalyst, the media emergence of black comedians spelled the end of the jester. In the early 1960s the end occurred as *the fool became an emancipator*.[45] The first one came in the form of a sly satirist, Dick Gregory, who was the first black stand-up comic to make his appearances before a white audience; the place, Chicago. His instantaneous popularity propelled him onto talk shows, where, suddenly, whites who had never before watched a black humorist listened as Gregory playfully excoriated them: "I sat-in for three years at this restaurant," he gently but mockingly declared in a line that was widely repeated, "until I found out they didn't have what I wanted."[46]

Gregory was quickly followed by other black humorists and comedians, some seasoned troupers who had performed only before black audiences, who made their way into white establishments, the coffeehouses, college campuses, nightclubs, television talk shows, and lecture circuits. Suddenly there was an outpouring of African-American humor never before heard by the majority of Americans. Whites found themselves on the firing line; they had become, in effect, the butt of the joke. "The American Negro's New Comedy Act" was the way Louis Lomax phrased it in a *Harper's* article in 1961.[47]

Within the short span of several years in the early sixties, black comedians capped what the civil rights movement had begun. Sambo ceased to have any large meaning in the media as blacks turned the tables and employed humor to criticize their centuries-old tormentors. Many of the jokes derived from the movement itself, but also dated back to the slave past, when humor was extensively used as a means of racial amelioration and retaliation. Not only was the humor heard over the airwaves, particularly television, but the remarks of the comedians were reported in the popular magazines, including *Time, Newsweek, TV Guide,* and Sunday *Parade,* as well as newspapers and literary magazines. Moreover, their routines were recorded on long-playing records sold in white outlets.

By the mid-1960s, "Moms" Mabley, Redd Foxx, Pigmeat Markham, Dusty Fletcher, George Kirby, and Timmy Rogers—skilled comics who had been restricted to the black theatre and clubs for virtually their entire careers—were being seen on television, and their quips and stories were reported in the popular press. Younger performers—Bill Cosby, Godfrey Cambridge, Flip Wilson, and Richard Pryor—also came quickly into prominence in the late 1960s and early '70s. Their presence in the print, electronic, and visual media altered racial perceptions by making whites more aware of African-American sensitivities and antagonisms. Whites read "My Favorite Jokes" in *Parade* magazine, which printed the materials of George Kirby, Dick Gregory, and Timmy Rogers.[48]

Open challenge, and biting as well as chiding admonishment, confronted whites from the humor pulpits in the mid-1960s, buttressed by jibes within the civil rights community. Author Imamu Amiri Baraka, nè Leroi Jones, and several friends purchased a watermelon from a passing vendor and ate it in full view of rush-hour motorists in Washington, D.C.; black laundry workers in Rocky Mountain, North Carolina, refused to clean Ku Klux Klan robes, which the KKK protested by picketing the cleaners; Dick Gregory playfully threatened to picket the U.S. Weather Bureau unless it name a hurricane after a black woman, "Beulah" (which eventually it did); Godfrey Cambridge teasingly observed that flesh-colored Band-Aids "didn't have me in mind"; and black students mimicked whites at college who were trying to move in the black style.

In the mid-sixties, in the space of two years, a considerable number of anthologies of folklore and humor appeared. Awareness of the complexities and power of black humor was suddenly extended by works by such as Langston Hughes and Arna Bontemps, *The Book of Negro Folklore* (1965), Philip Sterling, *Laughing on the Outside* (1965), Langston Hughes, *The Book of Negro Humor* (1966), and Richard Dorson, *American Negro Folktales* (1967). Hidden from view, denied by whites, the richness and power of the collections came as a surprise. Even the sophisticated humorist Ogden Nash expressed astonishment over the assortment and nuances of black humor. In his review of *The Book of Negro Humor,* he wrote that "the range of humor was a surprise. One would not have expected so many kinds, from so many sources. There are the contemporary comics. . . . There are jokes having to do with jive and the blues. There are anecdotes from the pulpit. There are stories from Orleans and Harlem.[49]

Multiplied across the country, this outpouring echoed as a chorus of militancy in humor. Afro-Americans defied, indeed, taunted whites to enter into the sanctuaries of laughter. A heavy portion of the comics' routines contained a mocking condemnation of racist attitudes and practices. People who had once been jived in private now found themselves the butt of jokes from the stage and on television. Jokes that had been confined to the inner reaches of the black community had made their way into white society. Powerful figures were mimicked, ridiculed, and skewered. Before he was the victim of an assassination attempt that left him paralyzed, George Wallace—he who had blocked the path of a black student trying to enter the University of Alabama in the mid-1960s—was one such target:

> Governor Wallace went for his annual medical checkup. The doctor examined him thoroughly and told him to return for the results in a week.
>
> A week passed and Wallace came in for the doctor's report. "Well, Doc, how'm Ah doing?" The doctor looked at him carefully and said, "Gov'ner, I've got good news and bad news."
>
> "Good news and bad news?" repeated Wallace. "All right, give me the good news first."
>
> "The good news, Gov'ner, is that you got cancer."
>
> Wallace blanched. "That's the good news—that Ah got cancer?" he asked incredulously. "Well, if that's the good news, what in hell is the bad news?"
>
> "The bad news is that it's sickle cell anemia."[50]

In addition to giving a sense of power over oppressors and events, the humor of militancy also reflected a high degree of self-acceptance. The final nail in Sambo's coffin was the open evaluation by the performers of black life itself. Mocking features of black behavior effectively undercut whatever notion remained of blacks as fools. Cambridge stated on more than one occasion that one of his aims was to acquaint whites with the black world. It was essential to let "people see the truth of our lives, like, for example, the way Negroes are afraid of each other too. . . . We must bring things out into the open."[51] Peering inward, the new generation of comics in the 1960s baited blacks, too, particularly the middle classes who attempted to melt into the background. To Louis Lomax, this was an important development in African-American humor: "Negroes are now laughing at themselves," he noted in 1961, "and they are doing it without the old overtone of self-effacement. Much of the Negro humor is still tribal but it is beginning to take on a tinge of interracial status consciousness."[52]

In the early acts of Gregory and Cambridge, the pretensions of the black middle classes were limned. Cambridge observed that the black who moved into an all-white neighborhood wasn't afraid of whites' bricks or bombs: "He's afraid that another Negro will move next door to him." Gregory's comments were especially scathing. "You should have been with me when I moved into that all-white neighborhood. You know who showed up that first day on my porch? The Negro delegation. This one Negro, Dr. Jones, he says 'You gotta be careful in this neighborhood, and cool, 'cause they're watching us.' I said, 'What you-all doing, stealing something?' He said, 'No, you know what we mean. They're going to look for you to depreciate your property.' I said, 'Buddy, they just charged me $75,000 for a $12,000 house. I'll depreciate this whole block if you let me.'"

Folk expressions reflected the same perspective. When a priest asked a Harlemite, "Are you Catholic, my son?" he replied, "Lord, no, ain't I got trouble enough just being black?" And a dialogue between an unemployed black man in Chicago and God best illustrates what poet Marianne Moore said was a clue to the most serious part of one's nature—one's sense of humor:

> "Tell me, Lord, how come I'm so black?"
> "You're black so that you could withstand the hot rays of the sun in Africa."
> "Tell me, Lord, how come my hair is so nappy?"
> "Your hair is nappy so that you would not sweat under the hot sun in Africa."
> "Tell me, Lord, how come my legs are so long?"
> "Your legs are long so that you could escape from the wild animals in Africa."
> "Tell me, Lord, what the hell am I doing in Chicago?"[53]

Between these layers of humor could be heard the sounds of other events that, because of their scope and perceived threat to the social order, by themselves would probably have ushered Sambo from the mass media as well. The tumultuous actions of protesting blacks in over a hundred cities, beginning in Harlem in 1964 and extending to the end of the decade, their looting, burning, and police pelting, called attention to black frustrations in urban areas—and spelled the end of nonviolence as a tactic in the quest for civil rights. The cry of Black Power with its emphasis upon separatism, beginning barely two years after the Harlem riot and extending into the 1970s, undercut the thrust of interracial harmony that had been the quest of the civil rights movement—and thoroughly frightened whites. The media—in print, over electronic airwaves, and on the movie screens—alarmed the white community with their portrayal of blacks as savages. Indeed, even the slogan "Black Power" was enough to render Sambo totally meaningless, so menacing was the picture of ferocious blacks. The paternalistic white image was certainly terminated by these events. Notice had been pointedly served by the comics, the rioters, and separatists that redefinitions were in order.

Together, these activities laughed and pushed Sambo offstage and into the shadows of history. In one way or another, Sambo was removed from public view: he was yanked from library shelves across the country, so that by the early 1970s copies of *Little Black Sambo* and *Epaminondas and His Auntie* were no longer in public libraries; his blackface was removed from the annual Mummers' New Year's Day parade, forcing the marchers to prance in goldface; his minstrel performances were hooted from local stages in high schools and civic auditoriums; his antics on Saturday and Sunday mornings and late-night television reruns featuring grinning and scared-of-spooks chauffeurs and servants and slaves happy in song and smile were constantly protested and gradually disappeared; his jockey face was painted white as he staunchly held aloft his lantern on front lawns; his "Walken fer de Cake," an annual festival at the University of Vermont, featuring fraternal organizations competing in flashing colors and in blackface, was canceled after the NAACP threatened to picket the affair; both his name and figure were protested, litigated, altered, physically removed—all of which finally occurred to the Sambo pancake chain in the 1970s. Most symbolic, in the defamation suit brought by Lincoln Perry, a.k.a. Stepin Fetchit, he charged that a CBS black history documentary using clips from his films had depicted him as "the symbol of the white man's Negro."

The liberating element in most of these ricocheting events was humor itself. Not that Sambo had suddenly ceased to exist within the depths of the white mind—do cultural forms totally evaporate into historical vapor once removed from the material culture?—but that he could no longer be used as a lever of social control. Control had passed into African-American hands for the profoundly simple reason that, in having access to the mass media, they were quite able to project the kind of humor, the type of image they desired, a jester included. Sambo was gone, in short, because blacks had finally shoved and laughed him off the stages, the screens, the comic strips, the cartoons, the front lawns, the children's stories, the knickknacks, the advertisements, the radio and television programs. It had taken centuries.[54]

After such knowledge, what forgiveness? Think now
History has many cunning passages, contrived corridors
And issues, deceives with whispering ambitions,
Guides us by vanities.

—T. S. Eliot, "Gerontion"

Notes

1: An Epitaph Read Backward in Time

1. Walter Lippmann, *Public Opinion* (New York: Macmillan, 1922), pp. 88–89.

2. Mrs. Henry Rowe Schoolcraft, *The Black Gauntlet: A Tale of Plantation Life in South Carolina by Mrs. Henry Rowe Schoolcraft, 1852–1869* (reprint, New York: Negro Universities Press, 1969), pp. 26–30.

3. Byron Christy, *Christy's New Songster and Black Jester* . . . (New York: Dick & Fitzgerald 1863), pp. 9–17.

4. Clement Wood, ed., *The Best Negro Jokes* (Gerard, Kans.: Little-Blue-Books, c. 1920–30s), pp. 38, 6.

5. Robert Burton, *The Anatomy of Melancholy, What It Is, with All the Kinds, Causes, Symptoms, Prognostics and Several Cures of It.* (1621; New York: John Wiley, 1850), p. 337. For an important recent view of the relationship between humor and health, see Norman Cousins, *Anatomy of an Illness as Perceived by the Patient* (New York: W. W. Norton, 1979), pp. 82–85.

6. Sandra Billington, *A Social History of the Fool* (Sussex, England: Harvester Press, 1984), pp. 122–23.

7. Anton C. Zijderveld, *Reality in a Looking-Glass: Rationality Through an Analysis of Traditional Folly* (London: Routledge & Kegan Paul, 1982), p. vii.

8. Alan Gowans, *The Unchanging Arts: New Forms for the Traditional Functions of Art in Society* (Philadelphia: Lippincott, 1971), p. 15 and Chapter 1.

9. Lippmann, *Public Opinion*, p. 93.

10. Donald Bogle, *Toms, Coons, Mulattoes, Mammies & Bucks* (New York: Viking Press, 1973.

11. Ralph Ellison, *Invisible Man* (New York: Random House, 1947), p. 373.

12. Bernard Wolfe, "Uncle Remus and the Malevolent Rabbit," *Commentary*, July 1949, p. 31.

13. Stanley Elkins, *Slavery: A Problem in American Institutional and Intellectual Life* (Chicago: University of Chicago Press, 1959).

14. William Styron, *The Confessions of Nat Turner* (New York: Random House, 1966).

15. David B. Davis, *The Problem of Slavery in Western Culture* (Ithaca: Cornell University Press, 1966).

16. Eugene Genovese, *Roll, Jordan, Roll: The World the Slaves Made* (New York: Random House, 1972).

17. John Blassingame, *The Slave Community*, rev. ed. (New York: Oxford University Press, 1979).

18. George M. Frederickson, *The Black Image in the White Mind* (New York: Harper & Row, 1971).

2: As His Name Is, So Is He

1. Elizabeth Donnan, ed., *Documents Illustrative of the History of the Slave Trade to America*, vol. 3 (Washington, D.C.: Carnegie Institution, 1935; reprint, New York: Octagon Books, 1965), p. 343.

2. John Atkins, *A Voyage to Guinea, Brasil, and the West Indies* (London: Ward and Chandler, 1737), pp. 99–100.

3. Donnan, *Documents*, vol. 3, p. 8.

4. Theodore Canot, *Adventure of an African Slaver, Being a True Account of the Life of Captain Theodore Canot, Trader in Gold, Ivory and Slaves on the Coast of Guinea: His Own Story as Told in the Year 1854 to Brantz Mayer*, Malcolm Cowley, ed. (New York: Albert and Charles Boni, 1928), p. 311.

5. Donnan, *Documents*, vol. 1, pp. 197, 199.

6. Donnan, *Documents*, vol. 1, pp. 204, 231, 206, et al.

7. John Newton, *The Journal of a Slave Trader, 1750–1754* (London: Epworth Press, 1962), p. 110.

8. George Dow, ed., *Slave Ships and Slaving* (Port Washington, N.Y.: Kennikat Press, 1927; reprint, 1969), p. 295.

9. Dow, *Slave Ships and Slaving*, p. 172.

10. William Saroyan, "Random Notes on the Names of People," *Names: Journal of the American Name Society* (1953): 239.

11. Murray Heller, ed., *Black Names in America: Origins and Usage, Collected by Newbell Niles Puckett* (Boston: G. K. Hall, 1974), p. 7.

12. Helen T. Catterall, *Judicial Cases Concerning American Slavery and the Negro*, vol. 1 (Washington, D.C.: Carnegie Institution, 1926; reprint, New York: Octagon Books, 1968), pp. 55–56.

13. Alden T. Vaughan, "Blacks in Virginia: A Note on the First Decade," *William and Mary Quarterly*, 3rd ser., vol. 39 (July 1972): 471–75.

14. T. H. Breen and Stephen Innes, "Myne Owne Ground": *Race and Freedom on Virginia's Eastern Shore, 1640–1676* (New York: Oxford University Press, 1980), p. 69.

15. Catterall, *Judicial Cases Concerning American Slavery*, pp. 76–81; Robert Twombley and Richard H. Moore, "Black Puritan: The Negro in Seventeenth Century Massachusetts," *William and Mary Quarterly*, 3rd ser., vol. 24 (April 1967): 224–43.

16. "Census of Slaves, 1755," *Documentary History of New York*, vol. 3 (1850); "A Schedule of the Ancient Colored Inhabitants of Charlestown, Mass. on Record Prior to 1800" (privately reprinted from the *Charlestown Chronicle* of January 1, 1870).

17. Daniel Horsmanden, *The New York Conspiracy*, Thomas J. Davis, ed. (Boston: Beacon Press, 1971).

18. George Sheldon, *History of Deerfield, Massachusettes: The Times When and the People By Whom It Was Settled, Unsettled, and Resettled: With a Special Study of the Indian Wars in the Connecticut Valley*, vol. 2 (Greenfield, Mass.: E. A. Hall, 1896), pp. 889–93.

19. James Axtell, "The Scholastic Philosophy of the Wilderness," *William and Mary Quarterly*, 3rd ser., vol. 29 (July 1972): 336.

20. Ralph Hamor, *A True Discourse of the Present State of Virginia, and the Success of Affaires There till 18 of June 1614* (London: John Beale, 1615), p. 97.

21. J. L. Dillard, "The West African Day-Names in Nova Scotia," *Names*, vol. 19 (September 1971): 260.

22. Philip Curtin, "Ayuba Suleiman Diallo of Bondu," *Africa Remembered*, Curtin, ed. (Madison: University of Wisconsin Press, 1967), p. 37, n. 27.

23. Lorenzo Dow Turner, *Africanisms in the Gullah Dialect* (Chicago: University of Chicago Press, 1949).

24. Allen Walker Read, "The Speech of Negroes in Colonial America," *Journal of Negro History*, vol. 24 (July 1939): 25.

25. Dillard, "West African Day-Names in Nova Scotia," p. 259. See also Henry M. Sherwood, "Paul Cuffee," *Journal of Negro History*, vol. 8 (1923): 153–232; Katherine A. Wilder, "Captain Paul Cuffee, Master Mariner of Westport, Massachusetts, 1757–1817," *Bulletin of the Society for the Preservation of New England Antiquities*, vol. 63 (Winter 1973); 78; and especially Sheldon H. Harris, *Paul Cuffee: Black Americans and the African Return* (New York: Simon & Schuster, 1972).

26. Alex Haley, "My Furtherest-Back-Person—'The African'" *New York Times Magazine* (July 16, 1972), p. 131.

27. Dillard, "West African Day-Names in Nova Scotia," p. 260.

28. Ira Berlin, *Slaves Without Masters: The Free Negro in the Antebellum South* (New York: Pantheon, 1974), pp. 51–52.

29. Eugene D. Genovese, *Roll, Jordan, Roll: The World the Slaves Made* (New York: Random House, 1972), pp. 445.

30. G. I. Jones, "Olaudah Equiano of the Niger Ibo," in Curtin, ed., *Africa Remembered*, p. 79.

31. Lorenzo J. Greene, *The Negro in Colonial New England* (New York: Columbia University Press, 1942; reprint, New York: Atheneum, 1968), p. 256.

32. New bell Niles Puckett, "Names of American Negro Slaves," in G. P. Murdock, ed., *Studies in the Science of Society* (New Haven: Yale University Press, 1937), p. 489.

33. Trombley and Moore, "Black Puritan," p. 226.

34. Puckett, "Names of American Negro Slaves," p. 477, n. 2; Heller, *Black Names in America*, pp. 21–27, 60, 82–83.

35. Puckett, "Names of American Negro Slaves," pp. 471, 486, 487, n. 50.

36. Frederick Marryat, *Diary in America* (Bloomington: Indiana University Press, 1960), p. 272.

37. J. L. Dillard, *Black English: Its History and Usage in the United States* (New York: Random House, 1972), pp. 130–31.

38. Curtin, "Ayuba Suleiman Diallo of Bondu," pp. 35–39; Arthur P. Middleton, "The Strange Story of John Ben Solomon," *William and Mary Quarterly*, 3rd ser., vol. 5 (July 1948): 342–50.

39. Donnan, *Documents*, vol. 4, pp. 12–13.

40. Atkins, *A Voyage to Guinea, Brasil, and the West Indies*, pp. 170–71.

41. *Documentary History of New York*, vol. 3, p. 856.

42. Gerald Mullin, *Flight and Rebellion: Slave Resistance in Eighteenth-Century Virginia* (New York: Oxford University Press, 1972), p. 46.

43. "Eighteenth Century Slaves as Advertised by Their Masters," *Journal of Negro History*, vol. 1 (April 1916): 168.

44. Georgetown, S.C.: Frances M. Baxter, 1808.

45. London: Harvey and Darton, 1823.

46. Mrs. Henry Rowe Schoolcraft, *Plantation Life: The Narrative of Mrs. Henry Rowe Schoolcraft* (New York: Negro Universities Press, 1969), p. 108.

47. Puckett, "Names of American Negro Slaves," p. 485.

48. John Davis, *Travels of Four Years and a Half in the United States of America During 1798, 1799, 1800, 1801 and 1802* (New York: Henry Holt, 1909), p. 97.

49. Isaac Jefferson, *Memoirs of a Monticello Slave, as Dictated to Charles Campbell in the 1840s*, Rayford W. Logan, ed. (Charlottesville: University of Virginia Press, 1931), p. 20.

50. John James Audubon, *Delineations of American Scenery and Character* (New York: G. A. Baker, 1926), pp. 218–19.

51. Pierre van den Berghe, *Race and Ethnicity: Essays in Comparative Sociology* (New York: Basic Books, 1970), p. 5.

52. A. Smythe Palmer, *Folk-Etymology: A Dictionary of . . .* (New York: Henry Holt, 1883; reprint, Westport, Conn.: Greenwood Press, 1969), pp. 338–39.

53. *Earthquake Peru: A True and Particular Relation of the Earthquake Which Happened at Lima, 1746* (1748), p. 240; quoted in James A. N. Murray, ed., *Oxford English Dictionary on Historical Principles,* vol. 3, part 2 (Oxford: Oxford University Press, 1914), p. 73.

54. John Stedman, *Expedition to Surinam* (London: Folio Society, 1963), p. 34.

55. Noah Webster, *An American Dictionary of the English Language* (New York: S. Converse for White Gallagher and White, 1831), p. 721.

56. Frederick Marryat, *Peter Simple* (Boston: D. Estes, 1896), p. 31.

57. Samuel Johnson, *A Dictionary of the English Language* (London: W. Strahan, 1805).

58. *Encyclopaedia Britannica,* vol. 17 (Edinburgh: Adam and Charles Black, 1875), p. 319; my emphasis.

59. Gertrude Jobes, *Dictionary of Mythology, Folklore and Symbols,* vol. 2 (Metuchen, N.J.: Scarecrow Press, Inc., 1961), p. 1393; my emphasis.

60. *New Standard Dictionary of the English Language* (New York: Funk and Wagnalls, 1953), p. 267.

61. *International Thesaurus* (New York: Thomas Y. Crowell, 1962).

62. Mark Sullivan, *Our Times,* vol. 6 (New York: Charles Scribner's Sons, 1930), p. 369.

63. Samuel Eliot Morison and Henry Steele Commager, *The Growth of the American Republic* (New York: Oxford University Press, 1930). Also see editions of 1937, 1942, 1950, and 1958.

3: Ladies and Gentlemen: Your Attention, Please

1. Theodore Canot, *Adventures of an African Slaver, Being a True Account of Captain Theodore Canot, Trader in Gold, Ivory and Slaves on the Coast of Guinea: His Own Story as Told in the Year 1854 to Brantz Mayer,* Malcolm Cowley ed. (New York: Albert and Charles Boni, 1928), p. 73; Barbot in Lynne Fauley Emery, *Black Dance in the United States from 1619 to 1970* (Palo Alto, Calif.: National Press Books, 1972), pp. 3, 9.

2. George Francis Dow, ed., *Slave Ships and Slaving* (Port Washington, N.Y.: Kennikat Press, 1927; reprint, 1969), pp. xxii–xxiii.

3. Eugene D. Genovese, "American Slaves and Their History," *New York Review of Books,* December 3, 1970, p. 34.

4. Frederick Douglass: *The Life and Times of Frederick Douglass Written by Himself,* rev. ed. (1892; reprint, New York: Collier Books, 1962), p. 54.

5. Frances Anne Kemble, *Journal of a Residence on a Georgia Plantation in 1838–1839* (New York: Harper & Bros., 1863), pp. 127–29.

6. Frances Trollope, *Domestic Manners of the Americans,* Donald Smalley, ed. (New York: Alfred A. Knopf, 1949), p. 7.

7. Frederick Law Olmsted, *A Journey in the Seaboard Slave States, with Remarks*

on Their Economy (1856; reprint, New York: Negro Universities Press, 1968), pp. 607–609, 552–553.

8. Kemble, *Journal of a Residence*, p. 127.

9. George Rawick, *The American Slave: A Composite Autobiography*, vol. 6 (Westport, Conn.: Greenwood Press, 1972), p. 135.

10. *Narratives of Ex-Slaves*, Social Science Source Documents, no. 2, (Nashville: Social Science Institute, Fisk University, 1945), p. 170.

11. Rawick, *The American Slave*, vol. 2, part 2, p. 210.

12. Rawick, *The American Slave*, vol. 1, Alabama Narratives, pp. 279, 96, 100, 206, 51.

13. Solomon Northrup, *Twelve Years a Slave*, Sue Eakin and Joseph Logsdon, eds. (1853; reprint, Baton Rouge: Louisiana State University Press, 1968), pp. 52, 165–66.

14. Rawick, *The American Slave*, vol. 2, part 2, p. 63.

15. Douglass, *Life and Times*, p. 147.

16. Mrs. Henry Rowe Schoolcraft, *Plantation Life: The Narrative of Mrs. Henry Rowe Schoolcraft* (New York: Negro Universities Press, 1969), p. 22.

17. Edwin Adams Davis, *Plantation Life in the Florida Parishes of Louisiana, 1836–1846, as Reflected in the Diary of Bennet H. Barrow* (New York: Columbia University Press, 1943), p. 381.

18. Rawick, *The American Slave*, vol. 1, p. 20.

19. William H. Russell, *My Diary North and South* (Boston: T. O. H. P. Burnham, 1863), p. 126.

20. Frederal Writers Project, *Slave Narratives: South Carolina* (Washington, D.C.: Library of Congress, 1930s).

21. Charles Lyell, *Travels in North America in the Years 1841-2; with Geological Observations on the United States, Canada, and Nova Scotia* (New York: Wiley and Putnam, 1845; New York: Harper & Bros., 1842), vol. 1, p. 144; vol. 2, p. 269.

22. Olmsted, *Journey in the Seaboard Slave States*, pp. 24–26.

23. Timothy Flint, *Recollections of the Last Ten Years, Passed in Occasional Residences and Journeyings in the Valley of the Mississippi* (Boston: Cummings, Hilliard, & Co., 1826; reprint, New York: Alfred A. Knopf, 1932), pp. 135–37.

24. *Seeing America and Its Great Men: The Journal and Letters of Count Francesco dal Verme* (Charlottesville: University of Virginia Press, 1969), pp. 50, n. 127.

25. Rawick, *The American Slave*, vol. 2, part 2, p. 215.

26. Federal Writers Project, *Slave Narratives* (1936–1938), vol. 16, part 1, p. 243; vol. 4, part 2, p. 348.

27. Douglass, *Life and Times*, pp. 147–48.

28. Olmsted, *Journey in the Seaboard Slave States*, p. 91.

29. Flint, *Recollections of the Last Ten Years*, p. 136.

30. Edward C. L. Adams, *Congoree Sketches: Scenes from Negro Life in the Swamps of the Congoree and Tales and Scip of Heaven and Hell with Other Miscellany* (Chapel Hill: University of North Carolina Press, 1927), p. 52.

31. Olmsted, *Journey in the Seaboard Slave States,* pp. 450, 394.

32. Thomas R. R. Cobb, *An Inquiry into the Law of Negro Slavery* (1858; reprint, New York: Negro Universities Press, 1968), p. clvii.

33. Kemble, *Journal of a Residence,* pp. 161–62.

34. Harriet Martineau, *Retrospect of Western Travel,* vol. 1 (London: Saunders and Otley, 1838), p. 271.

35. Martineau, *Retrospect of Western Travel,* p. 270.

36. Rawick, *The American Slave,* vol. 2, part 2, pp. 265, 319.

37. Ibid., vol. 1, p. 248.

38. Ibid., vol. 2, part 2, p. 212.

39. Gerald W. Mullin, *Flight and Rebellion: Slave Resistance in Eighteenth Century Virginia* (New York: Oxford University Press, 1972), p. 92.

40. Max Eastman, *Enjoyment of Laughter* (New York: Simon & Schuster, 1936), p. 132.

41. Rawick, *The American Slave,* vol. 1, p. 104.

42. Ibid., pp. 107–108.

43. Lyle Saxon, Edward Dreyer, and Robert Tallent, *Gumbo Ya-Ya* (Boston: Houghton Mifflin, 1945), p. 240.

44. Kemble, *Journal of a Residence,* pp. 67–68.

45. Rawick, *The American Slave,* vol. 1, p. 387.

46. J. F. D. Smyth, *A Tour in the United States of America,* vol. 1 (London: G. Robinson, 1784), pp. 40, 47–48.

47. Harriet Martineau, *Society in America,* vol. 2 (London: Saunders and Otley, 1837; New York: AMS Press, 1966), p. 316.

48. Smyth, *A Tour in the United States,* pp. 48, 40.

49. Michel Guillaume Jean de Crèvecoeur [J. Hector St. John] *Sketches of Eighteenth Century America,* Henry L. Bourdin, Ralph Gabriel, Stanley T. Williams, eds. (New Haven: Yale University Press, 1925), p. 148.

50. Schoolcraft, *Plantation Life,* p. 27.

51. John Bernard, *Retrospections of America, 1797–1811* (New York: Harper & Bros., 1887), pp. 126–35.

52. Cited in Bruce Erno, *Dominant Images of the Negro in the Ante-Bellum South* (dissertation, University of Minnesota, 1961), p. 242.

53. Martineau, *Society in America,* vol. 1, pp. 152–53.

4: *And Performing Today . . . Jim Crow, Esquire!!*

1. John Bernard, *Retrospections of America, 1797–1811* (New York: Harper & Bros., 1887), p. 126.

2. Washington Irving, *Knickerbocker's History of New York* (New York: Capricorn Books, 1965), pp. 103–104.

3. James Fenimore Cooper, *Satanstow: or The Littlepage Manuscripts: A Tale of the Colony* (New York: Burgess, Stringer and Co., 1845), vol. 1, pp. 65, 70.

4. Lorenzo J. Greene, *The Negro in Colonial New England* (New York: Columbia University Press, 1942; reprint New York: Atheneum, 1968), pp. 248–49; Lynne F. Emery, *Black Dance in the United States from 1619 to 1970* (Palo Alto, Calif: National Press Books, 1972), pp. 142–43.

5. Irving, *Knickerbocker's History*, p. 104.

6. Roi Ottley and William J. Weatherby, eds., *The Negro in New York: An Informal Social History, 1626–1940* (New York: Praeger Publishers, 1969), pp. 9, 25–26.

7. Carl Wittke, *Tambo and Bones: A History of the American Minstrel Show* (Durham, N.C.: Duke University Press, 1930), pp. 9, 20.

8. Ira Berlin, *Slaves Without Masters* (New York: Pantheon, 1974), p. 62.

9. Greene, *The Negro in Colonial New England*, pp. 248–49.

10. "Journal of Josiah Quincy, Junior, 1773," Massachusetts Historical Society Proceedings, vol. 49 (1916): 456–57.

11. Alexis de Tocqueville, *Democracy in America*, vol. 1 (Vintage, 1955), p. 374.

12. Hugh F. Rankin, *The Theatre in Colonial America* (Chapel Hill: University of North Carolina Press, 1965), p. 117; Frederick W. Bond, *The Negro and the Drama* (College Park, Md: McGrath Publishing Co., 1940), p. 20; and Alan W. C. Green, *Legacy of Illusion: The Image of the Negro in the Pre–Civil War North, 1787–1857* (dissertation, Claremont Graduate School, 1968).

13. Robert Munford, *"The Candidate: or, The Humours of Virginia Election," A Collection of Plays and Poems* (Petersburg, Va., 1798), Act I, scene i.

14. Samuel Breck, *Recollections of Samuel Breck with Passages from His Notebooks (1771–1862)*, H. E. Scudder, ed. (Philadelphia: Porter & Coates, 1877), pp. 182–83.

15. John Murdock, *The Triumph of Love; or, Happy Reconciliation* (Philadelphia, 1795).

16. John Murdock, *The Politician, or A State of Things* (Philadelphia: privately printed, 1798), pp. 19–20.

17. Naomi Goldstein, *The Roots of Prejudice Against the Negro in the United States* (Boston: Boston University Press, 1948), p. 142.

18. Hans Nathan, *Dan Emmett and the Rise of Early Negro Minstrelsy* (Norman: University of Oklahoma Press, 1962), p. 49.

19. Ralph Keeler, "Three Years as a Negro Minstrel," *Atlantic Monthly*, July 1869, p. 81.

20. G. B. Samson, *The Western World and Japan: A Study of the Interaction of European and Asiatic Culture* (New York: Alfred A. Knopf, 1951), pp. 279–80; William L. Neumann, *America Encounters Japan: From Perry to MacArthur* (New York: Aper Colophon Books, 1963), p. 37.

21. Robert C. Toll, *Blacking Up: The Minstrel Show in Nineteenth-Century America*

(New York: Oxford University Press, 1974), p. 124; William F. Stowe and David Grimsted, "White-Black Humor," *Journal of Ethnic Studies,* vol. 2 (Summer 1975): 82.

22. Constance Rourke, *American Humor: A Study of the National Character* (New York: Doubleday Anchor, reprint; 1961), pp. 85–86.

23. Ibid., p. 81.

24. "Do Come Along Ole Sandy, Boy," *The Negro Forget-Me-Not Songster, The Only Work Published, Containing All the Negro Songs That Have Ever Appeared* (Philadelphia: Turner and Fisher, 1950s), p. 20.

25. Reprinted in Sterling A. Brown, Arthur P. Davis, and Ulysses Lee, *The Negro Caravan* (New York: Dryden Press, 1941), p. 574.

26. Oscar Handlin, *This Was America* (New York: Harper & Row, 1949), p. 205.

27. Rourke, *American Humor,* p. 74.

28. Ibid., pp. 74–78.

29. Ibid., p. 74; my emphasis.

30. Hans Nathan, *Dan Emmett and the Rise of Early Nego Minstrelsy* (Norman: University of Oklahoma Press, 1962), Chapters 3 and 4.

31. John Pendleton Gaines, *The Southern Plantation,* (Gloucester, Mass: Peter Smith, 1962), pp. 108–109.

32. Toll, *Blacking Up,* pp. 42, 51.

33. Stowe and Grimsted, "White-Black Humor," pp. 82–83.

34. William J. Schaefer and Johannes Reidel, *The Art of Ragtime* (Baton Rouge: Louisiana State University Press, 1973), pp. 7–8.

35. Kenneth S. Lynn, *Mark Twain and Southwestern Humor* (Boston: Little, Brown, 1959), p. 101.

36. Newman I. White, "The White Man in the Woodpile," *American Speech,* vol. 4 (February 1929): 210.

37. Robert Sheerin, "The Origins of the Song 'Dixie': An Interview with Daniel D. Emmett, Its Composer, in 1895," in Robert R. Thomas, ed., *The Old Farmer's Almanac* (Dublin, N.H.: Old Farmer's Almanac, 1967), p. 110.

38. "Negro Minstrelsy—Ancient and Modern," *Putnam's Magazine,* January 1855, pp. 74–79.

39. "Tambo and Bones," in George C. D. Odell, *Annals of the New York Stage,* vol. 4 (New York, 1927), p. 372.

40. Samuel Clemens, *The Autobiography of Mark Twain* (New York: Harper & Bros., 1959), pp. 58–60.

41. Brander Matthews, "The Rise and Fall of Negro Minstrelsy," *Scribner's Magazine,* June 1915, p. 759.

42. H. G. Spaulding, "Under the Palmetto," *Continental Magazine,* vol. 4, 1863, p. 73.

43. John C. Dancey: *Sands Against the Wind: The Memoirs of John C. Dancey* (Detroit: Wayne State University Press, 1966), p. 118.

44. William McFerrin Stowe, Jr., "Damned Funny: The Tragedy of Bert Williams," *Journal of Popular Culture*, vol. 10 (Summer 1976): 5.

45. *Minstrel Guide and Joke Book* (Frank Tousey, 1898), pp. 20–23.

46. *Darkey & Comic Drama* (Chicago: Dramatic Publishing Co., 1898): *The Newsboys and Bootblacks: The Minstrel Show (Chicago: T. S. Denison and Co., 1919).*

47. J. C. Furnas, *Goodbye to Uncle Tom* (New York: William Sloane Associates, 1956), pp. 281–82.

48. *Report of the Superintendent to the Advisory Board of the Federal Industrial Institution for Women, Alderson, West Virginia, Bureau of Prisons,* "Correspondence" and "Memorandums" (January 30, 1933, May 26, 1937, and May 19, 1935).

49. *Minstrel Shows: At Ease, II* (National Archives, USO Camp Shows, Inc., 1942), pp. 138–41.

50. Ibid., 144–46.

51. Work Progress Administration, *56 Minstrels,* publication no. 39L, National Service Bureau, Federal Theatre Project (February 1938).

52. Arthur Leroy Kazer, *The Chain Gang Minstrel* (New York: Playhouse Plays–Fitzgerald Publishing Co., 1933), pp. 5–6.

53. *The Arts,* WPA Files, National Archives, series 1933–44.

54. Interviews with Mort Lewis, November 1970 and May 1971. Lewis kindly made available a portion of the written materials of the committee.

55. *Minstrel Shows: At Ease, II,* pp. 3, 9–10.

56. Mort Lewis, *Comedy Acts and Minstrel Show Material* (Washington, D.C.: The Infantry Journal, Inc., 1943), p. 11.

57. Script, October 5, 1942, pp. 6, 13–14.

58. *Life,* July 5, 1943, pp. 8–10, 93–100.

59. *Hollywood Reporter,* annual, September 1946.

60. Traverse City *Record Eagle,* April 10, 1971, p. 4; April 21, 1971, p. 4. I am grateful to Walter Beardslee of Northwestern Michigan College for providing information about these events.

5: Impressions in Boldface

1. Edgar Allan Poe, "The Gold Bug," *Collected Works of Edgar Allan Poe,* vol. 3, Thomas O. Mabbott, ed. (Cambridge, Mass: Harvard University Press, 1978), p. 821.

2. Kenneth S. Lynn, *Mark Twain and Southwestern Humor* (Boston: Little, Brown, 1959), p. 101.

3. John Pendleton Kennedy, *Swallow Barn, or a Sojourn in the Old Dominion* (reprint, New York: G. P. Putnam, 1853), pp. 452–55.

4. William R. Taylor, *Cavalier and Yankee: The Old South and American National Character* (New York: George Braziller, 1961), p. 303.

5. William Gilmore Simms, *The Yemassee: A Romance of Carolina* (Boston: Houghton Mifflin, 1961), pp. 100, 282–83.

6. Harriet Beecher Stowe, *Uncle Tom's Cabin: or, Life Among the Lowly* (New York: Doubleday, 1960), pp. 379–80.

7. Stowe, *Uncle Tom's Cabin*, pp. 379–80.

8. Recounted to author by Mel Bernstein.

9. "Ingenuity of a Negro," *Hagerstown Almanac*, in Joseph Cramer, ed., *Griggs City and Country Almanac* (Philadelphia, 1831), pp. 24–25.

10. Ivy L. Lee, *Memories of "Uncle Remus": Joel Chandler Harris as Seen and Remembered by His Friends* (privately printed, Christmas 1908), p. 17.

11. Paul M. Cousins, *Joel Chandler Harris: A Biography* (Baton Rouge: Louisiana State University Press, 1968), p. 26.

12. Bernard Wolfe, "Uncle Remus and the Malevolent Rabbit" (manuscript), p. 39. Wolfe generously allowed me access to his notes.

13. Julia Chandler Harris, *The Life and Letters of Joel Chandler Harris* (Boston: Houghton Mifflin, 1918), p. 146; my emphasis.

14. Harris, *Life and Letters*, pp. 164–65.

15. D. A. Walton, "Joel Chandler Harris as Folklorist: A Reassessment," *Keystone Folklore Quarterly*, vol. 11 (Spring 1966): 26.

16. Ray Stannard Baker, "Joel Chandler Harris," *Outlook*, November 5, 1904, p. 598.

17. Joel Chandler Harris, *Uncle Remus, His Songs and His Sayings* (New York: D. Appleton, 1911), pp. vii–viii.

18. Cousins, *Joel Chandler Harris*, pp. 132–33.

19. Harris, *Uncle Remus*, p. xvii.

20. Ibid., p. xiv.

21. Julia Chandler Harris, *Life and Letters*, p. 501.

22. Wolfe, "Uncle Remus and the Malevolent Rabbit," pp. 12, 44.

23. Pamela Colman Smith, Introduction, *Annancy Stories* (New York: R. H. Russell, 1899).

24. Martha S. Gielow, *Mammy's Reminiscences and Other Sketches* (New York: A. S. Barnes, 1898), pp. vii–viii, 15, 53–54.

25. "Notices," in Gielow, *Mammy's Reminiscences*.

26. Smith, Introduction, *Annancy Stories*.

27. H.A.F., "So Funny," *Chatterbox*, vol. 2, J. Erskine Clarke, ed. (Boston: Estes & Lauriat, 1877), p. 10.

28. Rayford W. Logan, "The Negro as Portrayed in Representative Northern Magazines and Newspapers," in Barry N. Schwartz and Robert Disch, eds., *White Racism* (New York: Dell, 1970), p. 392.

29. Lawrence Milton Bott, "The Negro as Displayed in Harper's Magazine,

1901–1924," (thesis, Howard University, July, 1951); Rayford W. Logan, *The Betrayal of the Negro* (1954; reprint, New York: Collier Books, 1969), pp. 242–45.

30. An excellent analysis of the book is Elizabeth Hay, *Sambo Sahib: The Story of Little Black Sambo and Helen Bannerman* (New Jersey: Barnes and Noble, 1981).

31. Sara Cone Bryant, *Epaminondas and His Auntie* (Boston: Houghton Mifflin, 1938).

32. Annie Vaugh Weaver, *Frawg* (New York: Frederick A. Stoles, 1930), pp. 11, 13, 18, 36.

33. Inez Hogan, *Nicodemus and his New Shoes* (New York: E. P. Dutton, 1937), title page.

34. Ellen Tarry, *Hezekiah Horton* (New York: Viking Press, 1942, 1944, 1945, 1952).

35. *Blue Diamonds . . .* (New York: Astor Publishing House, 1855), p. 1.

36. Samuel S. Butler, *Wit and Humor by Uncle Sambo* (Edwards, Miss.: New Light Steam Print, 1911).

37. Marion F. Harmon, *Negro Wit and Humor* (Louisville, Ky.: Harmon Publishing, 1914).

38. James D. Carrothers, *The Black Cat Club: Negro Humor and Folklore* (New York: Funk and Wagnalls, 1902).

39. Ibid., p. 7.

40. Edward V. White, Preface, *Chocolate Drops from the South* (Austin, Tex.: E. L. Stack, 1932).

41. Sam Boykin Short, Preface, *'Tis So* (Baton Rouge; Jack Walsh, 1952.)

42. P. B. Power, *Sambo's Legacy* (Philadelphia: American Sunday-School Union), p. 61.

43. Samuel A. Beadle, *Adam Shuffler* (Jackson, Miss.: Harmon Publishing, 1901), p. 23.

44. Orrie M. MacDonnell, Preface, *Sambo: Before and After the Civil War* (Macon, Ga.: J. W. Burke, 1924).

45. *Senggambien Sizzles: Negro Stories* (Dallas: Banks Upshaw, 1945), p. 20.

46. W. N. Hinkle, *Funniest Darkey Stories* (St. Paul: Keller Publishing, 1931).

47. O. M. Morris, *150 Latest Jokes* (Dallas: O. M. Morris, 1940s).

48. *Hi-Jinks,* October 1925, p. 50.

49. *Reader's Digest,* November 1943, p. 88.

50. Ibid., June 1942, p. 114; originally in *Colliers.*

51. *That Passing Laughter: Stories of the Southland* (Birmingham: Southern University Press, 1966).

52. Jerome Dowd, *The Negro in American Life* (New York: Century, 1926), pp. 357, 358, 401, 402, 404, 406.

53. Dorothy Scarborough, *On the Trail of Negro Folksongs* (Cambridge, Mass.: Harvard University Press, 1925), pp. 232, 162, 161.

54. *Report of Committee 3, Course G-1, "The Use of Negro Manpower in War"*

(Washington, D.C.: Army War College, November 12, 1936), quoted in *Knowledge into Action: Improving the Nation's Use of the Social Sciences* (Washington, D.C.: National Sciences Foundation, 1969), p. 18.

55. Kenneth W. Stamp, *The Peculiar Institution* (New York: Alfred A. Knopf, 1956).

56. Ulrich B. Phillips, *Life and Labor in the Old South*, (Boston: Little, Brown, 1929), p. 194.

57. Ulrich B. Phillips, *American Negro Slavery* (New York: D. Appleton, 1928), p. 291.

58. Ralph Gabriel, *The Course of American Democratic Thought* (New York: Ronald Press, 1940, 1956), pp. 7–8.

59. Francis Pendleton Gaines, *The Southern Plantation: A Study in the Development and the Accuracy of a Tradition* (Gloucester, Mass.: Peter Smith, 1927), pp. 224–27.

60. Samuel Eliot Morison, *The Growth of the American Republic* (New York: Oxford University Press, 1930, 1937, 1950, 1958).

6: Prismatic Projections

1. "Negro Life in Cartoons" (January 26, 1961), Picture Collection, New York Public Library.

2. *Brudder Bones Stump Speech and Joke Book* (New York: Ornum Publishing Co., c. 1850s).

3. G. A. Thompson ("Uncle Nic"), *Coonah Town Sassity and Other Comic Stories in Picture and Rhyme* (Chicago: Laird & Lee, 1903), p. 106.

4. See Harry T. Peters, *Currier & Ives: Printmakers to the American People* (New York: Doubleday, Doran, 1942).

5. Albert Bigelow Paine, *Mark Twain: A Biography* (New York: Harper & Bros., 1912), p. 772.

6. Francis Martin, Jr., "Edward Windsor Kemble, A Master of Pen and Ink," *American Art Review*, January–February 1976, pp. 58, 61; Beverly R. David, "The Pictorial Huck Finn: Mark Twain and His Illustrator, E. W. Kemble," *American Quarterly*, vol. 26 (October 1974): 331, 334–35.

7. E. W. Kemble, *Kemble's Coons* (New York: R. H. Russell & Sons, 1896).

8. *"Nine Niggers More" Songbook*, Aunt Louise's Big Picture Series (McLoughlin Bros., 1883).

9. For an extensive overview of the music situation, see William J. Schaefer and Johannes Riedel, *The Art of Ragtime* (Baton Rouge: Louisiana University Press, 1973), pp. 161–75.

10. For information relating to the history and character of the postcard, see George and Dorothy Miller, *Picture Postcards in the United States, 1893–1913* (New

York: Carkson N. Potter, 1976); Marian Klamkin, *Picture Postcards* (New York: Dodd, Mead, 1974); Jefferson Burdick, *Pioneer Post Cards* (Franklin Square, N.Y.: Nostalgia Press, 1964); Frank Staff, *The Picture Postcard & Its Origins* (New York: F. A. Praeger, 1966); Nan Robertson, "Wonderful Times for Postcard Fans," *New York Times*, March 2, 1979, C-16; and Edwin Newman and Leonard Probst, "Wish You Were Here!", *Atlantic Monthly*, August 1979, pp. 84–90. Various postcard collections exist in the Library of Congress, in Afro-American museums, and in personal hands. With few exceptions, the postcards analyzed in this chapter are in the possession of the author.

11. Martin, "Edward Windsor Kemble," pp. 55, 57.

12. *Boston Globe*, August 20, 1984, p. 22.

13. "Negroes in Advertising," New York Public Library Picture Collection.

14. There have been showings of these objects in the 1970s and '80s and articles about various collections around the country. Memorabilia collections have been displayed at The Gallery in Los Angeles, February 7–19, 1975; Dartmouth College, February 15–March 7; Queens College, New York, June 30, 1984.

15. Arthur Asa Berger, *The Comic-Stripped American* (Baltimore: Penguin Books, 1974), p. 27.

16. Ibid., pp. 42–43.

17. New York *American-Examiner*, 1911.

18. *American-Journal Examiner*, 1905.

19. Photographs by Frank B. McCrary and Lloyd Branson, "Photos of Black Children," UCLA Special Collection.

20. Mark Sullivan, *Our Times*, vol. 5 (New York: Charles Scribner's Sons, 1933), p. 487.

21. Tufts Dental School, *The Explorer* (Andover, Mass.: Andover Press, 1924), pp. 101, 91, 47.

22. J. Stanley Lemons, "Black Stereotypes as Reflected in Popular Culture, 1880–1920," *American Quarterly*, vol. 21 (Spring 1977): 112–13.

7: The Camera Eye

1. Daniel J. Leab, *From Sambo to Superspade: The Black Experience in Motion Pictures* (Boston: Houghton Mifflin Co., 1975), opening illustration.

2. Scripts, *In Old Kentucky* (Metro-Goldwyn-Mayer, 1927), University of Southern California Manuscript Collection, p. 12.

3. Camerson Shipp, "Al Jolson: America's Minstrel Man," *Coronet*, May 1948, p. 102.

4. Script, *High Sierra* (Warner Brothers, 1941), UCLA Film Collection, p. 23.

5. Script, *The Littlest Rebel* (Twentieth Century–Fox, 1935), UCLA Film Collection, pp. 5, 28, 6, 25.

6. Script, *Mississippi* (Warner Brothers, 1936), UCLA Film Collection, pp. A-1, A-5-6, B-14, B-16.

7. Script, *High Sierra* (Warner Brothers, 1941), UCLA Film Collection, p. 23.

8. *Bullets or Ballots* (1930).

9. *Belle of the Nineties* (1934).

10. *Johnny Come Lately* (1943).

11. *Shadow of the Thin Man* (MGM, 1941).

12. Twentieth Century–Fox press release, mid-1930s.

13. Newspaper clipping, UCLA, Johnson Negro Film Collection.

14. Ruby Berkley Goodwin, "When Stepin Fetchit Stepped into Fame," *Pittsburgh Courier,* July 6, 1929, feature section, p. 1.

15. Ibid.

16. Leab, *From Sambo to Superspade,* p. 89.

17. Script, *Stand Up and Cheer* Twentieth Century–Fox, 1934), UCLA Film Collection, pp. 36, 38.

18. Script, *Steamboat 'Round the Bend* (Twentieth Century–Fox, 1935), UCLA Film Collection, pp. 50–51.

19. Script, *Judge Priest* (Twentieth Century–Fox, 1934), UCLA Film Collection, pp. 4, 7–9.

20. *Los Angeles Times,* November 20, 1985, p. 3.

Three studies of African-Americans in films have amply covered the subject. The most extensive work has been done by Thomas Cripps in *Slow Fade to Black: The Negro in American Films* (New York: Oxford University Press, 1977).

Cripps's research and observations are most authoritative and provide the most definitive picture to date. They will most probably remain that way into the foreseeable future.

The other works, however, are extremely significant for their approach. Donald Bogle, *Toms, Coons, Mulattoes, Mammies and Bucks* (New York: Viking Press, 1973), and Leab, *From Sambo to Superspade,* provide salient perspectives of black performances during this early period of moviemaking. Bogle adroitly sums up the situation, arguing that through their parts, their appointed stereotypical characters, blacks accomplished an almost impossible task. "They proved single-handedly that the mythic types could be individualized and made, if not into things of beauty, then at least into things of joy. . . . Without scripts to aid them, and generally without even sympathetic directors or important roles, black actors in American films were compelled to rely on their own ingenuity to create memorable characters. As a result, blacks created comic worlds all their own in which the servant often outshone the master" (pp. 48–49).

8: The Radio Ear

1. Erik Barnouw, *The Golden Web: A History of Broadcasting in the United States,* vol. 2, *1933–1953* (New York: Oxford University Press, 1968), pp. 91, 110–11, 121.

2. Script, April 25, 1944, p. 19.

3. Script, May 9, 1944, pp. 14–15.

4. Script, April 4, 1944, p. 3.

5. Edward T. Clayton, "The Tragedy of Amos and Andy," *Ebony*, October 18, 1961, p. 66.

6. Hallmark, Contemporary Cards, 35KB 217-7.

7. Charles J. Correll and Freeman F. Gosden, *All About Amos 'n' Andy and Their Creators Correll and Gosden* (New York: Rand McNally, 1929), pp. 9, 13.

8. Script, August 16, 1928, p. 1.

9. Script, June 26, 1936, p. 21.

10. Script, July 3, 1928, p. 4.

11. Script, May 22, 1928, p. 1.

12. Script, May 25, 1928, p. 2.

13. Erik Barnouw, *A Tower in Babel: A History of Broadcasting in the United States*, vol. 1, to 1933 (New York: Oxford University Press, 1966), pp. 225–28.

14. Arnold Rose, *The Negro in America* (New York: Harper & Bros., 1944), pp. 300–301.

15. Script, January 12, 1926, p. 1.

16. Orrin E. Dunlop, "Amos 'n' Andy: The Air's First Comic Strip," *Literary Digest*, April 19, 1930, p. 42.

17. Script, February 6, 1932, p. 4.

18. Script, March 28, 1937, UCLA Manuscript Collection, pp. 1–2, 6–7, 11–12.

19. Script, October 17, 1932, p. 31.

20. Script, May 2, 1937, pp. 16–19.

21. Hal Humphrey, "Benny, Rochester Defy Stereotypes," *Los Angeles Times*, November 11, 1968, p. 27.

22. Arthur Frank Wertheim, *Radio Comedy* (New York: Oxford University Press, 1979), p. 131.

23. Script, November 3, 1932, p. 2.

24. Script, March 29, 1942, p. 11.

25. Scripts, December 17, 1944, pp. 4–5; December 24, 1939, pp. 7–8; June 26, 1938, pp. 14–15.

26. Scripts, March 22, 1942, p. 11; November 19, 1944, p. 14; February 20, 1940, p. 3; October 5, 1941, p. 13.

27. Scripts, March 8, 1942, p. 5; April 26, 1942, p. 16; February 4, 1945, p. 13.

28. Scripts, February 18, 1940, p. 6; November 7, 1938, p. 10.

29. Scripts, February 20 and 27, 1938, pp. 10, 12; April 27, 1941, p. 10; January 16, 1938, p. 11.

30. Script, March 30, 1941, pp. 6, 1.

31. Scripts, February 11 and 18, 1940, pp. 20, 18.

32. Script, April 3, 1938, p. 3.

33. Scripts, April 14, 1940, p. 9; March 27, 1938, pp. 14–15; December 31, 1939, pp. 17–18; March 27, 1938, pp. 14–15.

34. Script, December 26, 1937, p. 1.

35. Script, April 27, 1941, pp. 10–11.

36. Script, December 24, 1944, pp. 3–4.

37. Script, February 11, 1949, p. 2.

38. Script, June 4, 1939, p. 19.

39. Script, January 2, 1938, p. 11; November 13, 1938, p. 7.

40. Scripts, January 2, 1938, p. 11; December 25, 1938, p. 31.

41. Scripts, June 20, 1937, pp. 12–13; February 6, 1938, pp. 4–5; January 20, 1941, p. 21.

42. Leslie Fiedler, *An End to Innocence: Essays on Culture and Politics* (Boston: Beacon Press, 1948), p. 151.

43. Scripts, May 1, 1938, pp. 17–18; May 29, 1938, p. 5.

44. Script, May 3, 1942, pp. 3–4.

45. Script, January 29, 1939, pp. 15–18.

46. Scripts, May 10, 1942, p. 14; December 12, 1948, p. 19.

47. Script, May 9, 1948, p. 3.

48. Script, February 4, 1948, p. 12.

49. Ibid., pp. 11–12.

50. Script, March 28, 1948, pp. 1–2.

51. Script, April 29, 1945, pp. 2–4.

52. Script, January 1, 1950, pp. 22–23.

53. Irving Fein, *Jack Benny: An Intimate Biography* (New York: Pocket Books, 1977), p. 10.

9: The Fool as an Emancipator

1. Joseph Boskin, "Good-by, Mr. Bones," *New York Times Magazine*, May 1, 1966, p. 30.

2. James Baldwin, *Notes of a Native Son* (Boston: Beacon Press, 1955), p. 27.

3. Richard Dalfiume, "The Forgotten Years of the Negro Revolution," *Journal of American History*, vol. 55 (June 1968): 106.

4. Leonard C. Archer, *Black Images in the American Theatre* (Brooklyn, N.Y.: Pageant-Poseidon, 1973), pp. 208–209.

5. Erik Barnouw, *The Golden Web: A History of Broadcasting in the United States*, vol. 2 (New York: Oxford University Press, 1968), p. 162.

6. Arthur Frank Wertheim, *Radio Comedy* (New York: Oxford University Press, 1979), pp. 154–55.

7. Royal D. Calle, "Negro Image in the Mass Media: A Case Study in Social Change," *Journalism Quarterly*, vol. 45 (Spring 1968): 57.

8. "*Gunsmoke* Producer Tells Negro Policy," *Los Angeles Times*, November 21, 1960, p. 72.

9. Archer, *Black Images in the American Theatre*, p. 260.

10. Eldridge Cleaver, *Soul on Ice* (New York: Delta Books, 1968), p. 196.

11. Rheinhold Niebuhr, *Discerning the Signs of the Times* (New York: Charles Scribner's Sons, 1946), pp. 111–12.

12. *Jet*, April 28, 1966, p. 30.

13. Langston Hughes, *Fight for Freedom* (New York: W. W. Norton, 1962), p. 189.

14. B. Richardson, "That's All Right—Birmingham, Alabama," *Freedomways*, Fall 1964, p. 74.

15. Reed Sarratt, *The Ordeal of Desegregation* (New York: Harper & Row, 1966), pp. 328–29.

16. Ibid., p. 329.

17. Speech at Neighborhood Unitarian Church, November 5, 1964.

18. Robert Shelton, "Singing for Freedom: Music in the Integration Movement," *Sing Out!*, December–January 1962, p. 51.

19. John A. Williams, *This Is My Country Too* (New York: Signet Books, 1964), p. 150.

20. Howard Zinn, *SNCC: The New Abolitionists* (Boston: Beacon Press, 1964), p. 26.

21. *Time*, May 17, 1963, p. 23.

22. Richardson, "That's All Right," p. 74.

23. *Freedom Riders Speak for Themselves* (Detroit: News and Letters Pamphlet, 1961), p. 15.

24. Zinn, *SNCC*, p. 165.

25. Anne Moody, *Coming of Age in Mississippi* (New York: Dial Press, 1968), pp. 337–38.

26. Ossie Davis, "The Wonderful World of Law and Order," in Herbert Hill, ed., *Anger and Beyond* (New York: Harper & Row, 1966), p. 156.

27. *Newsweek*, June 6, 1966, p. 28.

28. *Time*, January 3, 1964, p. 13.

29. Ralph Ellison, "Hidden Name and Complex Fate," *The Writer's Experience* (Washington: Library of Congress, 1964), p. 4.

30. Robert Penn Warren, *Who Speaks for the Negro?* (New York: Vintage Books, 1965), p. 48.

31. James Farmer and Malcolm X, "Separation or Integration: A Debate," *Dialogue*, May 1962, p. 15.

32. Williams, *This Is My Country Too*, p. 148.

33. Merrill Proudfoot, *Diary of a Sit-In* (Chapel Hill: University of North Carolina Press, 1962), p. 79.

34. Nicholas Von Hoffman, *Mississippi Notebook* (New York: David White, 1964), p. 30.

35. Warren, *Who Speaks for the Negro?*, p. 227.

36. Diane Nash, "Inside the Sit-ins and Freedom Rides: Testimony of a Southern Student," in Matthew H. Ahmann, ed., *The New Negro* (Notre Dame, Ind.: Fides Publications, 1961), pp. 47–48.

37. Author's Notes, SNCC worker, Los Angeles, February 1964. See also Hughes, *Fight for Freedom*, p. 185.

38. Author's notes, Herbert Hill, labor secretary, NAACP, March 1965.

39. Author's notes, Interracial Conference, UCLA, March 1966.

40. Author's notes, Mary Jane Hewitt, associate director, UCLA Extension, October 1968.

41. Author's notes, graduate student, University of Southern California, March 1962.

42. Author's notes, Mary Jane Hewitt, April 1968.

43. Author's notes, Washington, New York, Los Angeles, 1962–66.

44. *Time*, January 3, 1964, p. 27.

45. Enid Welsford, *The Fool: His Social and Literary History* (London: Faber, 1935), p. 326.

46. Boskin, "Good-by, Mr. Bones," p. 90.

47. Louis Lomax, "The American Negro's New Comedy Act," *Harper's*, June 1961, p. 41.

48. *Parade*, January 11, 1970; August 20, 1972; March 18, 1973. See also "Communicating with Laughter," *Time*, April 6, 1970, pp. 56–59; Robert Higgins, "Black can be beautifully funny: Flip Wilson's gentle spoof of race relations makes his point without puncturing anyone's skin," *TV Guide*, January 17, 1970, pp. 36–40; and many newspaper articles, including Percy Shain, "Godfrey Cambridge: a man of many talents," *Boston Globe*, January 19, 1970, p. 16; McCandlish Phillips, "Dick Gregory Hones Humor at Village Gate," *New York Times*, June 11, 1970, p. 50.

49. Ogden Nash, *Los Angeles Times*, Calendar section, March 13, 1966, p. 33.

50. Author's notes, graduate student, seminar in Afro-American studies, February 1972.

51. Boskin, "Good-by, Mr. Bones," p. 90.

52. Louis Lomax, "The American Negro's New Comedy Act," *Harper's*, June 1961, p. 44.

53. Author's notes, recounted by Mary Jane Hewitt, April 1968.

54. Many of the jokes, quips and tales listed in the chapter were culled from different quarters and also recorded in various humor anthologies. Studies that concentrate on this topic include Norine Dresser, "The Metamorphosis of the Humor of the Black Man," *New York Folklore Quarterly*, vol. 26 (September 1970): 216–28: and Robert Brake, "The Lion Act is Over: Passive/Aggressive Patterns of Communication in American Negro Humor," *Journal of Popular Culture*, vol. 9 (Winter 1975): 549–60.

Index

245